"The real reason Kelman, despite his stature and reputation, remains something of a literary outsider is not, I suspect, so much that great, radical Modernist writers aren't supposed to come from working-class Glasgow, as that great, radical Modernist writers are supposed to be dead. Dead, and wrapped up in a Penguin Classic: that's when it's safe to regret that their work was underappreciated or misunderstood (or how little they were paid) in their lifetimes. You can write what you like about Beckett or Kafka and know they're not going to come round and tell you you're talking nonsense, or confound your expectations with a new work. Kelman is still alive, still writing great books, climbing."
—James Meek, *London Review of Books*

"The greatest living British novelist."
—Amit Chaudhuri, author of *A New World*

"What an enviably, devilishly wonderful writer is James Kelman."
—John Hawkes, author of *The Blood Oranges*

Books available by the same author

NOVELS
A Disaffection
How Late It Was, How Late
Mo said she was quirky
Dirt Road
God's Teeth and Other Phenomena

SHORT STORY COLLECTIONS
If it is your life
A Lean Third
That Was a Shiver
Keep Moving and No Questions

NONFICTION
Between Thought and Expression Lies a Lifetime:
Why Ideas Matter (with Noam Chomsky)
The State Is the Enemy: Essays on Liberation and Racial Justice

KAIROS

In ancient Greek philosophy, *kairos* signifies the right time or the "moment of transition." We believe that we live in such a transitional period. The most important task of social science in time of transformation is to transform itself into a force of liberation. Kairos, an editorial imprint of the Anthropology and Social Change department housed in the California Institute of Integral Studies, publishes groundbreaking works in critical social sciences, including anthropology, sociology, geography, theory of education, political ecology, political theory, and history.

Series editor: Andrej Grubačić

Recent and featured Kairos books:

The State Is the Enemy: Essays on Liberation and Racial Justice by James Kelman

Between Thought and Expression Lies a Lifetime: Why Ideas Matter by Noam Chomsky and James Kelman

Taming the Rascal Multitude: Essays, Interviews, and Lectures 1997–2014 by Noam Chomsky

Beyond State, Power, and Violence by Abdullah Öcalan

Building Free Life: Dialogues with Öcalan edited by International Initiative

The Sociology of Freedom: Manifesto of the Democratic Civilization, Volume III by Abdullah Öcalan

The Art of Freedom: A Brief History of the Kurdish Liberation Struggle by Havin Guneser

The Battle for the Mountain of the Kurds: Self-Determination and Ethnic Cleansing in the Afrin Region of Rojava by Thomas Schmidinger

Mutual Aid: An Illuminated Factor of Evolution by Peter Kropotkin, illustrated by N.O. Bonzo

For more information visit www.pmpress.org/blog/kairos/

All We Have Is the Story

Selected Interviews
1973–2022

James Kelman

KAIROS

PM

ISBN: 979-8-88744-005-7 (paperback)
ISBN: 979-8-88744-006-4 (hardcover)
ISBN: 979-8-88744-007-1 (ebook)
Library of Congress Control Number: 2023930616

Cover by Drohan DiSanto
Interior design by briandesign

10 9 8 7 6 5 4 3 2 1

PM Press
PO Box 23912
Oakland, CA 94623
www.pmpress.org

Printed in the USA.

Contents

Acknowledgments

It was not possible to establish all rights and permissions on these interviews. James Kelman is grateful to the publishers in question for their generosity, and to the individuals who conducted the interviews.

1

1973

Interview by Anne Stevenson

Anne Stevenson (1933–2020), the UK-based American poet and essayist, was a close friend of Mary Gray Hughes (see below). This article originally appeared in the *Scotsman* newspaper July 1973.

I met Jim Kelman over a pint on a crowded pub near Gariochmill Road in Glasgow, where he lives with his wife and two small daughters. Jim's first book of short stories, *An Old Pub Near the Angel*, has just been published in the United States by the Puckerbrush Press of Orono, Maine, so it seemed appropriate to talk to him over a hubbub of voices and the acrid smell of smoke and spilled beer.

Quiet-spoken, fair, with large, expressive eyes, Jim considers himself a Glaswegian, although after being brought up in Drumchapel he has lived in California, London, Jersey and Manchester. I asked him if the material for his stories, most of which are about working-class people and written with exceptional depth and tenderness, was provided by his own life.

"Yes," he said. "I want to write about real people, real things. I'm not interested in theories. A story can only be real if written through your own experience."

We were surrounded by university students celebrating their release from exams, so I asked him whether he thought a university education would be of much help to his writing.

"No, not at all. I don't think anyone should go to university before at least twenty-five. (Kelman is twenty-seven.) They don't know enough. It's training them to be officers before they've learned to be men."

"But you, yourself? Do you think now you'd like more education? Would you go to the university as a mature student?"

"Me? No. I don't write for educated people particularly. Of course I'm interested if they read my books, but I'm also interested in their reasons."

"Who do you write for, then?"

"People," he said. "Ordinary people who might pick up the book on a newsstand. Of course, I don't expect many people will pick up this book, because they don't know about it. Half the booksellers I've approached won't take it. It's published in Maine by a small press and is only known by other writers. Writers are classless, or should be."

"And yet you write mainly about working-class people."

"I write about the working classes because I was brought up in a working-class family. I'm published in America because an American writer, Mary Gray Hughes, liked my stories. She couldn't have known anything about working-class Glasgow. I feel I have a lot in common with black writers who have to write from the point of view of class. They can't do otherwise. But that doesn't mean you write for a class, if you write about it."

"I see what you mean," I said. "Tell me about your family and schooling. What made you want to write stories?"

"I was born in Govan, but we moved to Drumchapel, Number One Scheme, in 1954. My father is a craftsman, a picture-framer known to Glasgow artists, and he taught me to know good workmanship.

"Drumchapel was a good place for a child to grow up, lots of fresh air and space. My brother was at a school in Hyndland, so I went there too. That was before there was a school in Drumchapel.

"I left school at fifteen to be an apprentice printer and was a member of the printers' union. Then my father moved with the family to Pasadena, near Los Angeles in California. He thought there would be opportunities there, but after a while he got to hate the American system—master/slave relationship, he called it—so he came back to Glasgow. Two of my brothers stayed in the US—one older, one younger—but I returned with my father and my mother, and two younger brothers. We didn't have much money. The printers' union wouldn't have me back, so I went to work for a shoe factory in Govan. Then I was a sales assistant, a storeman and twice a bus conductor.

"In 1965 I went to Manchester, where I worked in factories, occasionally doing twelve-hour shifts, six days a week. I remember working a straight twenty-hour shift once. It didn't pay very well. In 1967 I came back to Glasgow and worked on the buses until August that year, when I headed for London. There I worked as a porter and on building sites and other things. For a while I picked potatoes in Jersey. Eventually I had to do a moonlight from there back to London."

"Where you met your wife?"

"Yes, we met in 1969. Marie's from Swansea, a secretary. Shortly after we met, we married, and when we found she was going to have a baby we came back to Glasgow."

"Why?"

"Accommodation's cheaper. We couldn't have afforded to live in London. I was working on the buses until last year, when I stopped and went on the broo so as to have more time to write."

"And you've wanted to be a writer all your life?"

"Well, no, I wanted to be a painter, but I wasn't good enough. I must have been twenty-one when I wrote my first stories. One was called 'He Knew Him Well,' about an old man who died without anyone knowing him. Another was called 'Abject Misery,' about having no money and no job."

"Those are included in your book, aren't they? I've noticed quite a number of your stories take place in slums or pubs."

"That's because I live in a slum and drink in pubs."

"When did you begin to take your writing seriously?"

"It was in 1971. Philip Hobsbaum was giving an extramural class in Creative Writing at Glasgow University. I went along. He liked my work and encouraged me. When the American writer Mary Gray Hughes visited Glasgow last year, he showed her my work."

I asked finally about his plans for the future.

"I've no fixed plans. I'll probably keep writing, though I have to get a job again in January. My wife's supporting us now, but in January it'll be my turn. I can't write for television or radio. I'll keep writing stories. I began a novel last year and had about sixty thousand words down on paper, but it turned out wrong. I've started another."

"Aren't stories difficult to get printed?" I suggested. "Wouldn't it make sense to write for the media, since they pay well?"

"Media isn't real," Jim replied. "If I had to write something not real I'd drive buses again. Does that sound ridiculous?"

"I don't think so. What writers do you like then?"

"Mostly contemporary Americans. Mostly American women writers. Especially, I think, Katherine Anne Porter, Flannery O'Connor, Mary Gray Hughes and Tillie Olsen. But of course, men too. Sherwood Anderson, Isaac Singer, the Russian Isaac Babel."

"For somebody without a formal education you seem to have read quite a bit," I said.

"You don't need a formal education to read," Jim said.

We drank to that.

2

1974

Interview by Jack Haggerty

Thanks to Tom Brogan for finding and posting online (in 2015) the following interview that Kelman cannot recollect ever doing.

Jim Kelman is a young Glasgow writer, presently living in Maryhill, who has just published his first book of short stories recently, *An Old Pub Near the Angel* (Puckerbrush Press, Orono, Maine, USA). Although born and bred in Govan, he was brought up largely in Drumchapel back in the '50s, drifting since then between London, Jersey and Manchester—even a brief spell in Pasadena, California.

I wanted to talk to him most especially about his boyhood in Drumchapel, what he remembered, how everything grew bad, sights, sounds, images, funny stories, the whole bit. Good copy for a reporter, great material for a creative writer. Over the telephone he said fine, come up at any time, we'll go for a pint maybe and talk.

The flat in Garioch Mill Road, Maryhill, seems very cramped and gives the impression of being crowded with that old-fashioned sort of furniture built by craftsmen, finished with care. Much more agreeable than some of the shoddy workmanship turned out today; much more pleasant an atmosphere to sit back in and talk, the firelight making everything slightly luminous, reminding you that everything has a softer surface.

"I've never actually published anything about Drumchapel yet," said Kelman, sitting in the front parlour. "Not yet. But I will. It's got to come into it at some time. With a housing scheme there's so much possibility, so much to write about.

"The *Scotsman* newspaper did an interview with me recently and I was later asked how about writing a sort of feature piece on Drumchapel. Actually I made a start on it, but never finished it. You see, it sort of developed into something else. It became a conversation between two Drumchapel women, housewives. One stays there, the other wants to move out … one day I'll come back to it and make a play out of it maybe."

While Kelman was talking, his two baby daughters kept spilling into the room, climbing up on his knee, wanting to be kissed, to say goodnight to the visitor before they went to bed.

Kelman is married to a secretary from Swansea, holds down a job as a bus driver to keep the wolf from the door. He's only twenty-seven, but is shaping up for some fine things as a writer. Lots of people think so—Philip Hobsbaum, the poet and lecturer at Glasgow University, an American writer called Mary Gray Hughes—everyone except society that is.

The only good writer is a dead writer, or one who makes a lot of money. Certainly Kelman can't go down the dole and register for work as an unemployed author. Recently he was turned down for an Arts Council grant, so he has to do his writing at all sorts of odd hours. Sometimes into the far watches of the night.

"When I was a boy in Drumchapel I never thought about being a writer," he said, "though I suppose I must have read a lot. I can't remember what. I wanted to be a painter up until I was twenty-one, when I realised I wasn't good enough. One of my earliest stories was called 'A Question of Balance,' which was about a newspaper boy in Drumchapel, which I was for a spell.

"I do think a lot about Drumchapel. Like the reasons it could have been better. So many mistakes were made, so many administrative mistakes. It's a place that breeds cynicism, even in the young people. Cynical seventeen- and fourteen-year-olds. You've got to fight your way out of that. What did I do when I was that age? Played cards all the time. Went on long walks up to the Old Kilpatricks. But even when we went there we used to get chased by the farmers and gamekeepers—especially if they caught you swimming in the lochs … there were clearwater lochs almost behind every rise in the ground 'way up there.

"From my house, up in Scheme One, on Glenkirk Avenue— or Stonedyke as the lower middle class like to call it," he grins, "we've had this fantastic view. The Campsies, the Old Kilpatrick Hills, Belside Hill, the Renfrew Hills."

When he isn't working on a short story, or musing over the novel he recently began, Kelman spends much of his time up in the Old Glasgow Room in the Mitchell Library. He has dug deep into the history of the Colquhoun family from Garscadden, some of whose exploits back in "ye old days" of the estate would make the original Tom Jones blush. Drumry, he says, is mentioned as far back in the annals as the fourteenth century.

"What I'm after," he explains, "is a general consciousness of the place, of Drumchapel. And there are things that the community should be conscious of—there's history on the doorstep out there, but I mean the kids don't know anything about it, they don't get taught about it in their schools. For example, do you know that the Lord Treasurer of Scotland, Sir Robert Livingstone of Drumry, was executed in 1447? This is the kind of thing I'm getting at, man."

He stops to roll himself a cigarette, leaning forward in his chair. Although by his output of spoken words Kelman could hardly be described as laconic, he somehow evinces that quality. Things that are left unsaid. The man who has noticeably more on his mind than he expresses. You could spend a whole evening with him, getting him to talk at length,

7

listening with an ear to his heart, yet come away not knowing too much about him. That's how it often is with writers. No point complaining.

"Talking about history," he begins again, "one of the things the Corporation should never be forgiven for is that in 1910 they knocked down a barn in Drumry. It was used as a bothy for some workers, but the thing is it had carved in Saxon characters over the door the name Laurence Crawford. Saxon figures! Think of the price Americans would pay for something like that today!

"Laurence Crawford, of course, was father of Captain Thomas Crawford, who captured Dumbarton Castle, later acquiring the estate of Jordanhill. That was a long while ago.

"Working-class people have no history. They have no real sense of history. Really, they're living only in the present ... or else they put history down to every conceivable superstition under the sun. Look at the way a man will ignore the historical facts of 1690 for example. No matter how you tell them, how much historical truth you present them with, they won't believe that King Billy used mostly Catholic mercenaries for his army at the Boyne, or that he received a blessing from the Pope. They have a way of blocking these things out.

"One of my short stories, 'Nice to be Nice,' is concerned with this theme. Let me try to explain. Supposing a young student were to come to a Glasgow working man who's getting on in years. And the student tells the old man that he's been conned his whole life. Now the old man is hardly going to accept that his life has been useless, or admit that all his life he has been a slave, no better off than a chattel; a pawn ... it's very sad to see the man who hasn't come to this realisation, who's still trapped—like the working man who votes Tory maybe. Who has no clue how much the whole system is conning him."

Politics aside, Kelman can call to memory moments from his childhood, as clear as looking into a rockpool, never forgetting its shape, its colour, details of its damage. There's also a

8

feeling of joy and liberation, like running water, which will always remain with him.

He remembers, for instance, tearing up Drumchapel's old Gunsite Hill (all gone now, alas to make room for Tallant Road) and hiding under the huge tarpaulins draped over the anti-aircraft guns which sat on the crown of the hill beside the army barracks, obsolete and useless, built for another age.

"That was before Southdeen was there," Kelman reflects. "I remember we used to hang on to the big barrels of the guns—that would be about 1955 or so. The guns must've been in pretty good nick, because we had to hide from a soldier once who was there to guard it or something ... and at the bottom of the hill, where Kinfauns Drive is, there was Ross Farm!"

He remembers, too, a pitch battle which developed between Drumchapel's new settlers and the natives who had always lived there—the tinkers.

"It was always between the tenants and the squatters," he recalled, "and it started off with just the kids, until the men got involved. But there were a few stones thrown well amiss and then it fizzled out—I've no idea how it happened."

He laughs. "The tinkers always intrigued me, the way it does when you're a wee boy ... we saw them like Red Indians, very mysterious."

In those days the famous Colquhoun family still owned the Garscadden estate down by the vale of Linkwood (where the three high-rised flats are today). Kelman remembers playing a game of catch-all or hide-and-seek one summer's evening when dusk was dropping. He hid himself, in the deepest part of the estate, watching out for the gamekeeper, when he chanced upon two pale headstones which sat spookily between the high stable walls and a spinney of whispering trees.

"The other boys had probably given up the ghost and gone home for supper," he said, "so you can imagine how I felt on coming across these two gravestones. They were the graves of a horse and a dog. I was so fascinated that I stole myself back the next morning when it was light just to make sure I hadn't imagined it. I wonder if the stones are still there today? The animals must've been beloved family pets, I suppose ... in those days the estate was almost idyllic, there were pear trees and apples trees ..."

Recently, under the guise of being a newspaper reporter, Kelman made a few investigations about the white church down in Old Drumchapel—he's always been by turns amused and disgusted at the "villagers'" snobbish attitude to the folk living in the scheme.

"They recently built an extension to the church for a discotheque," he explained, "and they were trying to get as many of the village children to go as possible. The caretaker I spoke to told me that if they got most of their children to go then they could clean out the riff-raff. That's what he said! They only needed twenty names and then they could say the books were filled, excluding most of the kids from the scheme.

"In the same white church, during the blitz in the last war, a lot of Clydebank people sheltered in the basement. One night a bomb fell leaving only a couple of walls standing, but everyone escaped unhurt. I wonder if any of your readers were there when it happened? Maybe if they remember anything about it they could get in touch with me. I'd be very interested to hear a first-hand account."

When we closed the interview we went down to a pub on the street corner for a pint. He talked briefly on some of the technical problems of his craft. He really cares about words, seeing it as a skill like his dad, who was a picture-framer known widely by Glasgow painters. But his father's trade was at least recognised by the world, they paid you a living, enough to subsist on anyway.

"Change?" Kelman asks. "You mean financial change? No, no, I don't think so. Change will be for the worst perhaps. There's just no way. It's almost impossible to live and write in this country. I may move with the family to Canada in a couple of years. Maybe. But I don't really know. There's no way."

He wasn't complaining. It was the way it was. He accepted it. He was happy just to be able to write when he could. It was something he couldn't live without. Walking off into the dark raw night he looked very like a bus driver who had to get home and get some shut-eye before tomorrow's shift. Which was true.

3

1984 & 1985

Two Interviews by
Duncan McLean

These interviews were first published in the *Edinburgh Review* in 1985.

The first conversation took place on the morning of March 1, 1984, a couple of weeks after the publication of *The Busconductor Hines*, James Kelman's first novel. He was working at the time as Writer in Residence for Renfrew District Libraries, and we talked in the office he had use of in Paisley Central Library.

The second conversation took place near the end of July 1985. After reading an advance copy of *A Chancer*, which wasn't actually published till September 26, I visited Kelman at his home in Cumbernauld. We talked in the afternoon, and again late in the evening.

The idea was that our conversation would record something of the way Kelman was thinking at the time of publication of his first two novels.

Part 1: March 1984, Paisley
Duncan McLean: Here's an extract from an article Neil Gunn had published in the *Glasgow Herald* [now the *Herald*] in 1941: "Glasgow needs 'a working class novel written from the inside.' This would show not a catalogue of horrors, but a revelation of the higher virtues, of periods of hardship bravely endured, of the usual human ills, flashes of irritability, of happy

times and good nights, a whole lot of gossip and not a little sentimentality."

James Kelman: That's very good, you know. I haven't read Neil Gunn at all. At one time I would have been surprised at that but not really now because I was reading an article by Naomi Mitchison about her relationship with Neil Gunn, and I didn't realise he was a good socialist. I didn't know anything about him. But yeah, that's a good kind of statement to make. [*Pause*] Refer it to me though.

DMcL: Well, is *Hines* "written from the inside" of the Glasgow working class? And is it a "revelation of the higher virtues?"

JK: Eh, the second part of your sentence is political, right. You see if I start to reply, in a way, it's as though—well, it comes from the outside and relates to the first part of your question. It's from the inside, of course, aye, because it's told in the form of a sort of interior monologue, it's not written in the "I-voice," so in that sense it has to have been written from the inside, otherwise it would have been found out too easily. So I think that would answer the first part of the question okay. Now the second part of the question. If I was to start to discuss it in those terms I would be discussing it from the outside of that culture anyway, which I'm not. It would be a mistake, for instance, to assume that because someone was a writer therefore they're no longer a part of that culture. Because that would assume that "culture," the culture of art, is somehow divorced from working-class culture, and that isn't true. I think, for instance, that that quote of Gunn's would assume that. Well, from what Gunn says, "a revelation of the higher virtues" ... in one sense the "higher virtues" would be art, art and culture, and in that sense art and culture is obviously just a part of working-class culture.

DMcL: You mentioned a wee while ago that *Hines* is written in a sort of interior monologue. Isn't it actually closer to an interior dialogue?

JK: There's a couple of technical things going on in the book, you see. I can't really describe it as an interior monologue, nor is it a dialogue, because either the character could be schizophrenic or else the narrative voice could be schizophrenic, or else the narrator ... contained in the narrative voice is a dialogue between narrator and central character. And that isn't happening either. I don't think any of those things are happening, I mean, I just said "interior monologue" as a quick description of what can happen with the "I-voice." But everything ... eh ... there's different kinds of writing as you know, different forms of writing. It's hard to ... what was the question again?

DMcL: Well, if it isn't interior monologue or interior dialogue what ...

JK: Those things are occurring within ... there's a lot of different things, different business going on, the only thing that doesn't go on ... well, there's an "I-voice" about three times in the book ... in reference to the main character, or perhaps it is the narrator, I don't know. There's nothing technically, for instance, that would disassociate ... it's very possible, you see, that Hines could be writing the novel. I mean that is technically possible within the framework of the novel. Nothing that happens happens outwith the perception of Hines. Absolutely nothing. So Hines could have written every single thing, in a way. I'm starting to refer to myself in the third person, "Kelman had two cups of coffee between half nine and ten o'clock this morning." A lot of people refer to themselves in the third person. I could describe it as a first-person novel written in the third person. There's a lot of tricks you can do in prose. You find when you're doing a short story there's different things, a lot of different things, you know you don't realise how powerful you can be until you start getting involved. A lot can be done in it.

DMcL: I suppose another side of it then is when Hines is "no longer able to tell whether he was speaking or thinking."

JK: That is another side of it, yeah. That is a technical thing. Eh, aye, it's an illusion, aye. Difficult to do that! I mean just in a very practical way in my prose there's not, for instance, any quotation marks to distinguish dialogue. Now if I had used quotations—inverted commas—for dialogue, it means I couldn't have done it. It would have been impossible, because the transition has to be done through the narrative, right, and it has to sort of switch from a sort of dialogue into narrative voice without the reader being precisely aware of where it happened. Okay? But I mean you couldn't do that with quotations, because right away you'd see where the quotation ends and where the narrative begins, wouldn't you. It just wouldn't be possible. People might think, "Oh look at that, Kelman doesn't use quotations! Gallus!" But it's not that at all. There's a good technical reason why a lot of writers don't. I mean there's no reason why they do or don't use quotation marks, they can use a dash or whatever. But it doesn't matter what they use, it doesn't matter. Beckett, for instance, doesn't use quotation marks for a reason. He works between voices quite a lot. But it's a hard thing to do, you know. It's not easy.

DMcL: Lewis Grassic Gibbon put his speech in italics. He didn't use quotation marks either …

JK: The thing is not to use anything, you can't use anything. My knowledge of Grassic Gibbon is too slight. I don't read Grassic Gibbon. I haven't read his novels. I've kind of glanced at them. I've read a couple of short stories by him, a long long while ago. So I don't know enough about his work to talk about it technically, although I know he was doing some good things.

DMcL: I've got here that famous bit of his essay where he explains what he's trying to do in his prose, technically. He tries to "mould the English language into the rhythms and cadences of Scots spoken speech, and to inject into the English vocabulary such minimum number of words from Braid Scots as that remodelling requires." Now, that sounds to me pretty much like what you do.

JK: Yes, I've no grumbles with most of that. I think it's fine. I knew that quotation before. I can't remember where I read it. I read a biography of Grassic Gibbon and I've read some of the things out of that *Scots Hairst*.* So that's good. I think that he was a man of his time. He was a near contemporary of Joyce and Kafka. That kind of thing was going on throughout literature and it's good that somebody in Scotland was aware of it too and working in prose ... only a good socialist could make that statement.

DMcL: So you didn't get involved in that kind of experimentation with prose through Gibbon at all?

JK: No, no, I mean—no, it's a tradition. It's part of a tradition in literature. It isn't always something you get at university. You get the other tradition there, the mainstream tradition, probably because of politics, you know, I don't think I'd ever read any Scottish writers at all when I started writing. I'd read very few English ones either. I usually read, eh ... I'm talking about when I was twenty, in my twenties, I only read European writers and American writers, you know, Russians, Germans.

I didn't go to uni until I was twenty-eight. I used to write when I was on the broo and stuff like that. And I really didn't like literature at all—English literature. It's not a question of it boring me, because I hated it, I hated the class assumptions that were being made by anybody who was involved in English literature as I thought of it, and still think of it, to some extent, because some of the reactions that my novel will get because of its language, for instance, show real class prejudice. The prejudices can be quite phenomenal. People who think they are critics, until they're met with something below the belt.

DMcL: How would you have reacted to a novel like *Hines* when you were twenty? Or what are twenty-year-olds now, like you were then, going to make of it?

---

* Lewis Grassic Gibbon, *A Scots Hairst: Essays & Short Stories*, ed. Ian S. Munro (London: Hutchinson & Co., 1967).

JK: Eh, I don't know. Depends on what their background is to some extent. I mean, if they're growing up, that English literature can contain stories … that working-class culture may be a part of literature, and that literature can be a function of ordinary life. Because normally it isn't. The things I like to write about and that I was interested in when I started to write, you know, like snooker, going to the dogs, standing in betting shops, getting drunk … these things weren't part of literature unless Russian, European, American. It didn't happen in English literature. In English literature the working class were always servants and you never saw anybody apart from, say, in Scottish literature there were ghillies. But they didn't live actual lives, they were all stereotypes. So I mean I hope—no, not I hope—the stories I write … I hope, eh well, in my opinion, they're about things that aren't usually found in literature. Or if they are, it's great, I'm certainly not jealous about it in any way. "My wee area … my wee … it's the largest area in Britain!"* But as far as literature is concerned it's dead, and has been for a long while. There may have been people who've done this without me noticing—Grassic Gibbon, Neil Gunn. I'm glad to hear that. It doesn't mean I'm going to rush away and read them, as a matter of fact, but I think it's smashing. One of the things that set me back on my heels was to discover I wasn't alone. You know the short story of mine, "Nice to be Nice" … I was in a pub with Anne Stevenson, an English poet—an American who writes English poetry—she assumed that I'd read Tom Leonard's poetry but I had never even heard of Tom Leonard and it was really good to get Tom's poetry, which was the *Six Glasgow Poems*. And I mean I stopped writing phonetic transcriptions of dialect after that because he was obviously much better than me and much more involved, in ways different to me. So that was great to meet someone like Tom. And to meet

---

* The old Strathclyde Region was the largest region in Britain at that time.

Alasdair Gray and people who were involved in different ways, who were treating literature as though—well, just assuming their own right to do it … Tom's poem where it's perfectly fine to be watching *Scotsport* on television and drinking a Carlsberg Special Brew, listening to Nielsen in the background.* That type of thing … that poetry being possible for anyone who has an ordinary upbringing is just impossible, because people who watch *Scotsport* don't fucking read literature. So that type of thing—American writers, eh, I can't think of any … although Sherwood Anderson I used to like a hell of a lot, stories like "I'm a Fool," great, I thought they were great. I remember reading that when I was twenty or something, maybe younger, and really being knocked out by it. A story about boy who goes away to work in a stables. At that time I still—well, I had just given up the idea of being a jockey. [*Laughter*] Those kind of stories. I remember reading *The Cincinnati Kid*, for instance, being knocked out by that, my teens, the idea that a story could be written about a poker player, I mean again this is totally … this doesn't happen in literature! I found that kind of stuff really good, and it led me on, say, to Kerouac and people.

DMcL: So was it after reading those people that you started to write your own stories then?

JK: Eh …

DMcL: Was it because of them that you started?

JK: I don't know really, except having time, I can't think of any motives or causes, except having time to do it and, eh

---

* *Scotsport* was a weekly television programme centred on Scottish football and Carlsberg Special Brew, a very strong lager; both would be seen as markers of "working classness." There were few things more abhorrent to Tom than the elitism that presumed great art was beyond anyone other than the European upper classes. In this poem of his a man is watching Scottish football on television with the volume turned down, while drinking strong booze and listening to the music of Carl Nielsen—probably the Fifth Symphony! I recall Tom's great delight about Nielsen's instruction for side drums during this to play as though to drown out the orchestra.

... I don't honestly know, because at one time I would have preferred to have been a painter, I thought I was going to be one.

DMcL: How did you get into the "other tradition"?

JK: Through mainly Tom Leonard, I suppose, because Tom was very influenced by Carlos Williams. I don't think I knew there was another tradition, not in English litera-ture—I came at it through European writers, apart from some Americans like Anderson and those great women short story writers, Katherine Anne Porter and people, who were tremendous, and doing something different with language that you don't usually get in English literature. I didn't know maybe it was another tradition, that was through Tom—Carlos Williams, who had consciously fought against, say, the Eliot influence, who was wanting to make the most important thing in literature the voice—something that Eliot was opposed to. For Eliot there is The Voice of Literature, right, and that voice isn't of course our voice, that voice is the voice of BBC Radio 3. And that would apply in America as well, and throughout the Commonwealth. Throughout the English-speaking world there is the ONE voice, The Voice of English Literature. It's not your voice, unless you've managed to go through uni and start to speak like you come from Hampstead Heath. Writers like Carlos Williams fought against that, so that language becomes involved with the ear. I mean the only people I ever read were prose writers; I never read poetry at all. I still don't read much. Do you read Charles Olson at all?

DMcL: No.

JK: An American poet who was one of the tutors at the Black Mountain thing, you know, with Creeley and all them. Olson, whose poetry I find difficult, but I like a lot of wee things he says in essays, talking about "the pulse," for instance, the rhythms of the writer being the pulse, and the way the blood goes through your head; that is your syntax, as a writer, poet or prose writer. That kind of thing is anathema to mainstream English literature but it is the only good side of literature. The rest is rubbish—mainstream writing, it's total rubbish. Just look at the stuff it's produced. Take the great contemporary English writers, say, of the last forty years. They're all fucking hopeless! I mean they're embarrassing, people like Golding and that, they're second-raters, Waugh and Graham Greene and all them, they're fucking second-rate. You'd be laughed out of world literature if you put forward the work of people like Philip Larkin; it's junk, total second-rate junk. And that is all that The Voice of English Literature has produced. Eliot's stuff, it's barren, totally barren; it gets rid of people and produces "culture," the voice of A Culture, the voice of The Culture.

DMcL: And like you were saying earlier, that is the voice that isn't relevant to most folk, the culture of the universities.

JK: Aye, but it props them up at the same time. Jobs for the Literary Boys. It plunders literature too. It's not only barren creatively, it plunders literature as a whole. I mean all the resources belong to the universities. I remember in my honours year writing an essay on that. The whole of the resources of literature belong to the university critics, more or less, the academics, all the books, the libraries, everything, even the stationery—every single thing belongs to people who either work for or within universities or else have degrees in English literature. They own literature, they own its resources, they own, for instance, Tipp-Ex. I mean I've got to take a job like this* to get anything. A writer like Alasdair Gray, people like that, they don't have typewriter ribbons! They don't have fucking paper, they don't have anything! I mean the ones that do have that—go into any university department, access to stationery—everything. None of them has anything to do with the actual thing, they're all fucking vultures! I remember Bernard MacLaverty and I going down to London for the launch of the first Firebird and the bus gets in early to Victoria, say about half five in the morning, so we're walking about and so then

---

* Creative Writer in Residence.

we went to the British Museum, and you're only allowed into that place ... you had to have a certificate or a letter from somebody from a university to say you were worthy of entering it. I mean you could have gone along there with six of your own books inside and said, "Look, I've got six books in this fucking place and I can't get in." And they'd say, "Oh sorry, you've got to have a letter from a university authority." They actually ... the same with Glasgow University Library, I mean that's probably the best library ... well, as far as I'm concerned there are things I'd love to get my hands on, manuscripts, books. But I can't, I can't get into that library, I mean you've got to be a university person to get into it—even to use their photocopiers. I mean, say if I finish a novel, right, what do you do with it? I mean it's going to cost you ten or twelve pence a page to get it photocopied. If you're in the university you can just get it done for nothing. The basic economics. It sounds petty to anyone who has access to stuff but it's everything to someone who doesn't. That is a class thing: people don't understand what to-be-without is. They don't actually understand things like, eh ... I did an interview on radio—which was hopeless—the other day. The guy interviewing me was a nice fellow, a nice middle-class fellow but he didn't understand certain basic facts of life; number one, that somebody like Hines doesn't have any choice. He's not on the broo because he's a masochist, or on the buses because he wants to be on the buses instead of being a university lecturer on twenty grand a year. The guy couldn't really appreciate—and this is one of those class things that people who are economically secure don't understand—what not-to-be-secure actually means. They don't understand what it is to be on the broo. They don't understand any of these things except as temporary phenomena. They don't realise that it can be a permanent situation from which there is no get-out, you know, your prospects won't improve next year so you can't borrow money on the strength of that, it's the strength of nothing, there's nothing ...

DMcL: You were attacking the uni there and the class thing within it, and I would join in with you on that, but I mean you've been through uni, I've been through uni, so aren't we being hypocritical or cutting our own throats or something?

JK: No, there's a very important distinction here. It's an important one to be aware of, otherwise you're in danger of giving literature away to those who think they own it already. It's like that kind of Stalinist Communist point of view that would say, "Fuck all art because it belongs to the bourgeoisie." Now usually the people who say that are themselves bourgeoisie anyway and it's a real kind of condescending thing to say, as if they don't want the proletariat to be contaminated by art, as if somehow it doesn't belong to them anyway, in the first place. So even though such people can be sort of well-intentioned, in effect what they're saying to the people who think they own literature, "Oh aye, it's yours." And it's important to realise that literature doesn't belong to any one class at all; literature belongs to mankind. It's a universal. One of the things that has been said about the way I use language is that it's a kind of attack on literature, or somehow a negation. But it isn't at all, it's just an attack on the values of the people who own it, who think they own it. So, for instance, when I use *fuck* all the time they think it's an attack on literature but it's not, it's an attack on their values. Literature doesn't belong to anybody. It's important to recognise that distinction. When I was at uni I was studying literature but that doesn't mean you become part of the establishment, only if you want it to be. Anybody who wants to study literature is entitled to do so; it doesn't belong to the universities, it doesn't belong to anybody. When you're going to university you're not going to study what it is to be one of the middle classes—not unless you want it to be. Part of the trouble is that when you go there you suddenly realise you're being forced into assuming certain attitudes and values. I mean they force you into saying that Eliot's a good writer, and if you really hate everything he stands for you want to be able to say, "If he is a good writer that means that writing is fucking rubbish. I don't want to study the concept of literature at all." I mean I spent four years trying to find an argument for that, really. Ultimately what I wanted to say was, "Right, okay, Eliot is a good writer but he's a bad artist." I wanted to get to some kind of position like that, you know. I wanted to be able to define things and say, "Right, what does it mean to say this is a good poem?" I don't accept the criteria of the Great Critic who can look at the words without looking at—well, I don't know, without looking at what? Can a fascist write a very good poem? Is it possible to say that Eliot is a great artist? Or someone like Evelyn Waugh: can he be a great artist, a great literary artist? To me the university system in this country, or the university system with reference to literature, hinges on that. And if it can't answer the question ... well, I don't think it can, not satisfactorily, because I think their answer is, "Yes, he is a great artist." I mean how the fuck can anyone who is a total fascist be a great artist! Eh? I don't want any part of that art. Well, I say I don't want any part of that because—the Stalinist line again, which is to deride it. I mean a lot of great upheavals, say "cultural revolutions," is because people have recognised that, or rather they've recognised that it's a logical extension of a certain kind of argument that art is rubbish. They've accepted that. So they go and burn books and burn paintings: "All artists are fucking bourgeois wankers," you know, and fair enough. But the trouble is in doing that they're giving art away. It's so stupid, a stupid thing to do. Because I'm involved in writing I don't want to do that, because I know that writing can be great and can be the most honest and truthful profession. I mean, I don't want to give Kafka away to people who live in Morningside or give Joyce away to Bearsden* ... Sherwood Anderson or Carlos Williams. They're welcome to

---

* Morningside, Edinburgh and Bearsden, near Glasgow, are used as examples of wealthier middle-class suburbs.

keep Eliot if they want. It's important to see that literature does not belong to a class, it does not belong to the universities. It doesn't belong to the schools either. Like Tom Leonard, when he was asked by the *Glasgow Herald* why he uses *fuck* in his poems, he said he uses *fuck* so his poems wouldn't be given out in classrooms. [*Laughter*]

DMcL: Aye, I remember thinking as I was reading *The Busconductor Hines* that this was the first time about, or one of those rare times, when there was a realistic amount of swearing in a piece of literature.

JK: Well, even the way that question was said, for instance, what makes you think it's swearing? You see when you use the term "swearing" it's a value. I don't accept that it is "swearing" at all, you see. How can you even talk about it? "The use of the four-letter word"? It's not satisfactory. You have to be specific. "Let's have a discussion on the use of *fuck* and *cunt* and *bastard* and *shite*." Because there's no way of really talking about them in any kind of objective sense. It's not swearing. It cannot be. There are so many different parts to the argument. I mean basically it's a linguistic argument, an argument about how language is used. Swearing is an act of verbal violence, and I'll give you an example, something I heard from a teacher who had these two wee lassies in the class and suddenly one turns round and batters the other one. And the teacher calls up the culprit and says, "Right you, what did you do that for?" And the wee lassie says, "Please miss, she called me a wee fucking *c-o-w*." Now the thing is that *cow* is the swear here, the act of verbal violence, it is not the *fucking*; *cow* is the swear word. So when you grasp that point … the argument has altered, words like *fuck*, *cunt*, *bastard* and *shite* are just part of language and have to be treated in the same way that the study of language treats other words. You can't separate them off and say, "Well, these are swear words, they're outwith the argument." They're not, they're part of it. So when we talk about language we include them, we talk about things like "verbal acts" … "actions." We have to be more systematic, be more serious about it. Obviously if I say, "Look at the sun, it's fucking beautiful," then I'm not swearing, obviously, I'm doing the exact opposite. So in that sense I object to taking part in a discussion that hinges on the use of such "swear words" in literature, because right away you've begged the question of what those words are, and you're involving me yet again in a value system that isn't your own to deny. I mean I deny this fucking thing but suddenly you find that you've affirmed it. The very fact you're talking about "swearing" means you've affirmed it. It's like if I'm a good athe- ist, which I am, and you say, "Do you deny God?" and I say, "Oh aye, I deny God," well, that's that whole business of how can you deny it without affirming it. You want to be able to use Russell's way out by saying, "I deny there is an object such that it ..." You know, the existential quantifier: "I deny the existence of a being such as that called 'God,'" or whatever the hell it is, there's that way of doing it and that's important.

Another thing in terms of class and four-letter words—I'll call them that—in literature ... say about fifteen years ago you had this stupid carry-on where you weren't allowed to use *fuck* unless you were talking about the act of screwing, you know, having sex. Now it was never ever used—I never ever heard it used—that way in my life until I started hearing Kenneth Tynan on television talking about D.H. Lawrence. I'd never ever heard that. In my experience nobody ever used the word *fuck* in that way. But suddenly people say, "I don't mind you using the word *fuck* as long as you use it properly," which is an absurd way to talk about language altogether. It's almost the type of thing someone involved in Scottish literature would say. It's totally absurd, and totally authoritarian. But that became the way of talking about "swear words," you know, a real class thing.

With four-letter words the same applies as with any words, the same rule any writer has to abide by: "Don't repeat yourself unless you can get away with it." And if you're using the word *fuck*, which most people would, three times in each sentence, you can only do it if you do it so well that nobody notices. The same applies to the word *and* or the word *wall*: you can't use the word *wall* in successive sentences unless you want the second one to be very emphatic; you must have a reason for doing it. The same applies to "four-letter" words. Eh … aye.

DMcL: Anyway, I just thought I'd mention that I thought you had the four-letter word proportion about right, for the first time.

JK: I don't think it is usual to meet books written from a working-class experience that is total; total in the sense that the character can be at the same time an intellectual and still be a bona fide member of the working class, somebody who is working on the buses and the possibility of university doesn't arise. In fact for Hines maybe it has and he's rejected it on another level. Remember that his pal the bus driver is wanting to get his "Highers" and there's the possibility that he might manage to do that but the character Hines won't—there is no possibility of him doing that. It's still possible to be an intellectual and, say, to read black Penguins, the Classic Series, and remain a bus conductor. That is possible. It makes life total. It means that his mind … there are no pockets of it within our culture that haven't been opened. You can't work round the character because it's written from the inside, and written also from within our culture. Usually it's self-conscious but this is not self-conscious in that sense; that form of irony here doesn't exist. Usually you get a form of irony between the writer and the reader; the working-classness of the character is revealed ironically.

DMcL: Have you got anything planned to go on to next?

JK: Aye, there's a long … I've started a … I kind of stopped writing for ages because, well, I chucked smoking last June and find it impossible, well, almost impossible …

DMcL: What, to write without smoking?

JK: No, to exist without smoking. [*Laughter*]

DMcL: How long had you been writing *Hines* for?

JK: I started it years ago. I keep finding old versions about the place. When we moved house I found versions dating way back. I did the bulk of it one time I stopped smoking. I had to start smoking again to finish it! This long thing I'm involved in just now, it's difficult because I need to be able to sustain it. So I need to work on it at all hours, through the night, whatever, work and sleep; I can't be bothered doing this job but I have to for the cash. When you've no money what it means is you've no money. Sorry, I'm in the middle of it, it's difficult. I've finished page 43 plus there's another twenty or thirty early ones that can be incorporated. So that would take it up to about eighty pages, and there's no sign of it stopping. And I'm enjoying it. There won't be a single *fuck* in it. Well, I'm saying that, which maybe I shouldn't because you're cutting off possibilities. At this moment it seems unlikely because it's very ornate language I'm using. I'm trying to handle a universal situation; the trouble is the present keeps bursting in. It's vaguely a fantasy.* It's about . . . well, it's trying to do a kind of university thing, because I felt I should do that.

DMcL: Just to show you could?

JK: No, I think it's important to use that experience, and if I don't I'm falling into the trap of what I was criticising other writers for: thinking somehow the university experience isn't mine or isn't part of the culture as a whole, but is only a part of middle- and upper-class culture. You should be able to go to university and still be a member of the "working class," in quotes, if you want to be. In a sense that's like literature: all learning should be available to anybody, you shouldn't necessarily have to come out of there getting one of those fifteen- or twenty-thousand-pound-a-year jobs for the rest of your life, unless you want to do that. It's important to be able to write about university without being coy, being able to use it as an

---

* The earliest attempts at what finally became *Translated Accounts*. The title in progress back in the 1980s was *Coagmentum*.

assumption of a way of existence, so I quite fancy doing it, I quite fancy the types of irony I'll be working in; being able to make some heavy statements, in a way. The thing that comes immediately to mind is Swift, getting into the type of irony he would use in *A Modest Proposal*. I would like to get into that way of seeing the world.

Part 2: July 1985, Cumbernauld*

DMcL: *A Chancer* is very different from *The Busconductor Hines*, isn't it?

JK: Aye, aye. Well, it's early work. Part of the problem in writing it was writing it as the thirty-eight-year-old Kelman, whereas I began writing it when I was your age,† and it's diffi-cult because of what you know and the sort of thing you're aware of being able to do. So you can't get as excited in it and it becomes very difficult to try and be wholehearted, you're wanting to give him a kick all the time, the character, and you can't do it. You can't even get really intellectually involved with him, it's not possible. So trying to retain faith with it as a work is difficult, trying to capture the verve and the sparkle and the spirit of it, occasionally managing it but in a slightly distanced way, say towards the end, certain things that would give me satisfaction now as individual chapters which I could handle now but not back then. Such as the boy playing football, right, when he's actually having to play football, which is difficult to do—sport's always difficult—and there's this big winger Tammas is up against. When I was first writing the novel I couldn't handle that, I had to kind of get by in some way, which is slightly underhand but perfectly permissible in writing. A chapter ends with a man heading off to a street battle involving his trade union. Then the next chapter begins, "When he came

---

* Kelman and family were living in Cumbernauld from 1984 to '86, then returned to Glasgow.

† Duncan was twenty-one years old during the 1985 section of the inter-view. He edited *A Chancer* at the age of nineteen.

back ..." and you think, "Fuck, what happened with the amazing bit in between!" The sort of thing Dickens would never do, right, he would have to go and write the whole section. There's always bits you can skip over as an artist. In *A Chancer* I would have skipped over some of those bits earlier on—I did skip over them; Tammas playing football was one of them.

DMcL: In *Hines* I thought the best bits were all the internal workings in his head. In *A Chancer* it was the sort of set-pieces, like the confrontation with the bobbies or else just at the exact middle when for one of the first times Kirsty and Vi and Tammas walk together down to the pond, trying to spot the rats; and also maybe the best bit of all was the bit when Tammas goes to visit Cathy when Vi isn't in and there's the "holding of hands" bit, the "Is something going to happen here?" bit. I mean, is that the kind of thing you're talking about?

JK: I never write "set-pieces" and object to the use of the term in relation to my work. When you are involved in a novel there are always problems to solve, technical problems. In *Hines* you have different ones to do with transitions within the narrative, moving from third party to first, and back again; these things are difficult and because of that it's exciting—even apart from the story where you want to find out what your character does. In early versions of *The Busconductor Hines*, for instance, the confrontation with the union doesn't happen. He chucks the job and goes on the broo. But it didn't work and I had to take it all back out. So the story drives you on but the technical stuff is equally important. It draws you to the desk. "How the hell do I get by that ... how do I get through this ... maybe I'll have to write it all out ..." And so on, but it can be really good and you see that was missing to a big extent in *A Chancer* because I'd got over these problems a while ago. The problem then in *A Chancer* was staying absolutely concrete, to do nothing that was abstract, nothing that was internal; there are a couple of internal sections in it but they're technically irrelevant, or redundant: they don't have to be there.

DMcL: A few questions present themselves. For one thing *Hines* was obviously a very internal book, the technical problems were to do with internal things, whereas in this one the technical things were to keep it all external. So why did you do two completely different things?

JK: Where?

DMcL: Well, why was one completely internal and one completely external, or nearly?

JK: Fair enough. A lot that goes on with the character Hines is intellectual, intellectual exploration, in a sense, to do with ideas. Hines is involved in ideas and normally ideas are a function of conversation. The sort of conversation that happens at uni and can happen elsewhere, but not to the same extent. If you're working in an ordinary job, say as a bus conductor, you can get these conversations but they happen in a different way; you can't take it for granted this is a part of life; there's wee games and rituals that go on, like Jeff Torrington writes about in "The Last Shift." That type of thing, with the Walt Whitman book—Jeff and I discussed this often, where you're a closet reader, if you come out the closet in a job like that you're not gay, although you might be, but what you are is A Reader of Penguins, modern classics. Somebody might spot a book in your pocket, "Hey what's that? Is that the *Lives of the Saints* sticking out your pocket! Aye! Oh…" And then you start discussing Lindisfarne or something. [*Laughter*] Usually that's a dialogue. In *Hines* there's the sense that it happens between him and his pal, Reilly, although it never quite does. Whereas in *A Chancer* that is not really possible…

DMcL: Well, I don't know, he does seem to read quite a lot.

JK: He reads all the time; he's always got a book on the go. But there's no dialogue; he's not got anybody really to talk to among his pals—the football player is the likeliest. When I was his age there was maybe one guy I could speak to about writing but it wouldn't have been on because there was other things to talk about, other things were central: making money, finding a job, hitting various places, you know, because at that age from seventeen through till I got married I was doing the jobs and stuff my characters do in *An Old Pub Near the Angel*, working down in England or whatever. How to get by, that was the main thing. But when you're at uni ideas are central; ideas to do with philosophy and politics. It only happens when you've a degree of security—a fixed abode, you can sit around and chat. In temporary jobs, temporary accommodation, you don't have the time, don't have the space and it's difficult writing about that type of internal life, it really is, you can't do it within an ordinary narrative voice. I can't do it without an amazing irony, because the type of things you're taking for granted are things to do with class.

The problems Jeff Torrington has had trying to write are the same that I've had, exactly the same. Most other writers don't recognise them as problems, they don't realise the difficulties you have talking about art. I would say there are about eight guys I've met in all the jobs I've had whom I could talk to in that way. Like Jeff—you were talking about Jeff talking about Hegel—one guy I knew lived up the stair from me and Marie. It was just after we came back to Glasgow—Frank McGoohan. Frank and I got drunk a lot. Some guys who drink too much are readers because when they're skint they have to do something. Frank read when he wasn't drinking and spoke about it. He was a good bit older than me but he was really involved in literature, he used to make good comments on Keats and folk. But there isn't too many like this, the type of guy like Owen in *The Ragged-Trousered Philanthropists* who just takes it for granted the right to that kind of intellectual questioning. You see, if you're trying to write a character like that, you can't do it, not from the outside; you end up with a pile of sociological explanations of "How is it possible for someone who left school at fifteen and works as a general labourer able to discuss Hegel?" It's a logical absurdity in mainstream English literature, the existence of a guy like that; it just isn't possible. But it happens in other cultures, like for instance, Yiddish, the teachings there, everything about the Jewish religion, all the stories, it's all part of the literature. If you're a member of that religion then you're a member of that culture—that great sweep—you're privy to it. It just doesn't happen in our culture. Even the servants in theirs, in Yiddish culture—maybe this is sentimental or something and just shows a lack of knowledge—but the servants and the peasantry all seem to know the great writers and scholars. It's assumed that they'll know about them and be able to talk about them in the same way as somebody who is really wealthy. Learning and culture isn't just a function of wealth and the economic power of the top members of that society.

Even taking it as a general point in our culture, it's always assumed that people low down the economic scale are not involved in art and have no awareness of philosophy, no interest in the history of ideas. Those things are supposed to not be a part of their culture. Now, to try to write a novel within an ordinary working-class framework—and to write it as a whole person, i.e., to do what all writers do, think about stuff, think about ideas, discuss ideas—you're back to having to give explanations as to why it's even possible for you to think in that way about these things. So either you have to use enormous, very deeply structured ironies, or else it's not really possible. I don't see how it is. You have to find some way round it. That's how it was for me anyway.

DMcL: Do you mean if you're going to write a novel about the working class and you want to show that you're writing it from the inside, you have to make the person you're writing about capable of having these ideas and reading books and things to prove that you are like him in that you are capable of writing a book?

JK: No, that comes afterwards. I think it's valid to think that but to me that's not a writer's question. Or rather, it can be a writer's question. But it shouldn't be. It's a critic's question, in a sense, because it is something that is asked after the event. No, it's not that, it's to try and make an authentic ordinary voice—an authentic member of the working class. That story of Jeff Torrington, "The Last Shift," some of mine are similar: when you read it you just naturally assume that you can talk to the central character on any subject under the sun. If you want to ask him about Hegel and he doesn't know anything about Hegel it doesn't mean Hegel has never been available, it just means they haven't read him. That type of thing, that part of culture, of high culture, is available, part of their own culture and not something that is cut off like an a priori thing. The best analogies would probably be with black writers, the kind of jump that gets made by white people first coming upon black writers; the shock they get to realise that these black writers are totally aware of what they're aware, that their background includes, say, Nietzsche, and what they regard as the "ordinary" intellectual background, "ordinary" meaning traditional European, high European. So that wee shock, "Christ, he knows the same as me," and maybe thinks about it the same way, that black writer in Africa is the same as this white working-class writer in Britain.

DMcL: But you might read this black writer and see that the writer has read the same as you but the person he's writing about hasn't necessarily read the same as you.

JK: I'm not talking about that. I'm talking about the subject, the characters, not the actual writer. One of the things that goes on in English literature is the wee dialogue between author and reader about character. All the wee signals and codes. You were talking earlier about the Aberdeen writer William Alexander, where you have a transcription of dialect in the dialogue, done in a phonetic style, and the narrative is done in ordinary Standard English, right? Now that, of course, is a game going on between writer and reader; "reader" and "writer" are the same, they have a shared background, they speak in the same "voice" as the narrative, unlike these fucking natives who talk in phonetics. English literature is based on that relationship between writer and reader and the person in the middle is the character. In the average novel written about a working-class character the assumption is that the character doesn't know as much as the writer and the reader. The character in phonetics is only ever found in dialogue and is never intellectually aware, never a thinking presence, never ever found in narrative except when described from the outside; they don't have any "thought process." Maybe they don't have one!

This is why so many working-class writers seem to fail so often—apart from the fact they're boring—you can't even ask, "Is there anything I can see here? Anything I'm not seeing?" All you have is a writer who has sold out. That's their "entire" culture, they've dumped the lot in the dialogue—"entire" is minus the "intellectual" of course, which is only ever found in the narrative. There's no point even looking at their work because the depth of the sell-out is just so great. There's nothing.

DMcL: Let's talk about the opening sentence of *Hines*—in particular about its punctuation. You know what I'm talking about—the fact that it's two sentences separated by a comma.

JK: I know that opening sentence of *Hines* quite well. I spent a lot of time on it. You cannot make it a semi-colon; you can't make it a colon: it's got to be a comma. The principal part of that sentence is the first one, which is "Hines jumped up." There's no cause or effect. It's a picture of a fact. The fact is: somebody has jumped up. It begins the whole thing, the character jumps up, stands to attention. There is this movement going on. Then you start the analysis, if you want to do that, "Why did he jump up?" It so happens he jumps up because his wife is about to lift over a pot of boiling water—an inadequate pot. That is the spark of life. In terms of drama that is all that is necessary, nothing else. It can't be a semi-colon because that puts too much emphasis in it, you know, it's got to be something that's so "everyday."

I remember Alasdair Gray saying about reading it the first time and finding it horrendous and hair-raising, that opening section, whether it would all come to pass okay, it was terrible; if this girl was actually going to fill the bath without scalding herself. I don't even think I could read it like that. But it's exactly the kind of thing I was after, that drama, the drama of that moment, from something that is so mundane, so "everyday." It's like a factory story, something people do every day of the week, it's just part of life. But somebody who's not involved suddenly sees it and, "Christ, is this what this person does every week for £45?" Like say a worker at the coal-face who risks the kind of death that most people would regard as an amazing nightmare. But that's what they do. Part of their job is to take the sort of risks that nobody would take for less than say fifty grand if they were middle class—my one-page story, "Acid," as a for-instance. I mean in one job I nearly lost my hand—a factory in Manchester. I've still got the scar to prove it, blah blah. But it can be something you do every day in your working life, it's just part of the job. It's very very hard to get the drama of that, because the whole thing seems to be a boring way of living, and it is, very very boring. Somebody watching on the outside might go, "Oh Christ, how on earth can they keep doing that, day in day out, on and on and on?"

DMcL: Like in the copper rolling-mill in *A Chancer*?

JK: Aye, that kind of idea, although there's more leeway in that. The opening to *Hines* is similar. There's no evaluation being made. It's just trying to set out a thing at its very basic, its most basic. When you've got the thing at its "most basic" that is the fact. In setting out the fact you have set out the danger because the danger is inherent within the fact, I mean the fact is itself hair-raising. If you can put forward that fact then you put forward the hair-raisingness of the experience, which is why I go after all these wee affects in *A Chancer*, such as no abstractions, keep everything concrete. It's only through the concrete you get the terror, you know—Carlos Williams too. Just state the thing, don't think in terms of ideas, if you get the thing properly then you've got it, and you'll have the horror. You don't have to say, "This is horrible." Just state it properly and it's there. That's what Kafka does. Kafka is the first person to do that. Nobody had done that before him. Or since! [*Laughter*] I know, for instance, that what I do in *Hines* Joyce does not do in *Ulysses*, but I really do think he would like to have done that. [*Laughter*] Honestly, I mean that. I'm talking about the transition, just in a technical sense. That does not mean I think I am "better" than Joyce or anything like that. I'm writing seventy years after him for a start, and he's been there before me. I'm talking about that particular transition from the world outside to the world inside—Zola going through Robbe-Grillet, straight concreteness, there's only facts being stated, no such thing as a value judgment. Objective reality. Going from there into an "I-voice." James Joyce would have loved to do that. I'm not kidding you. I think the person who comes closest is Alasdair in *Lanark*. That's why it starts off in the "fourth book," it's to do with the same problem. Beckett has it as well. I can only say it with too much shorthand here and it would just sound rubbish. But it's to do with "time." I think, for instance, that *Ulysses* is too long and it wouldn't have been as long if Joyce had had certain things at his disposal, certain technical movements, certain ways of working narrative.

DMcL: People like Anthony Burgess say that Joyce is the greatest master of English prose, or had the greatest technical control over English ever …

JK: The important thing is to have that mastery over prose. It's nothing to do with "English." Kafka was doing things that Joyce couldn't do. Kafka was doing things that Joyce was just not capable of doing. *The Castle* is far superior in terms of the sort of possibilities that are contained within any work.

The problem is to make the action happen while you're talking, where there is no space between telling the story and the story itself. It's to be able to say, "Jack struck the axe into Jill's head," in such a way that there's no past tense, and where Jill is "I." The problem is to get it to the act without any distancing, with no narrator, a straightforward statement as an enactment of the scene itself. One of the wee ways of getting to that is through the "I-voice," and that's been happening for two hundred years, it's what Goethe was trying in *Young Werther*. The person writing the story goes, "I walk through the forest and, aahh, Jack strikes the axe in my skull!" So the first thing you ask is, "Well, how did you write it down, if there's an axe in your head? Was that your dying breath?" That's a genuine problem in the sense that people have to tackle it. James Hogg has to tackle it—Wringhim,* I mean what happens there? Because that is the "I-voice," right, and you find the dead guy has written it all down and buried it at the crossroads or wherever, and somebody discovers it—the "editor." Lermontov uses it. Goethe does it in *Werther*. Goethe's the oldest guy I know who does it. He has a wee preface saying something like, "The following story was found by me, dear reader, I am the editor. And here now is a tale of a poor wretch ..." That allows his "I-voice" character to die, to commit suicide, to go mad; whatever! So you obtain that great immediacy. "Myself and the duke were fencing till suddenly he thrusts his sword"

end of story, the "I-voice" stops in mid-sentence.

Well, that's never happened to my knowledge but you get the point: you've achieved that immediacy. That's the goal. That's what leads Joyce into *Finnegans Wake*. Honestly, there's nothing else apart from that; to obliterate the narrator, get rid of the artist, so all that's left is the story, that's the thing.

---

* In Hogg's *The Private Memoirs and Confessions of a Justified Sinner*.

4

1989

Interview by Kirsty McNeill

This interview by Kirsty McNeill was conducted in London on February 20, 1989, the day of publication of *A Disaffection*. It originally appeared in *Chapman*, and a shortened version of the interview was used by the *Guardian* newspaper.

Kirsty McNeill: Is Patrick Doyle based on someone you know? Why a teacher?

James Kelman: It had to be someone committed in a way that would presuppose a working-class or lower-middle-class background; someone who also thought there was a possibility of change from within the system—a mainstream socialist. I've never believed in that. I've voted maybe twice or three times since I turned twenty-one.

KMcN: You don't believe change is possible from within?

JK: It isn't possible—not a case of "I don't believe"—it's not possible. The big American corporations and multinationals would never allow it, they control most of everything. If Kinnock was not a liar he wouldn't be there: someone else would be there who was a liar. It's a long while since socialists had any real say or power. In the '50s the CIA destabilised the Labour Party anyway. No, there is no possibility of socialist change. Doyle is like a lot of people who come through university without any real experience of working-class jobs. They think—and the educational process teaches them to think—that they can change the system from within. I think Doyle has only become aware of his own knowledge of the futility of things quite recently. He's led a fairly normal existence in the working-class-boy-goes-to-uni routine. I think his elder brother and sister-in-law are much more worldly than he is.

KMcN: Do you identify with Patrick Doyle in any way?

JK: In certain respects; but there again, I feel that with nearly all my work. I don't think there is anything in it which is expressly myself. I'm forty-two and that character is twenty-nine. For me there are possibilities that there aren't for Doyle. My interests are different from his. It would also be nice if this was said, as far as politics are concerned, that my own sympathies are quite a way to the left of Doyle's, libertarian socialist, anarchist—what the Labour Party would nowadays refer to as "loony." I regard Doyle as a fairly naive character—which perhaps I am but I certainly don't feel. But I don't suppose he does either.

KMcN: Your use of narrative voice with Doyle seems similar to *The Busconductor Hines*.

JK: I thought that initially but don't think that now. Formally I think this novel is a progression.

KMcN: In what ways would you distinguish the two?

JK: *Hines* is quite a difficult thing. I feel quite guarded about that actually. I think that things go on in *Hines* that are formally quite big and hadn't been done before; transitions of narrative. One of the things you do as an artist is find formal ways out of problems. I don't know writers who have done it in that way before, which doesn't mean it hasn't happened before; it might have, but I've never come upon it.

A Disaffection is a different set of problems. In a sense Doyle's consciousness is much easier because it can *assume* a certain further educational level, so the possibility of Doyle knowing what the writer knows can be taken for granted whereas it can't in *Hines* because that character is just an ordinary working-class person without a further education. In *Hines* I had to take out references, say to Dostoevsky— Camus is implicitly mentioned, implicitly—I had to take out those references because it didn't seem to be correct structurally. But only structurally. Most critics and commentators probably would think the reason is the guy's a bus conductor, and for me to have made such references would have been quite outlandish. That also explains why the formal things haven't been noticed in the novel, because the central character works at an ordinary, so-called unskilled, labouring job—very few contemporary critics ever conceive that a story about a bus conductor could be of formal interest to them. It becomes easier when they deal with a character like Doyle because he's a teacher and a professional type of person like themselves and therefore *bound* to know Camus, *bound* to know Dostoevsky. The usual elitism.

KMcN: Do you think that Doyle, as an instrument of control, feels impotent—beat in fact?

JK: I think he feels impotent but I don't think he feels beat. Maybe to see it like that would be to risk sentimentalising the character. I do think he's impotent, right, and I do think he's beat; but that isn't to say that that's what he feels himself. Again, it's paradigmatic of people doing jobs like in the social services, people who would regard themselves as left-wing: I regard this as a naive position to be in, that they should even be cynical or sardonic or something like that. And the idea people should ever be disillusioned by Thatcher I find kind of farcical. So I'm not like Doyle at all, personally, I've never been a teacher, I've never done anything like that. I went to university but left without getting a degree. (I don't actually know the situation there, it's quite a complicated carry-on.) I went for purely economic reasons: I was barred off the broo, you know, and I couldn't get any DHSS, so I just went for straight economics. I was twenty-nine. I went to Strathclyde who were then open to taking a writer who was published without "qualifications," whereas I doubt if Glasgow would have done it; but nor do I think Strathclyde would do it at the present time.

KMcN: You wrote an essay about the resources of litera- ture belonging to the universities; do you feel strongly about reclaiming this right?

JK: Yeah, that's the ultimate thing, that's the most concrete thing of all for an artist. If I say to people who operate within the English departments of the education system—and I mean critics and many actual writers as well as ordinary lecturers and teachers—"you have photocopying facilities and I don't, that's how much you are in control in this society; you are and I'm not," they think it's a kind of metaphor I'm giving them. Everything costs the writer money. That's the reality. But these people who get employed in departments of literature and English studies get access to all the resources and materials in the creation of literature—books, pencils, paper, typewriters, Tipp-Ex, word-processors etc.

Artists who are involved in dissent usually get nothing. That's the way it should be anyway, although people who are part of the establishment get surprised by that, they don't think it's a problem, not a real problem, an aesthetic one. The way I would dwell on that economic reality, they'd wonder about it and think I was being perverse or something. In a sense that sums up the political and economic state of our society. I mean if I say people are starving in Drumchapel or Castlemilk or Easterhouse or Bow or Brixton or Camden Town or someplace like that, they think you are making a "political" point—there's no reality behind it. The *fact* is that just now people in Britain are being killed in the name of society. That's concrete, that's the reality. Look at infant mortality rates in the last ten years. And poverty, nearly a million people in the Strathclyde region alone. Then the way official government policy gets transformed; the racism of the immigration laws into brutalised attacks on families, finally into murder—someone was murdered in Edinburgh four weeks ago, a racial murder. People are dying because of the politics of our society. Everywhere I go in London I'm confronted by Volvos, Mercedes and BMWs and Rolls-Royces—all parked on one street. The wealth down here, the price of a meal, and how much it costs for a jacket, say— compared to other parts of Britain just now, it's an obscenity.

KMcN: I was going to talk about the spotlight that will come on Glasgow next year with the 1990 European City of Culture. Tom Leonard has said it is just a lot of Sunday supplement nonsense consisting of a bit of sandblasting in the city centre while the unemployed underclasses remain out of sight in vast housing estates on the outskirts of the city.

JK: Yes, it's really quite obscene, it's so bad what's going on—it's almost like a paradigm of what's happening within mainstream socialism. The whole hype to do with the City of Culture comes from Glasgow District Council, i.e., establishment Labour Party. Now, Saatchi and Saatchi are doing the publicity and Rupert Murdoch is doing the printing, right? I mean it's even beyond saying, "This is disgusting," it's just sick. To argue that we should take the City of Culture seriously you have to be enmeshed in that particular value system. I don't want to be involved even in negating it if I can help it.

KMcN: You'll probably still be lumped in with it all, though.

JK: Only by implication. I've never been invited anywhere with any official connection to do with Glasgow since I've been published, never.

KMcN: Perhaps the acknowledgment will come now?

JK: If the invitations come the case will be I'll have to refuse them where before I never had the possibility.

Good art is usually dissent. I want to be involved in creating good art. One of the things that goes on with something like the City of Culture is the establishment—i.e., the right wing— saying to the yuppies and big business in general, "Don't worry about terrorism in our place, we can contain it." (And a crucial aspect of terrorism, in a sense, is subversion, is art.) "And we've negated art. Don't worry about art, there isn't any of it in Glasgow. Whatever there is we've bought it."

KMcN: And rendered it impotent.

JK: Yeah. They're saying, "It's like London here, you can go and parade your wealth and you don't have to worry about being stabbed."

KMcN: Are you in danger of being labelled a regional writer?

JK: I suppose so, yes, but you can get labelled in any way at all. I can't stop myself being labelled. It's like being labelled alongside Beckett: Beckett is major and I don't feel major at all. But I don't have any control over that sort of thing. I see myself very much as part of a tradition, and the idea of being regarded as an "original" I actually find embarrassing. I'm only involved in tradition, through prose, maybe through Scotland, in a way that people are perhaps not used to. But it's been going on for 120, 140 years, since, say, James Hogg—earlier. I'm doing it in a way they can maybe now relate to and so they say, "Oh Christ, this is new." It's not new at all, just that they've now discovered it.

One of the things the establishment always does is isolate voices of dissent and make them specific—unique if possible. It's easy to dispense with dissent if you can say there's "him" in prose and "him" in poetry and that sums up Britain just now. As soon as you say there's him, him and her there, and that guy here and that woman over there, and there's all these other writers in Africa, and then you've got Ireland, the Caribbean— suddenly there's this kind of mass dissent going on, and that becomes something dangerous, something that the establishment won't want people to relate to and go, "Christ, you're doing the same as me." Suddenly there's a movement going on. It's fine when it's all these disparate voices; you can contain that. The first thing to do with dissent is say, "You're on your own, you're a phenomenon." I'm not a phenomenon at all: I'm just a part of what's been happening in prose for a long long while, but the literary establishment of Britain has chosen not to notice—it's been a selection process—they've said, "We don't want this to be read. As far as we are concerned literature is to be T.S. Eliot, in prose Henry James, Evelyn Waugh etc.; in contemporary terms it's Ian McEwan, Martin Amis, William Boyd, Graham Swift, Salman Rushdie"—although for Rushdie this is maybe becoming a bit problematic.

KMcN: You've stated that you're trying to obliterate the narrator, to get rid of the narrative voice.

JK: Not every narrative voice, just the standard third-party one, the one that most people don't think of as a "voice" at all—except maybe the voice of God—and they take for granted that it is unbiased and objective. But it's no such thing. Getting rid of that standard third-party narrative voice is getting rid of a whole value system. You have to start examining every term. The example I would use is the term *beautiful*, or *pretty*, or *handsome*, or *ugly*. There is no possibility of using such a term in my work, not in the standard narrative, it's not a possibility. I can't even say *fat*, or *thin*, because to do that would be to assume a whole value system. None of my work will have any of that it in it whatsoever. This is an extreme example of the kind of formal problems you might have to get through; in a way to begin a story from nothing. In a sense I think the jump is similar to the *nouveau roman*, a similar type of thing, trying for a value-free text, total objectivity. Let's just go for the factual reality here. Any colouring that's going on to try and get rid of. Whether it's from a feminist point, a heterosexual male point, a middle-class point, any point at all. Get rid of it. So that nobody else is going to be oppressed or colonized by it. And that's what I was trying to do in *A Chancer*, to get something that was "Let me state a fact here." So nobody can say that's your opinion because you're working class or middle class. It has to be something that is so cold, so straight black and white, that no one can deny it as *fact*. So, in a sense, getting rid of that standard narrative voice is trying to get down to that level of pure objectivity. This is *the* reality here, within this culture. Facticity, or something like that.

KMcN: You also spoke of a "voice" common to "major" English writers of the last forty years or so—Golding, Waugh, Greene and the rest.

JK: They all use that standard narrative, they've all assumed that value system, they're all part of it. Maybe Golding has been aware of the difficulty, maybe early on he knew it as a formal problem he had to get over, I don't know, I've never found his work interesting enough to get to grips with. But none of them seems to have bothered working out that this "third-party voice" they use to tell their stories is totally biased and elitist, economically secure, eats good food and plenty of it, is upper-middle-class paternalist. It's their own view of the world anyway, they all hold it in common. And that's the main reason they've never worked it out in their writing, because they all share the same cultural experience, they never seem to have been alienated by literature at any time in their lives— not even as writers. So if they say, "There's a handsome man walking down the road," then everybody else in mainstream English literary circles knows precisely what they're talking about because everybody knows what "a handsome man" is. It's absolute junk. Take as an example "There is a big man." In this hotel here, a big man is seven feet tall. So what is a small man? Six feet? Now if you lived where I live in Glasgow you can maybe get called "big yin" and you might only be five feet nine inches tall, like Hines. So what does "a small man walking down the road" actually mean if it's coming in the traditional third-party voice of English narrative prose, especially when you get a context and you discover the guy's nearly six feet high? You have to start asking about the value system not only of the actual author but of the whole tradition of narrative prose itself. And then see if you're alienated or not.

KMcN: Does the traditional working-class novel fare any better in this respect, the likes of Sillitoe or John Braine?

JK: John Braine you can't take seriously. Alan Sillitoe is probably a trier. John Braine probably can't remember when he sold out he sold out so long ago, you know, he's like Kingsley Amis or something, his work's just junk basically. I doubt if Sillitoe's ever worked things out about narrative, the existential in literature and art, I doubt if he knows what it really is, and it's importance politically. You can't get to it through English or Scottish literature alone, you have to move through different cultures, other traditions maybe—you've got to really appreciate the significance of Gogol's "Overcoat" for a start.

KMcN: It's very much a man's world in your work. One critic has remarked that women are the soft, rounded characters in a harsh world. Is that how you see women's roles?

JK: I really don't know. Some of the best, most genuine criticism I get is from women. I find the relationships between men and women in the novels quite solid. They're structural in the sense that everything develops from them. I don't even think it's depressing or pessimistic that the male or female world should be like that. I do tend to think that's the way they are, but sometimes I think that's where the strength lies. But I don't feel guilty that certain things aren't happening in my work. I'm only forty-two and I've still got a long way to go.

KMcN: Who do you think is breaking ground as far as feminist literature is concerned?

JK: Kathy Acker is doing stuff, because she's getting attacked by everybody. Anyone who's getting attacked like that must be doing something right. She's been physically abused in the streets and her response to that—without being presumptuous—is "Why not? I'm abusing them." These people know her writing is a violation, I mean, literally, a physical assault, because some people read that work and are nauseated, an actual physiological change occurs in their system.

KMcN: And that makes the writing very potent.

JK: Well, suddenly it's art, because that's what art is— though not just through the physical maybe; it has to be more than that. I was interviewed recently and the person doing it was wanting to take it for granted that (and I'll here use a quotation by Auden) "writing doesn't essentially change things." What absolute junk. This was just about a week ago, during all those threats against Rushdie. And in different parts of the world right now writers are being jailed, tortured and occasionally murdered. This attitude is that of upper-middle-class, Anglo-American liberalism. When somebody raises that old chestnut you've got to ask, with Chomsky, how come you are at liberty to say what you've just said in the face of such overwhelming evidence against the position, what is your ideological stance, your relation to the people in power in society, and so on. That attitude puts across the assumption that this is the way *all* literature has to be, excluding the possibility that art and literature might not just be the property of that one wee drawing-room group, that it might be part of the political struggle out there on the streets. Maybe that's it: they don't think of literature as being on the streets.

KMcN: Maybe ten years of Thatcherism has lulled people into a sense of impotence regarding change, into apathy and pessimism.

JK: I don't think that's a tenable position. People do continually assert that kind of thing but it's similar to the last point. The media commentators who say, "Nothing seems to change," are above all hoping that nothing will change; they are trying to nurture a mass myopia, just like the refusal to see what's going on in the world—US terrorism in Central and South America, Asia, Africa, the Middle East. It's this refusal to see things—to bear witness to things—that are happening. And it's in favour of most of the liberal media people to say, not so much that these things are not happening, as that *if* they are then they cannot really be stopped, that we are powerless in the face of such realities; if they cannot change it's best to think they cannot happen—there must be a variety of ways of putting it, it's very sophisticated, all these ways of having bad faith. Essentially, it's ways of being in bad faith.

KMcN: Sue Wiseman once wrote that the question of Who Reads Novels, particularly experimental novels, is crucial. Does readership concern you?

JK: I don't agree with Sue on all of that point. To me the very existence of a novel like *The Busconductor Hines* is like introducing a person to a critic and asking the critic to agree that the existence of this person is a possibility. And if it is a possibility then all of their critical arguments about readership go out the window, they are redundant. As far as I am concerned Hines is a general, he isn't specific. Working-class intellectuals are simply a fact. That's the way things are. Once people from the professional classes are prepared to accept that fact then they will have begun examining what we mean by "intellectual" anyway. I mean, I would say that intellectuals read my work, which might seem an elitist point of some sort, but I don't think it is. People in the working class read my work, and in the middle class, and in the upper middle class, and also maybe in the upper class as well, I don't know. Reading books has got nothing to do with class. Neither does writing them. It's not even to do with educational attainment. There's something more at work than that. I left school at fifteen and was a published writer three years before I went to uni. Once again you've got to start asking why this kind of elitist mythology is still getting shoved down our throats. All you have to do to dispute the point is to go to the more shadowy reaches of the lower shelves of public libraries and look. But why are we still fighting this battle even now? In 1792 there was *Black Dwarf*—a libertarian socialist magazine—getting passed between say London and Glasgow. It was being read by weavers, lawyers, fucking labourers, blacksmiths, masons. Why are we still having to argue that the literate class isn't logically separate from the working class, that folk read and write literature from every social position? There's a straight ideological stance behind such reasoning, because the reality has been open to perusal for the past 150 years and longer, for anyone who's ever felt the urge to go and look.

KMcN: To turn briefly to *A Chancer*, was it difficult remaining sympathetic to a character who is in a way such a non-starter?

JK: He's only twenty; in my terms he's a boy. He is a reader. I think he's a trier. I mean, I've got a lot of time for him, respect for him. He's the hero of the novel. He's trying hard in a world where things are very difficult. The world that he moves in is naive. His family and all his friends are naive. My major feeling towards him is pity. His saving grace is that he is only twenty. The woman he's involved with is a bit enigmatic, two years older than him, given that she's been involved with an older man and has a kid five years of age. I think it works, the relationship between them. How can a lassie that's so sophisticated go for someone like him. He really chases her, you know. She's getting rid of him at the end. Maybe she's more knowledgeable than his immediate circle.

It wasn't a possibility to get inside Tammas's head. Again, I wanted to show things, to demonstrate them. To show necessities. The novel isn't written from his viewpoint so much as from over his shoulder. I can only show how people are in the way they react and respond to him. I can't induce a conversation so that he can say, "What happened to you?" so some sort of individual history can emerge. But I do have to find ways in, as a writer, because everything's hidden from him. But there is just about no way to get beyond it. Unless it becomes bad work. If you're sticking to writing as well as you can that means not interfering. If somebody doesn't tell something to somebody in my story then I can't jump in like Nabokov and say, "Tell it to me." The value of the work means that can't be done. *A Chancer* is difficult in some ways, but speaking as the writer, I've got a lot of respect for it. So fucking hard to do. I came back and rewrote it after *Hines*. It's like writing with one hand tied behind your back. How can you do that! The story of a twenty-year-old. He's just a young man in a situation he can't handle.

KMcN: He sees the old guy from the betting shop as some kind of hero figure.

JK: Yeah, I think he does. The danger for the writer is to collude, to actually *present* him as a hero figure. I tried to make him a bit of a shadow. It would be very easy for me to romanticise the figure.

KMcN: That scene where he tells Robert people like Phil don't just give money to anybody…

JK: I know the gambling world and that's true. I still gamble. People give money to gamblers who wouldn't give it to anyone else—I mean other gamblers, it's just a different culture. Any subculture is. Something with both luck and a game—i.e., not roulette—that produces a black economy. It's almost like a different world, a different value system altogether, murderer as hero, murderer as saint. And in order to grasp it you've got to go through a transformation. Conventional values have to go altogether. That gesture, stuffing money into the top jacket pocket, is classic. That kind of gesture doesn't happen in ordinary straight society. That's the way it is between the old man and Tammas, it's just a gambler giving another gambler money, gambling money—like that Paul Newman scene in *The Hustler*, no guarantee, no security. But giving someone a few quid is also insurance, because if you're skint next time they might have dough.

KMcN: The subculture of the gambling world is an escape for Tammas.

JK: Definitely, as an overview. The difficulty is in keeping a safe distance. I want to side with say the boy's sister and brother-in-law. The solution may be political. The politics are always off the page. Maybe that's the difficulty—keeping them off the page. Gambling can be good, it really can be an escape, leaving you compos mentis, unlike drink or dope.

KMcN: You say Tammas is a reader. What were you reading as a young writer?

JK: As a young reader, about fifteen years of age, I was reading Louis L'Amour the cowboy writer, and quite quickly going from there to Kerouac, I think—it wasn't a great jump. At certain points L'Amour was just writing good novels. Like the very early work of Harold Robbins or something. I was thinking of that in bed this morning, it immediately came to mind, Harold Robbins's first novel, it was *A Stone for Danny Fisher* (later made into the very best Elvis movie, *King Creole*—KMcN). How the fuck have I remembered that name for twenty-five years! It must have had something. Just say fifteen I was reading Louis L'Amour and seventeen I was reading Kerouac—and it was something as quick as that, because at nineteen I was working on the buses and reading Camus.

KMcN: Why do you spell *dowp* with a *p*?

JK: That's a really good point. It's Gaelic. In fact it's Gaelic for "arse," *d-o-w-p*, the *p* is just a glottal stop—sounding like *t* because it's a glottal stop. Where the point becomes really important is where it goes into the essence of a culture, and how that language is continually being transformed by all the different sources. "He's right hard," a character will say and this is straight Glasgow English, the whole gamut of Scotch Gaelic and Irish Gaelic right in there inextricably.

Maybe there's an underlying point in what you're asking. Do I use Scotch words, do I use them intentionally. Sometimes, I do, yes, occasionally, because I forget them—some just aren't in my own vocabulary. *Blether* is a good example. It's a common word in Glasgow but I don't use it personally; it just isn't in my vocabulary for some reason. So I don't mind going back afterwards and saying, "That word there should be *blether*." I've only done this kind of revision recently. Before I would never have tampered like that.

KMcN: You wrote the story "Nice to be Nice" phonetically.

JK: It took thirty to forty drafts for "Nice to be Nice." I don't know what I would've done if I had known Tom Leonard's work first, but I didn't know it until later. At the time I wanted to handle the story from a certain individual perspective—a Glaswegian male in late middle age. And the way in for me was through phonetics, as well as phrasing, but for my own purposes in prose the conventional standard spelling turned out to be fair enough later. This question of "phonetics" and so-called standard spelling needs more space and time than currently available here.

KMcN: You appear to have abandoned traditional narrative structure, with beginning, middle and end, in favour of the facticity you mentioned earlier ...

JK: There's a lot of ways of coping with that question. Ultimately, with me anyway, it's to do with politics. I think the lives of most ordinary people are fairly dramatic. All you've got to do is follow some people around and look at their existence for twenty-four hours, and it will be horror. It will just be horror. You don't need any beginning, middle and end at all. All you have to do is show this one day in maybe this one person's life and it'll be horror. And it's a case of artistic selection in the sense that—okay—you've got to know where to begin and where to stop. When to allow the camera to begin and when to cut the camera off. That will assume the artistic mind or perception behind it. But that's all. There's no need to be saying or thinking, "When's the murder or bank robbery going to happen?" No such abnormal event will occur—the kind of event that seems to motivate almost all mainstream fiction whether in book or screen form. In reality these events are abnormal. The whole idea of the big dramatic event, of what constitutes "plot," only assumes that economic security exists. The way that literature generally works in our society, you never have to worry about these everyday routine horrors, the things that make up everyday reality for such an enormous proportion of the population. In the Anglo-American literary tradition there's almost no concrete reality, no economic detail. All kinds of abnormal events and dramatic plots are required, there's got to be folk appearing out of closets, long-lost sisters and brothers, a father who's a murderer, all that sort of junk— there has to be something to lift it out of the "ordinary," because for them the concrete reality of "everyday life" contains no drama, because these writers never seem to have to worry about the next bite of grub, or where the rent's coming from. For 80 percent of our society life is constantly dramatic in a way that the 20 percent who control the wealth and power find totally incomprehensible. If you go up west from here just now, up around Piccadilly and Leicester Square, you see boys and girls begging. I mean that is horror, it's horror.

5

1990

Interview by *Variant*

This interview originally appeared in issue number 8 of *Variant*.

In January of 1990, a two-day event took place in Govan, Glasgow, entitled Self-Determination and Power. Organised by the Free University of Glasgow, *Scottish Child* magazine and the *Edinburgh Review*, the event was attended by over three hundred people over the two days (with many more turned away due to demand); this conference was one of the largest independent events of its kind ever seen in Scotland. Those attending included groups and organisations from tenants' groups, educational campaigning groups, anti-racist, women's aid, anti–poll tax, artists, writers and activists of all description. The keynote address on each day was delivered by Noam Chomsky, the American dissident thinker. Prior to the event, one of the key organisers—Glasgow writer and activist James Kelman—wrote:

> Chomsky's thesis, and that of the Common Sense phil-
> osophical view in general, is the apparently obvious
> point that people can think for themselves—apparently
> obvious because nowadays most ruling minorities
> tend to regard it as dangerously subversive. "Common
> Sense" takes the view that the reasoning skills which we

use in our everyday life are there to be developed and applied to any subject we want, and not just subjects like "foreign languages," "geology," "dog-racing," or "criticising TV programmes"—but subjects like a country's foreign policy, or the correlation between cuts in welfare benefit and infant mortality, cuts in welfare benefit and suicide, and drug abuse, alcohol abuse, gambling abuse, suicide, local crime and violence, prostitution, madness.

We interviewed Kelman at the time of the event about the ideas behind the event and the connection with Chomsky. Following that, we include excerpts from Chomsky's key address on the first day.*

James Kelman: About eighteen months ago I was writing a review-cum-essay on Chomsky's work and the deeper I got into it, the more I realised that there were parallels with something else I was reading, which was the work of George Davie, the Scottish philosopher. Basically there were lines coming together to do with Common Sense philosophy, which, to me, the way it operates, is that it provides a philosophical context for a political struggle. It connects with the Enlightenment period. There was also my own knowledge of the time. I've written a play near the period so I knew that around the mid to late eighteenth century not only was there a French Revolution but also that there were great things going on elsewhere, in Glasgow and other parts of Scotland. These connections were

---

* See *Variant* issue number 8 at https://www.variant.org.uk/vol1/issue8. html, which includes the relevant Noam Chomsky excerpts. Many years later Kelman worked with the full cooperation of Noam Chomsky to bring a fuller account of this major event, which Chomsky described as the best conference he had ever attended. See Noam Chomsky and James Kelman, *Between Thought and Expression Lies a Lifetime: Why Ideas Matter* (Oakland: PM Press, 2021).

interesting. The Common Sense idea seems to me basically the right to self-determination, the right to freedom.

When I was doing the Chomsky thing and getting into the technical side of his work I wanted to show how powerful it was. I had done a little bit of reading on it before and I wanted to draw some links. And when I was exploring his work there was something he said which made me realise that he wasn't aware of a certain part of the Scottish tradition in philosophy. This was all fairly recent to me and had only come through reading George Davie's work in *Edinburgh Review* magazine; I was seeing there were things in this country outside of the Anglo-American tradition in philosophy.

I sent some of Davie's work to Chomsky so he would get some idea of the Scottish tradition which has virtually been wiped out by the Anglo-American tradition, done in by it, for I think political reasons, an apology for imperialism—if David Hume makes a case for treating black people as inferiors then of course the West can go and exploit them and make slaves out of them. The first thing to do is say that this person is not a person, this person is something that resembles a person, but isn't—and then basic human (person) rights like freedom and self-determination just don't apply.

Chomsky got this work and I thought that this will mean something to him, he'll be interested.

There's another technical aspect to be mentioned here, Chomsky's approach to rationalism, and the Scottish tradition seemed to be offering a way out of that. By "rationalism" I mean an "innateness hypothesis," meaning that people are born with knowledge, forms of it, not got through being in the world. That's why Chomsky is on a radical limb even within his own field and that's why a lot of people regard what he does as anachronistic, a throwback to the early seventeenth century—Descartes especially. It struck me—as it still is the case—that the Scottish tradition offered the possibility of Rousseau-type principles of freedom, and "human nature, and didn't have to get bogged down in any "innateness hypothesis." I felt excited by the way all of these things were being drawn together. I sent the finished article off to him and made a case for him coming to Glasgow since he was going to be visiting Oxford in 1989. He couldn't make it then though.

I later discovered that someone else had offered Chomsky an invitation to Scotland at about the same time. This was Derek Rodger, the editor of *Scottish Child* magazine. Because the way that magazine operates meant that he was very open in coming in on it together with the Free University. It was Chomsky himself who set the date for January 1990.

6

1990–91

Interview by the *Shadow*, Glasgow

This interview appeared in volume 1, number 1 of the *Shadow* under the title "Kelman: From Disaffection to Dissident."

The *Shadow* spoke to writer James Kelman, author of *A Chancer*, 1985, and *A Disaffection*, 1989. Kelman's literary style and his prominent involvement in Workers City has attracted controversy. When we arrived at Kelman's flat we were treated with warm hospitality. When we entered Kelman's study we were confronted with books, books and more books. We were ensnared in a dense forest of literature. On the floor copies of *Artwork* and the *Keelie* were scattered about. His vast library could either be viewed as a student's dream or nightmare. We noticed no pictures or posters adorned the walls. Perhaps he views them as a distraction to his work. Who knows! After shifting and rearranging the furniture to provide space for the interview Kelman apologised for the "mess." Throughout the interview Kelman expressed his views in a frank, funny and down-to-earth way. He refused to pose for photographs and just let the photographer take spontaneous shots. Despite chain-smoking throughout the interview (a real smoker this man, filter-less cigarettes and a brass Zippo) Kelman conveyed the impression of not being totally at ease with the world. Some criticisms directed against him were merely regarded as an irrelevance. Kelman also claimed his house had been recently broken into. Nothing was stolen. In the same week this event occurred, three other members of Workers City had their places invaded. It not only sounded strange but sinister. Were the Special Branch attempting to intimidate Workers City?

The Shadow: According to the *Glaswegian*,* an ex-academic, David Daiches, claimed in a recent lecture that your book, *A Disaffection*, portrays a one-sided, dark and pessimistic picture of Glasgow. For instance, he states, "The rendering of Glasgow working-class speech is done with obscenity." Do you think this criticism is justified?

James Kelman: [*Laughs*] I don't really bother about this sort of criticism. I don't really pay any attention. It's an opinion. That's fair enough. I don't have any feelings about what he said, fortunately. [*Laughs*] There are criticisms that have been levelled at me. These are more important. I don't agree anyway. [*Laughs*] I cannot remember what the quote was!

TS: I quote: "The rendering of Glasgow working-class speech is done with obscenity." It's a pretty bad criticism.

JK: If that was a critical point it's junk! It shows a lack of understanding of how language operates. Is he a professor of literature?

TS: The *Glaswegian* claims he's an ex-academic.

JK: I suppose the serious point is what it reveals, the lack of understanding of how literature operates, of how language operates.

TS: We heard your book was short-listed for the Booker Prize but you never attended any award ceremonies. Why didn't you? We got the impression you wanted nothing to do with it!

JK: For one thing I was busy at the time. I had something to do in Glasgow the following day. I had other things on the

---

* A local weekly newspaper of the day.

same day. So it was difficult. I don't think it's an important thing to get involved in. It's important for the publisher, but not to myself. I've certain political views on the thing, you know, whenever the prizes are dished out they rely on private sector money, international corporations, so it appears to be suspicious—well, not so much suspicious as not important.

TS: Do you think it's only important to commercial interests, i.e., the bottom line is book sales?

JK: Yes, because it's being run by the publishing industry doesn't mean writers should regard it as important.

TS: How do you respond to the criticism that your characters are passive and that this impression adds strength to the conviction that you cannot change the system? For example why doesn't the schoolteacher in *A Disaffection* emigrate or attempt to change society? Perhaps it's an unfair criticism.

JK: No, it's a criticism that is often made, and it's a literary criticism. There are two types of criticism you can make. One is a literary criticism and one is a political criticism of the character. In that sense I would agree with you about the character. I mean, you can say to him, "Why don't you go out and do something?" That's fair enough. But it would be an error to confuse my views with those of the character.

TS: But your books appear to be written in such a way they subvert the English language. For instance, it's difficult to tell whether a character is speaking or thinking. You sometimes don't use capital letters at the start of sentences and miss out inverted commas. Is this a literary technique used to express a political view concerning the imperialism of the English language?

JK: I do use this as a device to expose and undermine the elitism of the English language. In most literature the narrative or story dominates and constrains the language of the characters. In my stories the characters are given more scope or voice and this subverts the narrative. Since most of the narrative is expressed in Standard English the best way to subvert it is to let a character express his voice in such a way that he breaks the rules of the English language. By removing inverted commas around speech, the voice of the narrator becomes submerged with the voice of the character and is not so authoritarian.

TS: How could you respond to the idea that Chomsky, like Habermas, is one of the last Modernists? That Enlightenment ideas are out of date, that Enlightenment ideas were responsible for the growth of fascism and Stalinism. Haven't Enlightenment ideas exhausted themselves in such a way that even communism is dead?

JK: I don't think that "centralism," or "democratic centralism," or anything that becomes like Stalinism or totalitarian represents the Enlightenment. Maybe they've come as a reaction against Enlightenment ideas. Maybe John Stuart Mill and Bertrand Russell, others like that, the Anglo-American line, maybe that leads to totalitarianism. It's not a genuine democracy, it believes you can make decisions for other people, which is maybe the opposite of Enlightenment ideas and the right to self-determination.

TS: Do you believe that those who have power or would have power think that people are too stupid to think for themselves?

JK: That's what the orthodox left thinks as well as the right. They are so very similar. That's why I'm saying there are often views more subversive than that so-called left-wing position. There's the need to make decisions for yourself and the right to determine your own existence. These mainstream parties don't take that line, whether left or right. The orthodox left says, "Let's go down and teach these people how to make a revolution." That's disgraceful, you know, that's the whole problem of that vanguard idea, that basic socialist-communist line. It's easy to see how problems develop. Chomsky quotes Rousseau about so-called uncivilised people. He says it doesn't matter how uneducated or uncivilised people are and what sort of living they would get from being part of a society which they don't control, they would give up all that for freedom; they would go back to their old way of life just for the sake of that, the need to be free. I think Enlightenment ideas have been done in by Anglo-American philosophy, for ways that are easily manipulated by other interests, whether capital or any other. It's set up an intellectual perspective that gives the right to nations to march into other nations, for imperialist aggressors to say, "We know what's good for you, here's missionaries, factories and whatever else we can think up." Self-determination doesn't exist. It comes in its extreme form in psychology with B.F. Skinner and all that right-wing behaviourist crap. It is a total aberration of Enlightenment ideas, the very opposite—more like the suppression of Enlightenment ideas.

TS: What do you think of Pat Kane's suggestion that the teaching of Scottish philosophy should be brought back into school and re-established within the Scottish education system as a whole?

JK: Yes. Some people on the left think it's a step back the way but I don't think they're grasping the arguments: aspects of the Scottish tradition in philosophy, they don't understand how important they are. Not so much that they're important but essential to it, and makes the tradition quite a radical thing, potentially, quite subversive, anti-authoritarian. Debates on Scottish education happened in the past, say between 1820 and 1930 and maybe on three major occasions a fight to stave off the move towards specialism, a kind of a rearguard action. Slowly but surely the English university system was creeping in, in place of the traditional generalist approach of the Scottish system. It's not some airy-fairy abstract notion. The English system educated people for functional roles, preparing the way for "specialists" who would be more useful in the marketplace, for business. But what this leads to is a kind of general ignorance: you lose your ability to make a judgment, so if you want to know something, call in an expert. The Scottish approach more concerned itself with educating people as citizens, introducing young people to philosophy was considered basic, questions on first principles, the "meaning of life" debates and so on. So if you are used to thinking about this, that and the next thing then you're better capable of making decisions and judgments; in other words you can think for yourself.

TS: In regard to what has become known as "the Elspeth King affair," do you think this represents a start to a more concerted onslaught on the identity and traditions of the Scottish working class? It's pretty sinister isn't it!

JK: Really sinister, yes. A lot of the present political situation is encapsulated by what's happened to Elspeth.* She's come to represent a crucial part of the social-historical identity of Glasgow which is being suppressed, done in, bought off, sold, dispersed and everything else, what the Labour Party's doing right now. You could maybe call it an aspect of Modernism rather than Postmodernism; outsiders come in and abstract things from inside a culture—the "assets," the paintings and sculptures in the local galleries all become "assets," there to be ripped off. They take what can be sold and they do in the rest. The People's Palace is an example and that's what the Labour Party councillors are doing, they come in, take what can be sold and do in the rest—people's history, working-class people, they don't want it on display, the real stuff, for instance, the Calton Weavers, executions and battles with the army, that's not what's wanted, give us Oor Wullie and the Broons, Billy Connolly's Wellington boots and crap like that. In forty or fifty years' time people will be saying what was "the Glasgow identity," because all its assets and historical heritage will have gone, been removed, sold off.

TS: Dug up and removed like the Gorbals community?
JK: Yes.

---

* See the essays in Farquhar McLay, ed., *Workers City: The Real Glasgow Stands Up* (Glasgow: Clydeside Press, 1988), and Farquhar McLay, ed., *The Reckoning: Public Loss Private Gain* (Glasgow: Clydeside Press, 1990).

[*Kelman then picks up a copy of the art magazine entitled* Artwork, *Scotland's independent arts and crafts guide.*]

JK: Believe it or not this magazine has been banned by Glasgow District Council. They tried to have it censored. They wouldn't allow it to be kept in the library and given out free. Look at it! Nobody would consider it the least bit radical. It's been hit because of David Kemp's* articles on the Elspeth King affair. The Mitchell Library had two hundred copies and they were going to be incinerated or whatever, until a guy from Workers City just went in and took them. [*Laughs*]

TS: Glasgow culture itself has been suppressed by the authorities but isn't the Labour Party there to represent the people?

JK: It all comes down to those in control. It's the way the party operates in Glasgow. In a sense it shows how weak they are. Pat Lally and these other gangsters can do what they like. It doesn't matter what the party says to them. All they can do essentially is make recommendations. They go ahead and do things that were never in the manifesto. A third of Glasgow Green! They just fucking sell it!

TS: They take a Thatcherite stance, authoritarian centralisation, where one person makes the decisions.

JK: Yes, it's like back to a situation where two or three people make a decision from a pub.

TS: People with their own social networks!

JK: It's not even like that. In some cases it's worse, and in others it's better.

TS: Do you think they're like the Roman emperors who want to leave something behind so that people will think nicely of them?

JK: Not really! That's very personal. It maybe applies to a couple. I don't think there's any general point here.

---

* David Kemp, writer and journalist, brother of Arnold Kemp, then editor of the *Glasgow Herald*.

TS: We're referring to the new "opera house."*

JK: I know what you mean but I don't think it's got to that stage. I do think they're involved in cynical manipulation, in patronage and deals, land deals and all that. I think it's more down-to-earth, and ultimately fraudulent.

TS: Who actually owns Glasgow Green? Is it the people or can the District Council act on behalf of the people in such a manner?

JK: Yes, that comes back to this centralised so-called socialism where these people are in power and suddenly it's two or three guys making all the decisions. The worst thing for them is genuine democracy. They honestly don't think that we've got the right to talk about this. They would shout, "Out of order!" Even the mammoth decision taken by Glasgow District Council to go ahead with a public meeting to decide whether to sell that part of Glasgow Green, they only took that very reluctantly. They were forced into it. That was a great decision! Totally unheard of. Lally's crew—the party leadership—was defeated, it was incredible!

And that was the bottom line, how actually worried they were about holding a public meeting. That means allowing in folk like Workers City—which is just a dozen people who meet for a pint in the Scotia Bar! [*Laughs*] In a sense but what Workers City represents is genuine democracy, because there is no party basis to it. That's why these people cannot do in the group, because nobody's concerned with party or power or patronage or anything like that. It's just like, "This isn't right, and this needs to be done," and finding ways of being critical. That allows Workers City in and allows ordinary working people to give an ordinary opinion. The District Council don't

---

* The new Glasgow Royal Concert Hall, then known as "Lally's Palais." Pat Lally was the Labour Party's leader of Glasgow District Council. The concert hall was seen as "his baby."

think ordinary Glasgow people have that right. They are absolutely contemptuous of that.

We took over their place, the City Chambers, almost two and a half months ago. This event received almost no publicity. It was an historic occasion. Two hundred people occupied the City Chambers! That picket-line had old-age pensioners in it. The councillors treated them with absolute contempt. Just outright laughter, that was what they did. It's like the way they've treated Michael Donnelly (curator's assistant at the People's Palace). These guys started singing "My Way" not behind their back but right in front of them, to provoke and intimidate absolutely, and they had the cops there too. Labour Party politicians, totally cynical of the rights of ordinary people.

TS: So how do you see ordinary people overcoming this?

JK: By doing what we've done. We're picketing at 12:30 today at the City Chambers. Just by actually showing what you can do in the streets is of value because there you are demonstrating you can change things on the streets. Just by showing how we can change it, that's us doing it.

TS: A negation of the ballot box?

JK: That's right. It's just campaigning on the street. Which is really all we've been doing. That shows it is still possible. However, we are not organised on a party basis. As soon as people begin to organise outside a party the troops are sent in, which is what's been happening with the anti–poll tax campaign. So on the one hand Workers City shows you can mobilise to change things—which is the opposite of *A Disaffection*, the point you were making, you can mobilise on the street. In this sense it is very basic.

7

1990

Interview by Chris Mitchell

This interview originally appeared in the Spring 1990 issue of *GUM* (*Glasgow University Magazine*).

James Kelman has been responsible for some of the most challenging and innovative Scottish writing of recent years. Following the publication of his third novel, he spoke to Chris Mitchell.

Chris Mitchell: One thing that stands out in your work is that you use regional dialects and phonetics.

James Kelman: Well, I don't regard my work as being in phonetics at all. I just occasionally use a phonetic transcription of a word because without that the word doesn't exist. To that extent, it's not even a phonetic transcription. To give you an example, the word *one*. In Glasgow you have at least three ways of saying the word *one*: "one," "yin" and "wan." Now each is used at a different time by the same speaker; each one is a word of its own, because there is a certain significance attached to each. So it would be a nonsense to say that *y-i-n* is a phonetic transcription of *o-n-e*. You don't say "Hey, Big One!" So to that extent I question the use of the term "phonetics." So I don't really use phonetics at all … well, occasionally I do. People think I do more than anything. As far as I can see, what I do is, I write in Standard English with a *syntax* based on a Glasgow speaking voice. Some people think it's phonetics or vernacular dialect, but it's not.

CM: But you pick up on ordinary conversations; for example you don't get full sentences, people stutter, hum and haw. This is what you want to capture?

JK: The reality of the individual largely revolves around the language of that individual. I'm stuttering now, only I'm doing it in a very professional way, which is through a series of pauses. Because when people are talking they happen to break when they speak, so a stutter is a kind of punctuation.

My work has always been to arrive at a certain thing to do with the way people use language, whether it's in the mind, or speaking, or written. I try to do it in such a way that they're interchangeable. I never use the phrase "regional dialects" (I'm using it now in quotation marks), you'd have to defend yourself, I'd really attack that position; usually, at best, it's a sort of inverted elitist position. So I reject it altogether.

I've always been after the same thing, and there's a certain basic class position involved as far as I'm concerned—that usually in English literature you don't get stories written about ordinary people by one of the people themselves. So that if you want to write a short story in the voice of the person within the group that the situation or event is occurring, then you have to find a way of doing that in the same language. So if the person's an ordinary Glaswegian, you have to be able to use the language that an ordinary Glaswegian uses. Now that's quite difficult to do, it seems straightforward but it's not at all. It's straightforward in other languages, but in ours it's quite difficult because of all the cultural taboos, the hierarchical nature of our language system. For instance, a man with my accent could never read the news on the BBC. That is the structural basis of our whole culture. And in a sense that goes through every short story ever written in English; it's in the same voice that reads the news. And anyone who speaks the way I do, they're never going to tell a story. So trying to get this voice is trying to get an enactment of the thought process, the voice of narrative prose. It's allowed me to write stories that it wouldn't have been possible to write in any other way.

CM: So in the novels, in capturing ordinary life, it tends to be episodic. There's no general structure: no beginning, middle, end.

JK: On a simplistic level, once you say that, you think it will be structurally unsound, but that's not the case with the two novels *A Chancer* and *The Busconductor Hines*, each has quite a tight structure—it can only be a retrospective thing, because the novel is created, it's not something you begin with, a big skeleton and then you fill in the bits between the bones. Some writers do that as far as I hear; generally I'm not interested in their work and find it boring—it surprises me they even have the energy to finish it, never mind expect people to read it. The writing that interests me is where there is a process of discovery and it's a creative process all the way through and that's what sustains the drama, the need to read every sentence because something surprising may happen. There may be a sense of things that are inevitable going on, but never that predictability which you get in bad art. Structure can be retrospective, and I regard my work as structurally sound. In that sense my work is existential, where the thing is made as it goes, but all art should be like that.

CM: I wasn't implying that they had a loose structure. The novels are consistent throughout because you're very much with the main character throughout the whole thing, but what happens to the character in the course of the novel tends to be episodic.

JK: Fair enough, yeah. But there can be a misunderstanding there that if you don't start with a structure then it doesn't have one. In good works of art the structure is developed in terms of itself. You don't plan the thing. You're working on it and you discover it.

CM: Some might say you're setting up a lot of difficulties for someone approaching your work for the first time. For example, the lack of quotation marks in dialogue—some may find this difficult to read.

JK: There's a lot of different aspects to this; some just relate to the technical side of it. It's difficult to use nothing to differentiate dialogue and narrative, as difficult for the writer as for the reader. Quotation marks are just a convention; what's important is the separation of dialogue from narrative. Whatever you use to separate them is just a convention. People are familiar with quotation marks, but if you read some people they use a dash before dialogue, like Joyce and others. Kerouac, it's just a convention.

CM: But all these conventions highlight dialogue, whereas you use nothing.

JK: In a novel like *Hines* for instance, it wouldn't have been possible for Hines to exist if dialogue could be distinguished from narrative. Part of what goes on in *Hines* is that at certain points there is an absolute ambiguity of where this language derives from—is the character talking, is he thinking or is it a third-party narrative? Now, that ambiguity is essential to that novel.

CM: I can see that about *Hines*, because of a lot of that novel is what goes on in Hines's head. But with *A Chancer* you don't get inside Tammas's head, you never really find out what he's thinking.

JK: Apart from one or two places ...

CM: In the betting shops, gambling ...

JK: Yeah, right.

CM: So why do you need to lose the convention there?

JK: I don't want any distinction between the narrative voice and the person who is in the dialogue. I want the person who tells the story to be from the same culture as the person who the story is about, and also that the syntax of the dialogue is the same as the syntax of the narrative. All that can only come about through starting afresh in a sense.

CM: Is this something you want to bring to bear on all your work?

JK: Yeah, because I want all my work to be straight Glasgow culture. I only want to be a writer who creates stories. It so happens I'm a Glaswegian. So I just want to be able to use everything that I can as a writer, and you should be allowed to do that. The only way that I can do that is to be able to have all the language at my disposal that a Glaswegian has. Usually that's the one thing you can't have as a writer in this country—the freedom to use the language of your own people. Most writers who write in English are cut off from their culture because of class; they can't tell a story about their father because their father says "fuck." So they have to tell stories about someone else's father, because he doesn't say "fuck." So because I don't want to write about Robin Day's father, I want to write about my own father, and he happens to be Glaswegian, I need to be able to use the language of my father and myself. You see, my father also reads Plato, and every time he says "Plato," he says "Fuck Plato." So I want to write this story about my father who says "Fuck Plato" all the time, which is really difficult to do. Not so difficult now, but it was almost impossible; to some extent when I started writing that was a logical absurdity, because it seemed a contradiction in terms to say the word "fuck" in conjunction with the word "Plato," because it seemed to cut across two cultures, the culture of the powerful and the culture of my father. So what I'm after is *all* of my culture, which includes the words "fuck" and "Plato." So that means I have to define everything IN TERMS OF MYSELF WITHIN MY CULTURE. All writers should be free to create stories, and most aren't.

CM: Somebody who perhaps did something along the same lines was Jack Kerouac.

JK: He probably knew the problem that I'm talking about, because he was involved with or liked certain American writers that were coming from the same position. They were trying to do, in a sense, what I've been trying to do—trying to get out from under a form of linguistic imperialism. Yorkshire, Manchester, Liverpool people, Cockneys, were all made to feel second class as well, all made to feel culturally inferior unless we assume the same language as those in power. It's important to keep that in mind, because often ordinary people are made to believe that they have no cultural history, that people like Plato don't belong in it. Somehow they've just got the last hundred years. First and Second World Wars; that's our history, when we're getting fucking killed, you know? Beyond five hundred, six hundred years back you might see that culture in terms of a universal culture.

CM: So, this overview of your culture, working class . . .

JK: It's your term, "working class" . . .

CM: Well, you've used it elsewhere . . .

JK: Well, okay, only because I'm happy to use it in the way I do. But if you use it you may use it in a way which I don't accept. Because usually when it's used in terms of literature it precludes things like Plato. I can write a short story tomorrow about Socrates, to me that's a working-class story. This is the problem with the term, it seems to suggest, "Oh, you're not writing stories about betting tracks and pubs now, so you're entering the middle class." That's just nonsense as far as I'm concerned.

The thing about convention is that it becomes very close to stereotype, cliché—in literature the convention is a Glasgow man is always a thief and is always drunk, an Irishman is always stupid and digs ditches, and so on. Writers who use conventions too freely get involved in stereotypes, racist and fascist. It's surprisingly easy to fall into these traps. The more conventions you use, the greater the danger of allowing something through without defining it. You should be defining each thing as an artist, discovering each object.

CM: So you want to carry on doing what you're doing?

JK: I'm just carrying on doing this. I'm happy just to create stories. There are overviews, but basically the things that I do well are the stories. Obviously I have political commitments and beliefs but they can't get in the way of the story, they have to be part and parcel of the story.

8

1992

Interview by *Socialist Review*

This interview originally appeared in *Socialist Review*'s November 1992 issue under the title "The Art of Subversion."

James Kelman is a writer from Glasgow whose novels and short stories have established him as a distinctive talent in Scottish writing. He is also a political activist. His latest book, *Some Recent Attacks*, a series of essays on culture and politics, has just been published. He spoke to Tommy Gorman and Dave Sherry.

Socialist Review: You are opposed to the censorship which has always existed in this country. Ironically some of your books are now being withdrawn from various secondary school libraries by the Labour-controlled Strathclyde Education Authority. Why has this happened and what do you think should be done about it?

James Kelman: To my knowledge five books have already been withdrawn from school libraries. Two of these books were written by me and one of them has been on the syllabus for twelve years. One of the other books which has been removed is *The Color Purple* by Alice Walker. I believe it's happening because the Labour council and the education officials have refused to stand up to one or two members on one particular school board. These individuals want to ban the books because they find them "obscene," "sexually explicit" and because they contain so-called "expletives." I've written to the education department seeking an official clarification. I'm still waiting for a reply. It seems that in the face of a moral crusade by one or two people, the local authority's response is one of fear.

It's now got to the absurd situation where every work of fiction published since 1970 has been withdrawn for scrutiny by two moral watchdogs. Who knows what their specialist subject is—literary criticism or moral rectitude? It's dangerous stuff and it's a mistake to find it funny. It's got to be seen in terms of the right-wing reaction taking place throughout Europe. We have to see what's going on and take a stand. Destroying people usually follows destroying art.

SR: You were critical of the council during the European Year of Culture. You're still involved in the Workers City group. What do you think about "The New Glasgow" image?

JK: I'm against the elitist notion which imposes "official culture" and invalidates local or regional culture. Local cultures are downgraded, made inferior or deliberately ignored or suppressed. It's not just happening in Glasgow, but all over Britain.

You have a group of professionals—all trained in the same places, with the same view of culture and art, people with so-called objective ideas about what is good and what is inferior. These people have control, so what you get—be it Newcastle, Belfast, Glasgow or Exeter—is that all those different regional and local cultures are being denied any validity. The people who control the art galleries, the museums, the events and the funding all belong to or subscribe to the same ruling-class culture.

SR: Is that why you and some other notable writers and artists were virtually excluded from the official events during the city's Year of Culture?

JK: The Labour councillors were elected by, and even claim to represent, the working people of this city. Yet they accept the official view that our traditions are somehow inferior. So they've been assimilated, if you like—they completely accept that the partnership between the arts and big business is healthy and they want to sweep the reality of Glasgow life under the carpet.

In 1990 myself and other writers were severely censured by a top arts administrator for embarrassing the city's "cultural workforce" and for bringing the city into disrepute. We were an embarrassment to their new image, partly because some of us were trying to show that the way ordinary people live is valid and relevant. It's not a question of being proud of it or being ashamed of it—it's just the way it is and that needs to be acknowledged.

The leaders of the council are either dismissive or frightened of art—so what they've done is sell or give it to the right wing.

SR: But there's a lot of "high" culture—opera, classical music, painting—that we can assimilate and learn from without becoming "bourgeois." Surely you're not against that?

JK: Not at all. That was standard propaganda against the Workers City position. The group was presented as a bunch of workerist philistines doing a hatchet job on the city which was probably the opposite of what we were about. But the city officials wanted to sell the idea of a partnership between art and big business. On the contrary, art and big business have never been allies, but art and subversion have.

SR: Are your stories like *The Busconductor Hines* and *Short Tales from the Night Shift* an attempt to show the other side of Glasgow?

JK: It just so happens that I write about what I know, what I'm familiar with. Like a lot of people I left school at fifteen, and started serving my time as an apprentice compositor. During my apprenticeship my family emigrated, but it didn't work out and we came back to Glasgow. I couldn't start back in the trade— the union wouldn't let me—so I worked in a whole series of ordinary jobs such as working in a warehouse, selling suits, making shoes, working on the buses.

I went to London and worked on building sites, went to Manchester and worked in an asbestos factory and picked potatoes in the Channel Islands. I came back to Glasgow and went back to the buses—in fact I had seven different spells on the buses, and the last time I was there I was involved in an unofficial strike in Partick garage. I started writing in the late 1960s and had work published in the early 1970s.

My last job was in an asbestos and rubber works, and the conditions were terrible. It was one of those places where you'd go into the toilet and you'd notice that the guy next to you had only two fingers on his hand. This was in the mid-1970s. I had two kids and my wife started working part time. I hated the job but I couldn't get back on the buses again. People I knew who were interested in my writing encouraged me to go to university.

SR: Which writers have influenced you and do you see yourself as part of a Scottish tradition?

JK: I don't see myself as a "Scottish" or "British" writer particularly. As a young writer there were no literary models that I could look to from my own culture. I'm not saying they didn't exist, but I couldn't find them. All the English writers I came across presented working-class people as stereotypes.

So I had to look elsewhere and I became interested in foreign language literature in translation—Russian and European writers like Chekhov, Dostoevsky, Kafka—and from reading them I found ways to write about the life of ordinary people. It was only after I had started writing that I met other people like me, who were working from their own Glasgow background. It's been said by academics and "literary" people that I have chosen to write about the subject of the working class—as if it was a choice! I'm only realising the freedom that other writers take for granted—the freedom to write from your own experience.

SR: One of the essays in your new book deals with "The No Tory Mandate in Scotland Argument." In it you successfully lampoon the kind of popular front politics which has characterised the leadership of the Scottish labour movement under successive Tory governments. A number of Scottish writers and artists have identified with Scotland United and Common Cause—what are your views about these campaigns?

JK: I won't say Scotland United is a joke, that would be taking it too far. Let's just say there is no good reason that I can see—historical or otherwise—to trust the folk in control. To say that certain issues need only be raised once Scotland is independent is a great mistake to my mind, and it ignores the reality of right-wing nationalism and xenophobia elsewhere in Europe. It's a dangerous time and we need to be clear on what we're about at the most fundamental level.

9

1992

Conversation with Jeff Torrington

This piece was published originally in the Glasgow-based *West Coast Magazine*. **Shortly afterwards Jeff Torrington's book** *Swing Hammer Swing!* **was awarded the Best First Novel section of the Whitbread Prize, and later the full prize itself as Book of the Year.**

James Kelman: Well, Jeff, if we can start with last things first, your novel, *Swing Hammer Swing!* When I met you—about thirteen years ago—you were working on a version of it.

Jeff Torrington: Aye, ever since I mastered joined-up writing I seem to have been churning out successive drafts of the thing.

JK: Can you roughly date ...

JT: When I started *SHS*? Somewhere in the '60s I suppose. The demolition of the Gorbals paralleled the demolition of each tottering version of the novel. The first intimation to the public that a literary turtle was on the way appeared in the first issue of *EMU*, an extramural uni magazine edited by Ann Draycon and James G. MacDonald. A couple of good poems by Liz Lochhead appeared in the same issue. You'd a short story in a later publication hadn't you?

JK: Aye, that's right.

JT: The novel excerpt appeared under a "Writing in Progress" tag but I think "Writing in Regress" would've been more apt. You know, all this chat about the multitudinous versions of *SHS* might create the false impression that I was continuously at work on this novel. This just wasn't the case. In reality it spent long periods of its existence in the deepest of comas.

JK: On reading those earlier versions I felt an affinity with them. I mean what I recognised was that you were encountering the same sort of technical problems. I was working on *Hines* at that time so I was able to recognise in your work similar difficulties, you know, finding the right voice, that kind of thing.

JT: Sure, there were problems in plenty. By the way, maybe I should mention here that another novel came to birth around this time. I called it *Open Wide Otto* and I can see how heavily influenced it was by Koestler's *Darkness at Noon*. It starts with Otto Osserman, a has-been poet, seating himself in a dentist's chair to have a tooth extracted ... anyway, how did I get onto this—back to Clay.*

JK: I was talking about the problems of finding a "voice" ...

JT: Aye, finding this mic's even harder! [*Laughter*] Structure ... getting it down onto the page. It amazes me how some folk blithely head-hop from character to character and seem to have no compunction about assuming a godlike role. Now I contend that although it would be extremely helpful to know the thoughts of a half a dozen characters in a single room, when you arrogate to yourself such omniscient powers then you've already said, "Ta ta real world—Hello Disneyland." No, the monofocal viewpoint is the only one I can comfortably assume, and, as you know, it bristles with problems of its own.

JK: Aye, and the funny thing is that a lot of folk don't seem to worry too much about these modes of approach, they take a sort of cavalier attitude to the problems which present themselves. In fact, they don't apparently see them as problems at all.

---

* Tam Clay, the narrator of Torrington's *Swing Hammer Swing!*

JT: Aye, that's right. For instance, when I settled on the "I-voice" for *SHS* I did so only after I'd experimented with other means of telling the story. The first-person narrative imposes hefty disciplines and restraints upon its user: head-hopping is definitely out. This doesn't mean though that the reader of first-person narrative work is necessarily doomed to be sealed up in the narrator's monomania—there are escape exits available. Take Kinbote in Nabokov's novel *Pale Fire*: although the narrator seems a plausible, even humorous bloke, it is evident from early on that he's a raving nutter. This, of course, is a secret signalled by the author to the reader behind the madman's back, so to speak. By the way, Jim, I recently read Stevenson's *Treasure Island* again, you know, just to see if the old delights could still be seen through the cracked specs of adulthood—just as Tam Clay tries to root out a few laughs from the *Beano*. The answer, in my case anyway, is a bleak no. But what is of interest is Stevenson's attempt to break out from the solitary confinement cell of first-person narrative when for a few brief pages he hops from Jim Hawkins's head so that he can describe certain crucial incidents which have befallen the goodies.

Christ, where have I got to?

JK: Eh, "I-voice," perspective etc.?

JT: I'll let you into a wee secret concerning Clay. Throughout the many versions of *SHS* it'd always been a possibility that Clay might snuff it. In fact I wrote his death scene in which he plunges through the roof of the Planet Cinema and falls "in a hail of mouldy stars and putrid planets." I won't try to be coy and say that his survival surprised me but I was pleased to see him walking away so jauntily at the end. It might be claimed that by adopting a first-person narrative that Clay's survival was assured. That was a presumption I was keen to foster so that Clay being killed would have a powerful impact—like aw they "white hats" getting offed at the Alamo, for instance. [*Laughter*]

JK: So the diary was to be used as your get-oot device?

JT: Aye, that'd been its original purpose. Clay's son, and not Clay himself, would turn out to be the narrator. But in the end I baulked at the use of such a hoary literary device. I decided though to retain Clay's diary-keeping since it served certain purposes that we might return to later.

JK: Okay. You mentioned publishing short stories. You used to have a nickname for them.

JT: "Scorpions"—sting-in-the-tail stuff. Real poison. Bad for the system. These Scorpions appeared fairly regularly in the *Edinburgh Evening Dispatch* back in the '60s and just might've been a contributory factor in that worthy paper's demise. The *Weekly Scotsman*, another of my literary spawning grounds, suffered a similar fate. You know, it was only the "surprise ending" that made these things saleable.

JK: Five-minute fiction?

JT: Aye, really dire. I wonder if anybody really read any of them.

JK: Did you attend writing groups at this time?

JT: Aye, one in particular, that of Edward Scouller, MA. His "Literary Appreciation" evenings were well attended in the '60s. I met some really smashing writers like Bill Oliphant, Pat Bailey and Jimmy Miller. Govan Workspace Ltd. have recently published a posthumous collection of Jimmy's tales under the title *Tenements as Tall as Ships*. I'm sure you'll like it, Jim. Shipbuilding—most of his stuff's set in and about the Yards. Jimmy Miller never got the recognition he deserved.

JK: His name's no familiar to me.

JT: He chucked writing for a time after entering into management training, a move which, no matter the gain to shipbuilding, was a great loss to Scottish writing, believe me.

JK: There was quite a lot going on in Glasgow at that time. I wasn't there then—I was down in London. I never came back till about 1970. It was an interesting period, eh? Alasdair Gray never attended, did he?

JT: Unfortunately not. The group met once a week in the Nurses Club in Bath Street. Scouller was a witty wee man, very professorial he looked with his mane of white hair and brisk mannerisms. His knowledge of literature was formidable and he sure didn't suffer fools gladly. Having submitted something for group analysis I lived in dread of it ending up in Scouller's "Trash File." As I recall, he dealt with submitted material along the following lines: only the awfy good and the awfy bad stuff were discussed—mediocre manuscripts were promptly returned, accompanied by usually helpful comments. My first submission did in fact end up in the mediocre category and Scouller's comment on it was: "This kind of stuff went out with the shooting of Dan McGrew. Write about what you know and I'm sure you'll do well."

So, I penned my first railway story. It was called "The Ghost of Mike Muldoon" and it was published by the *Weekly Scotsman*.

JK: Was that the railway story you read at the Paisley Group?

JT: Aye, it probably was. My first ever published tale appeared in the Glasgow *Evening Times*.

JK: And did you carry on with other groups?

JT: Aye, it was a good way of meeting other writers. But writing groups have a common danger—if you attend the same one too long there's a good chance you'll become what I call "groupised." You know, pausing in the middle of writing something to consider whether Wee Aggie or Churchy Adams will be offended by a four-letter word. In other words you find yourself keying into the general morality of the group. And that's the time to chuck it and go look for another group or better still manage on your own for a while.

Another problem I've found in writing groups concerns leadership, especially when the Supreme Scribe has gone off to bed to nurse a bad review or something. Who'll be the temp, shepherd us literary bleaters then? Usually the group member who's long suspected that justifying the Arts Council grant amounts to little more than the duplication of drivel and the ability to keep one's eyes open during the reading of "Aunt Milly's Magic Tammy." Aye, it can be a fascinating business this leadership problem.

JK: I know what you mean, you know, going to groups, hearing the way groups operate. For instance, if there was one English teacher in the group, somebody used to asserting his or her authority on the subject, that could be a disaster, the type of authority that would judge a story the way he or she would judge a composition in school.

JT: Talking about teachers, a funny thing—the majority of them who attended groups I was involved in tended to submit the dullest fiction. Of course their grammar was impeccable, not a split infinitive in sight. But it was as if their specialised knowledge inhibited them in some way.

JK: You'll remember John Harvie of the Paisley Group?

JT: I'm no likely to forget him.

JK: John was fucking great. I can write a story about anything, he said to me one day. Aye, even one about your shoe-laces. And the next week did he no come in with a beautiful wee tale about laces! D'you mind yon story of his about the auld guy going into this charity shop to buy a jaicket?

JT: Aye, and picks wan wae a daud of chewing gum stuck tae a button. D'you remember yon smashing wee story of his about the worthy out for a bit of a daunder and he becomes puzzled about how everything on the High Street seemed sort of out-of-kilter. It seems to him that the shops and the buildings are teetering on the verge of sliding into the gutters. Becoming anxious, he goes up to folk to ask them, "D'you no think that there's a queer slant tae things the day?" But he seems alone in his delusion. He staggers home to tell his wife to fetch a doctor. "Ya silly lump!" she exclaims. "There's damn all wrang wae ye— you've gone and lost the toorie aff yer tammy, that's aw!" John was a strict Temperance man, you know.

JK: Aye, a total teetotaller.

JT: But he'd still a great insight into pub life. In one of his tales there's this knockout line: "Beezer's heid clonked down onto the table. 'Jeez,' said Patchy Mclaurin, 'wan oclock already!'"

JK: Apart from humour he could write some powerful social history. His family was from Donegal. His granny figured a lot in his reminiscences. She used to walk these incredible distances. She lived somewhere down about Kilmarnock. When she visited John and his family in Foxbar she'd think nothing of walking the whole way back. Says John, "Aye, she'd hap her shawl aboot hersel and say: 'That's me away doon the road,' and she'd be off, no turning a hair at the miles that lay ahead of her." John Harvie's description of her sticks in the mind: "She was sitting on her chair and took up the space of a small cushion."

[*A wee pause for refreshments*]

JK: This might sound like a stupid question to ask: Are you glad that your novel was published late on rather than say ten years ago?

JT: I regret having wasted so much time, if I have wasted it, you know, when I could've been doing other things.

JK: That's a thing. From the luxury of having published three novels, right, the best advice you can pass on to people, well, maybe not advice but a reminder to folk who're toiling overlong at their first novel, you know, that they can always write another one. I had that wi *A Chancer*. Because it was my first novel there was always that feeling, you know, that everything had to be in it. Ance you'd finished it you suddenly found yourself involved in another novel. That sort of experience is important in a way because it means that you don't have to get everything into the first novel. You realise, "Fucking hell, I could do this all the time!"

One of the things I always find very stupid and is usually said by people who don't think very much about the subject is the Great Glasgow Novel. You know, as if somehow a person's whole body of work, you know, the idea everything can be done in the one novel, it's so facile and stupid, yet people persist in promoting it.

JT: I agree with what you've just said. As if there could be such a thing as the "definitive novel." It's about as unimaginable as a clockwork sundial. The point you were making—this obsession, aye, in my own case I'd put it as strongly as that, for it's surely obsessive behaviour to spend day after day, night after night, writing the same words over and over, with only minor variations—all for the sake of so-called perfectionism. You would've thought that an edict had been published which banned writers from publishing more than one novel in his or her lifetime! In my present home suitcases stuffed with the Clay saga not to mention plastic bin bags crammed squeakful of the stuff drive my wife, Margaret, to despair. A version even exists of *SHS* which is rendered entirely in American usage, so convinced had I become that the New World's brash culture was staking out a cemetery for the body-bagged remains of our own one. Maybe you recall the version, Jim—it was the one in which a film crew had set up in Scobie Street to make an avant garde movie. This offered the attractive contrast of Burnett trying to preserve a bridgehead for Hollywood nostalgia while the modernistic film director floods the street with all sorts of human monstrosities. Aye, you're right, Jim, I should've let the thing go and moved on to fresher work.

JK: Anyway, to change the subject, I remember when you were a member of the Paisley writing group telling me that you had to go to the Southern General's neurological unit for tests. You didn't say what was wrong but I deduced from your tone that it was something serious. When would that be about?

JT: Around 1981. I'd begun to notice I was making typing errors and that a tremble sometimes disturbed my left hand. My local sawbones sent me for tests. In a manner that was very brutal, a consultant said that he was 99 percent sure I had Parkinsonism. Subsequent tests proved him right. I didn't let on to my employer—I was in the car industry at the time—for I'm sure they'd have got shot of me—a trembly-handed telex op sending faulty build-codes to various stages of the assembly line was a liability that wouldn't have been tolerated. Anyway, this became academic when after declaring that the Linwood plant was to remain an integral and most important part of their operations the French owners shut the place down, throwing the entire workforce onto the dole.

JK: It must've been a difficult period for you. But you battered on with the writing just the same. Apart from the novel you were working on other stuff: car stories, railway stories and so on, is that right?

JT: Aye, and getting some of the stories published, which was encouraging.

JK: I'd imagine it must've been hard to concentrate under those circumstances. I mean, your life had changed in such a fucking dramatic way. Especially, writing a novel, you would have to put aside your own personal concerns to take up the trials and tribulations of Clay. I mean, were you conscious of the need to prevent leakage from your factual life getting into the workings of your fiction? How did that go?

JT: I suppose just as yon auld Greek, Heraclitus, says that nobody can step into the same river twice, then it must follow that no man nor woman can step twice from the same bed. As a consequence then we may say that owing to gradual changes, tiny disintegrations, the cellular casualties from the great Microbic Wars that rage within us, that never the same writer confronts his typewriter each day. Self-continuity is a myth, an assumption—a con in fact. I don't have a "factual life." Like everyone else I lead a thoroughly fictitious existence. Clay in a way plagiarises these fictive files, cribs from my emotive and intellectual ranges, draws, so to speak, from all of my available resources.

A long way round to answer your question, Jim, but I suppose what I'm getting at is that collisions with the brute facts of one's circumstances become something of a necessity. Damage limitation which strives to compartmentalise so-called "facts" from fiction does not, in my opinion, contribute to honest writing.

JK: Would you like to expand on that at all?

JT: Naw, you can fill the balloon with only so much hot air before it bursts: we'd best cut the string on this one, eh?

JK: Okay.

JT: Let's get away from writing for a bit. Aye, let's talk about Jeffrey Archer! I was reading a review of the man's latest literary tomb, sorry, tome, in which a well-known columnist who shall remain nameless—but not blameless!—states that while the man's writing is worse than bad he found the tale being related was so fascinating that he could scarcely tear himself away from the book. What d'you make of this separation of writing from its content?

JK: Well, to state a truism: good writing is good writing. The tale itself is integral with and fully dependent on its author's fluency of expression and mastery of his/her craft. Let's take a familiar literary device—the so-called "cliff-hanger." The dramatic energy surge derived from its usage depends crucially upon the writing itself, it is through the deployment of the writer's words on the page that dramatic tension is evolved.

JT: I'm with you on that. I remember seeing this movie in which the film's camera could be glimpsed in the bedroom mirror recording this woman's removal of about forty petticoats. For me that mechanical voyeur provides the perfect metaphor, it sums up the essence of what bad writing is, namely, authorial intrusion, allowing the machinery of the prose to rise through the creative surface. I'll risk your wrath by adding a further metaphor: good writing is not to be found on the written page in any discernible marshalling of words and phrases. Nevertheless, it is there, as subtle as a watermark which remains undiminished, and the stronger the critical light brought to bear on it then all the more strongly does it flourish its presence.

JK: When critics discuss the likes of Jeffrey Archer, Jilly Cooper, Frederick Forsyth or suchlike mainstream writers they always make the error of divorcing the story from the writing, you know. I remember once in the Paisley Group I felt I'd been slagging off people, especially Frederick Forsyth, without really justifying my criticism. There was somebody in the group who liked Forsyth and could scarcely believe that I didn't share his taste. So I brought in a Forsyth novel with the intention of using it to illustrate the fundamental flaws in this author's writing. As it happened I didn't have to look further than the book's first paragraph. It was incomprehensible. From the first sentence you started to ask yourself: "What's he talking about? What's going on?" The writing was so unclear. What you do with novels like that, and Archer's, all that kind of stuff, is to skip pages, you don't have to read every word presented: that's how most readers get through these bulky books.

JT: Aye, and just as there's writing to a set formula, so it's not surprising that there's formulaic reading. By that I mean readers of mainstream novels take up, say a Wilbur Smith novel, with certain expectations—that the hero or heroine will be forced to run over a by-now-familiar terrain in which only the land mines have been redistributed; that there'll be narrow squeaks aplenty; that the key character'll overcome his problems and live to tell the tale. I get very annoyed with this childish expectancy, this doltish need to have everything rendered in terms of "wee adventures." And if that isnay bad enough there usually occurs the egregious epilogue, you know, when a dumb Della Street says with a wrinkled infant brow: "What I don't understand, Perry, is how the hand grenade got into the victim's bra in the first place ..."

If the novel *SHS* gets any critical notice at all I suppose its apparent lack of resolution will receive prime mention. Too bad, is all I can say to those readers who want everything neatly tied up. The fact that Clay was currently reading the life of Pirandello should've been hint enough.

You know, Jim, it's been said that the novel's a dying art form and that its practitioners are merely indulging in a nostalgia for the antique pleasure of reading. The spate of comic books continues to increase, most of them seemingly pandering to the modern young adult's predilection for speedy delivery: fast food, fast cars, and even faster fiction. It's hard to imagine your present-day adolescent working his way through the solid columns of print which featured in the comics read by his or her grandparents. You know, *Hotspur*, *Rover*, *Wizard*, *Adventure*, *Girls' Crystal*. Mind you, when I started to outgrow such comics you could see even then the rot setting in—the graphic artists, having seized the covers of these magazines, had begun to penetrate their interiors.

JK: One of the things I think of that, Jeff, is the crucial necessity of book publishing continuing in this country. What's at stake is not only political integrity but public honesty as well. If there isnay going to be an honest media, right, no truthful media, no honest radio, no honest television, no honest filmmaking, no honest theatre, then writing and reading of books becomes a possible centre of resistance against the multiplying corruptions in present-day public life. That's basically what I feel anyway. Other than book publication there are no mediums available which can offer anything else but a feeble token resistance to the blight of censorship and anti-radicalism. One possible ally in the fight against authoritarian suppression of the media outlets could be alternative video, you know, maybe in the same way as you can get indie music, wee labels, that kind of thing. If that happens and you start to get the spread of honesty in video then maybe, aye, there'll be less reading about. But until that happens the need for honesty and truth demands the reading and writing of books.

JT: When I laboured to a heating engineer on the building sites I asked him what purpose an expansion loop served. He told me it was used to prevent pipes from bursting. He agreed that the device certainly added to the cost of pipe installation since it involved the conduit being forced to make detours in order to accommodate the loop. But because immutable laws of physics were in play and the water delivery system would abort without the loops then they were an expense that had to be bourne. It'll probably come as no surprise to you, Jim, that I'm about to hit you with another metaphor, a political one this time. The way I see it is that the more fascist and tyrannical a regime becomes the more permissive and liberal it seems to act. An oppositional press is allowed to criticise the government; much-publicised political amnesties are granted to formerly reviled dissidents; the State Theatre performs works which are thinly veiled satires against the regime—to such performances foreign dignitaries are taken. "See what we permit," say the despots. The reality of course is that all of those people, from the insurrectionist editor to the "pardoned" dissident, the playwright, and the actors, are all creatures of a series of political expansion loops. Unless these detours, which is all they represent, are allowed then the system will fracture through over-rigidity.

JK: I remember being asked by the British Council to do some readings in Germany. On the railway platform a council member—he was quite a nice guy—says to me, "We were asked why you were invited along to this." But he told them straight, he said, "It's far better to have your radicals within …" So they're part of that loop you're talking about as well, you know, although our National Controllers haven't been slow in identifying the likely eruptive spots in the system like Toxteth or Bristol, or wherever, to which they dispatch posthaste their incumbent Minister of High Hopes, along with the boys in blue; the troops. The Tories proved skilful too in creaming off working-class talent. Maybe the reason Thatcher got the establishment elbow was her increasing rigidity.

[*Pause*]

Well, Jeff—the tape's aboot done, you'll be glad to hear.

JT: Aye, so's the bevvy. Time for a pint. Cheers, then.

JK: Cheers, Jeff. It is.

10

1995

Interview by *Scottish Trade Union Review*

This interview originally appeared as "K Is for Culture" in the January–February 1995 issue of *Scottish Trade Union Review*. It ended with the following note: "Thanks to Tommy Gorman for his help in conducting this interview."

***Scottish Trade Union Review*:** Your recent writings have created something of a stushie amongst the literary establishment. You don't really set out to get up their noses, do you?

James Kelman: Well, it has to be said that usually I get good reviews from the actual literary establishment. I've been publishing now for twenty-two years and my work has caused a bit of controversy all the time during that period. Now obviously the Booker Prize thing brought an awful lot of stuff out the closet ... whether these prejudices are basically elitist, or racist, a lot of people felt very up front about being able to attack myself and by implication the community of people that they think I am part of and also write about, so I allowed them to come out and attack that quite blatantly and that's been a very interesting thing.

I certainly don't set out to get up their noses, although it's quite pleasant when you do. I never actually consider the audience at any time, whether good or bad. I just set out to write the story ... to make it ... to cleanse it ... so it stands properly and is not open to misinterpretation and any ambiguities. I just take great pains with each story so that every comma is my comma, every full stop is mine ... just so that everything is as precise as it should be, that's my only aim. In other words I just see the story, I don't see anything beyond the story. Once it's finished it takes care of itself.

STUR: Your writing has brought you fame and, some might say, notoriety. You previously refused to attend a Booker Prize giving, yet you did attend and accept the winner's prize this year. Can you explain this change of heart?

JK: Well, you know, I considered going the first time and didn't go ... and the same again this time, I considered going or not going and eventually did go for different reasons. I don't think it's a big enough deal to warrant acting on principle about it ... it's important to the literary establishment and that includes the whole bookselling industry but I don't regard prizes in that way at all for writers, I don't think it's as important to writers as all that really ...

STUR: An article entitled "Scotland the Depraved?" which says that Scotland's literary image is a nation of drunks, drug addicts and dropouts, quite clearly fits you within this framework and actually gives you the title of being the leader of this literary school. How do you feel about this type of criticism?

JK: Well, this is really a big ... huge sort of question ... I think the first thing is the establishment in Scotland, the political establishment, and that includes the media and people who kind of, eh, play the game, regard any artist in Scotland as being an unpaid member of the Scottish tourist agency. They regard artists as being part of their promotional team, and that they should put forward this image that will attract overseas investment. They think that any kind of dwelling on the reality of—for want of a better term—the working classes, the richness of that class or group or community of people, is bad for business. So writers like myself or Tom Leonard or Irvine Welsh or any writer or artist who seems to be dwelling on the culture of the working classes is a threat.

An obvious example was Michael Kelly, a fairly established figure within the Labour Party, being a former Lord Provost of Glasgow, where he took the trouble to write to the Scotsman saying something along the lines of "Well, I've not read Kelman's novel but from what I hear it's written in a language that you wouldn't want to read, because it's the type of thing you can hear daily from taxi drivers and plumbers." Basically what he is saying is it's not worthy of literature—so there you have an extremely elitist statement by a member of the Labour Party establishment in Scotland. And in a way that's a sort of general thing … it was an essential part of what was going on, say, since 1986/87, and came to a crescendo in the Year of Culture.

Most of the attacks on us were from the soft left in the establishment, Glasgow District Council or occasionally the Region. They were really upset by the independence of the artists and that independence is also a left-wing independence which, in a sense, is also the independence of the ordinary people and I think that the threat for them is that, although the structures tell them that they are in control of the people, occasionally they aren't. As for example we saw during the poll tax struggle where obviously it was the people that won that fight.

I think all our work really, the work of many of the artists in Scotland, is an attack on authority, is always an attack on authority … where that authority is left-wing as in this country, it's still an attack. I mean let's face it, the Labour Party establishment, of course, their claim to fame is that they'll manage the market economy better than the Tories. I mean, they're just in there showing that they're better managers. And they're also primarily engaged in appealing to the, say, the two prongs of late capitalist economies—in other words both industry and the city and finance—and trying to play that sort of game. So we don't fit in of course with any of that and they attack us in any way they can.

Another part of this that's also very important here—most of the top jobs in Scottish public life are held by English people, even those who are not English really ... people who have assimilated the values of the upper-middle-class elite in England. This is not a nationalist position or xenophobia about English people, it's a very clear political point. What you find is that the people who form the bulk of the [Scottish] establishment, these are a sort of comprador class you would say, from other struggles and other parts of the world. They're people who are kind of ... they've been bought, that's basically it, they've been bought. Artists like myself, and also political activists or cultural activists who are engaged in a way different to what they would like, would be attacked by this group of people that I am describing, kind of assimilationists, this kind of comprador class. They're upset by what they see as the dwelling on working-classness in the base material of my writing, for example. They actually ... it's almost like they're ashamed of it, you know ... just imagine, they're meeting all these people socially who were born and bred into this ... and they want to kind of show that there's no difference between them, or if there's a difference it's something to do with Highland mists or something like that. I think the fact is that they're ashamed because they implicitly accept their own inferiority. So many people, so many Scottish people who are in authority, or part of the authority structure, basically feel inferior to those who are genuinely upper-middle-class English, because they are genuinely that. So they get very upset when they discover that there's all this going on by people who are actually fighting or in struggle against it, because the bottom line is they've sold out, so they don't like to be reminded of it.

Also, just like any country under imperial rule—which is basically what Scotland has been, like so many other countries in the former empire—our education system is designed to teach us that we are inferior. Our kids are always taught that they're failures, they're taught that their language is debased, they're taught that their culture is debased. Of course in some countries this has happened in a much worse way than the likes of Scotland and Wales. For example, the Kurdish people—the children go through the education system and they're actually taught that they don't exist, you could say like in the way the Scottish Gaelic community were essentially taught that they didn't exist either. Their language didn't actually exist, never mind it was debased, whereas us, we are taught our language is debased. So it's a very complex thing about why people are so threatened within Scotland about what the artists in Scotland are doing. The implications of that throws the whole education structure into disarray.

STUR: So you would say that there is nothing wrong with the language of joiners, plumbers, welders?

JK: I mean, this is, it's so absolutely ridiculous and saying it's absolutely ridiculous is to give it the benefit of the doubt. Ultimately the establishment want—the best possible mode for them is—silence, they want silence. They can censor and they often do censor but they much prefer that people censor themselves and that people are silent. So there's this incredible onslaught all the time on ordinary people that your language is a debased thing and therefore we don't want to hear it, and it doesn't have the value of our language and it doesn't deserve to be heard.

You know, how can anyone's language be bad or not good enough? There is no such thing as a hierarchy of language or a hierarchy of culture or a hierarchy of art. That's real kind of elitist and right-wing propaganda and the problem is that an awful lot of people believe it. This is why let's say an ordinary kind of kid in Glasgow when you're at your parents', it's not only the teacher that gives you a doing for saying "doon" instead of "down" or "aye" instead of "yes," a lot of the times it's your mother: she also gies ye a slap and says now don't say that, you know … don't say "doon," you know. So I mean the level of propaganda that's been kind of imbibed by people to keep each other down is quite incredible, you know.

How is it possible to say that someone's language is wrong? Language equates with people's existence, it's like saying that someone's life is wrong. What does it mean when a politician says of an ordinary citizen that their life is wrong? What does it actually mean?

STUR: Is it possible to explain to us how in fact you go about building up your hopeless, unambitious, inarticulate characters and their social conditions?

JK: Well, right away, obviously, it's debatable whether or not that is the situation of my characters. In other words I don't necessarily think it's hopeless or unambitious or inarticulate at all.

But the question about how you build it up … I think I just try, like any writer should be allowed … I just want to work within my own experience really. That means like everything in my experience, including whatever I've read in life, or whatever I've watched on television but most importantly whatever I've come into contact with, or whatever, in my community, within my own community. So all you could say is that I just want to be able to work from within my own community, beyond that really it's to do with technique and method. I don't start up stories with ideas, I just actually begin a story from nothing, like the way a sculptor operates, I just begin from writing some words down and gradually I make a story out of it. The old Scottish term "makar" really, that's the way I see it. You make a story. You begin from the words, like a craftsman in that sense, and you just make a story. I don't begin with any idea of what that story will be, I just begin and go on from there.

STUR: There has been much comment in recent years about a renaissance in Scottish culture in general and literature in particular. Is there a Scottish cultural and literary "movement"? If so, how far is it political, left-wing or anti-establishment? And how far do you feel that you are a part of it? For example do you socialise with other Scottish writers in a regular way?

JK: Well, taking the last part first: yes, I see quite a few Scottish writers—not necessarily regular, but yes I do. I think, one thing—there's more generosity amongst writers than critics. I don't think writers are really in competition with each other … most writers get on with each other, or most writers I know anyway.

But okay, to take the other side of it, I think there is a growing self-confidence amongst people, and that's what's going on in Scottish literature. There is certainly not a literary movement as such, whatever there is. I think it's part of being confident, and that is like saying, "I'm not saying my language is any better than you, or my culture is any better than you but it's a valid language and valid culture, and as a writer I'll make use of my language." Just having that confidence to be able to do that, I think, that's the crucial thing that's happened.

Now that's taken a long, long time. I mean, there is a tradition of writers in Scotland who have been using or trying to use language in this way. That includes people like Fergusson and Burns, and right through the nineteenth century you'll find one or two (not many)—James Hogg, parts of Stevenson, even parts of Walter Scott as well, where there's an occasional confidence in language: so it's not something that's only happened in the last twenty-five years, you know …

STUR: Do you see yourself as a "Glasgow writer"?

JK: Well, the fact is I was born and bred in Glasgow. To some extent where you're born, well, that's an accident, it so happens I was born in the city of Glasgow so I'm a Glaswegian writer. I don't feel any particular responsibility from being from Glasgow. I could have been born anywhere. Anyway, there's been all these different cultural experiences here so the culture of Glasgow is really rich and varied, it contains many, many different cultures, a great many different ones, so there is no such thing as the "Glasgow writer" in that sense. There are only writers who live and work in Glasgow really, that's all.

STUR: Some critics characterise you as very much the "macho man" … is this fair? Are there any contemporary women writers whose work you admire?

JK: Well, there are many, many women writers whose work I admire. See, one of the things is that women have had, in writing, one of the most influential roles in literature, simply because women have had to fight against the existing value, and that value is a paternalist male value.

So some of the most important writers in the tradition that I think I am part of have been women. They're the ones that have had to subvert the whole paternalistic male-dominated value system which works within literature. So women have had to find ways of turning it on its head. So the writers at the root of the American realistic tradition have mainly been women, writers like Kate Porter, Gertrude Stein, right through later ones such as Flannery O'Connor ... there are so many really important writers who have been women and especially within this tradition of subverting the existing values of authority. So it would just be a nonsense for any writer to not be influenced by women, that's just nonsense ...

Now it's interesting that a lot of the "macho male writer" criticism (of myself) comes from liberal men who make it on behalf of women—in other words the typical liberal position: they are representing the views of what they regard as the victims.

There is the technical point of course, you know, and this is an obvious point to me, so much so that it makes it difficult to treat seriously criticisms about being macho—I intentionally work from the perspective of a male narrative voice, in other words, the voice that tells the stories that I write is a male voice. Now take the last novel [*How Late It Was, How Late*] as an example. This is very deliberately written in the voice of a man who could be an acquaintance of the central character, an acquaintance of the man that goes blind, and also he is telling the story to other men and the ideal setting would be in a pub. So you could say this story is told by a man to other men in a pub and he is telling the story about another guy, and this other guy is a guy who would normally be drinking in the same pub with the same people. In a sense I'm being condemned for what I set out to do intentionally. Much of the criticism is prejudiced … it doesn't actually look at the work, it begins from a prejudice about the work.

STUR: You are better known for novels and short stories, but recently you had a play on in Glasgow, Edinburgh and Dublin, *One, Two—Hey*, about a rhythm and blues band?

JK: That's actually the fifth play I've had on. This play was basically a collaboration between myself and George Gallacher of the Poets, the Blues Poets, one of the legendary Sixties bands, so it was a great thing to work on. It would be very expensive and very difficult for any company to put this on in Scotland because of the whole way theatre funding operates … it's geared towards amateurs and very cheap productions.

Our sort of play, with twelve people, with a lot of music and real musicians doing the music, you couldn't really put that on in Scotland unless you were within one of the big funded theatre companies, because they are the only ones that get that kind of dough. So we had to form our own company and put it on ourselves.

This is the first time I've been involved for five years and I mean normally I can't even get my own plays on in Glasgow.

This one wouldn't have been put on except the fact that we put it on ourselves and the Arches Theatre were good enough to let us tour it in there. It doesn't even matter if your play sells out—our play began selling out in Glasgow and in Edinburgh for the five days, but there was no possibility for us getting any help from Glasgow District and Strathclyde Region. There would be no money for us, but they would be very willing to spend upwards of £500,000 with something that fits in with their own political standpoint. I'm talking of course about the play about the First World War, because it happens to be a thing in their interest to commemorate and that whole kind of, what could you say, shitty way of operating really.

STUR: You were involved in Workers City, which is probably best known for its campaigns against many of the grand
schemes initiated by Glasgow City Council for 1990 Year of
Culture. Why was Workers City formed, and what results has
it had?

JK: It was always a wide range of people who didn't have
one political view. They did have certain political beliefs in
common, you know, things should be seen to be aboveboard
and that corruption should not operate. A great many of those
involved had been through various party formations and I
think one of the things in common was that people were just
sickened by the prevailing political systems and that includes
the left, the established left.

So I wouldn't presume to speak on behalf of Workers City
really. I didn't become involved with Workers City until something like February 1990 itself. I joined a picket at Glasgow's
Glasgow because it seemed a thing that I should be supporting.
A Glasgow guy, Farquhar McLay, had made a statement [in his
Keelie editorial] and had asked for support from people who
were in opposition to the European City of Culture year. Now
there was a great many people in opposition to that who were
not involved in Workers City and that includes writers and
artists. Away about eighteen months before the City of Culture
thing we held a huge big meeting one Saturday afternoon and
there was about eighty to a hundred people turned up for this,
this was either late 1988 or early 1989 and there was Alistair
Gray and a lot of visual artists and musicians, there was so
many people there. [In his statement] Farquhar was talking to
a lot of the artists he knew were not involved in Workers City
and were taking a kind of affirmative position outside it.

When we occupied the City Chambers, there was about
two hundred people there, you know. The same with other
issues—that horrible thing they did to Elspeth King and Michael
Donnelly, that was another case where hundreds of people, thou-
sands of people in fact, got involved in that campaign. There was

more people that wrote to the *Glasgow Herald* about that obscenity conducted by Glasgow's Labour authority than any other issue since Billy Graham came here in 1955 or something like that. Each campaign had different people involved in it.

Of course there is the one thing that I still haven't changed my view on, is the whole selling point from Glasgow Council and all of those behind the City of Culture year. I mean they described that as being a celebration of art and culture. It wasn't. It was an attack on art. It attacked art and it attacked artists, there is just no question about that.

STUR: You are not known as a campaigner for a Scottish parliament unlike many other people in literature and the arts. Are you opposed to a Scottish parliament?

JK: No, not at all, it's just that I personally don't campaign on behalf of it. As far as I'm personally concerned it's not a major issue. Because you don't campaign on behalf of one issue doesn't mean that you are in opposition to it. It often just means that you don't have the time or energy to commit to it because you are involved in other things.

Having said that, I don't think that a Scottish parliament is the answer to our social and economic problems in Scotland, especially if it's going to be controlled in the same old way, you know, controlled by those who believe that the British electoral system offers the means for radical change in society. So if we get a Scottish parliament through the benevolent grace of the British parliament, then I can't conceive of how that can be some kind of radical thing because otherwise we wouldn't be given it. I don't take part in it, that whole kind of parliamentarian political process, to me it's an absolute charade.

STUR: You are an active campaigner on behalf of those who suffer from asbestos-related illness. What made you so concerned about this particular issue?

JK: I came in contact with a couple of people who were involved in that fight full time really, ex-pipe-coverers and guys who had the asbestos-related diseases, and just became aware of what the issue was. It's rather like that lawyer who started so much of this campaign going in Australia, he could see what was happening in the courts and he couldn't believe it, his quote was "These people are dying, what the fuck's going on here?" That was actually the thing that came home to me: if these diseases exist then these people are dying. So here is a set of diseases people get because they go to their work, that's all, and no one is doing anything about it. The government's manufacturing the figures and the medical industry are not diagnosing and the lawyers are accusing them of malingering, the state's not paying benefits, no one knows it's happening, no one knows anything about these diseases. No one knows that the asbestos industry are themselves aware. They are going about killing people, and no one is doing anything about it. I just found my head reeling with implications and found that I couldn't do anything else than be involved really. It was just impossible not to be involved.

The campaigning group in Glasgow got no funding whatsoever, they got nothing, they just got kind of pennies here and there or some donations from individual trade union branches which usually meant that one person was interested and tried to do whip-rounds. There was no kind of organised assistance for these people at all coming from the labour movement—in fact, on the contrary, you could say they were being obstructive. I saw that there was a lot of basic stuff that I could do such as writing or how to speak the language of certain parts of officialdom. So gradually I became totally involved in that campaign, to the extent that I didn't do anything else for over a year, really, I was a full-time worker you could say ...

When you are involved in this campaign you become very aware of the structures of state. I mean, if you had given up terms like "class war," once you become involved in this sort of issue you very much are back to using them again and talking about things like "the working class," terms that we are not comfortable using these days. But when you are involved in campaigns like this you start to see in fact that the class war still goes on. And it's not that ordinary working people are on the attack, it's just that war has been perpetrated against them. You are just trying to defend yourself, in a sense, finding ways of organising against these attacks that are continually going on, and you find that the state, the British state, is operational on every front against you. All these different institutions such as the medical profession, the legal profession, the DSS, all these different aspects of state, are all kind of refining their own arms against victims of industrial disease. And it's refined to such an extent that people who are actually killing other people, there is no recourse under law to bring them to trial.

So what you find is that it's almost as though civil law has been set up by the State so that the State doesn't have to answer to criminal charges. In a sense this is what your awareness of the fight of people suffering industrial diseases is about. It's about things like murderers getting off scot-free—that's basically what it's about.

STUR: Are there any other issues that you have been involved in campaigning on behalf of?

JK: I have tried to help in issues around race ... the fight that black people have in Britain, for black people it's like the whole of the State is on the attack against them.

In an analogy, in the way that you are a victim of asbestos-related disease, you go to the doctor expecting the doctor to diagnose your disease. You find they don't do it and you've got to fight against it. Now similarly if you are a victim of racist assaults, or a member of your family has been killed by racists, you would naturally expect the police to look for the victims, or to say that you have been assaulted, or that a member of your family has been killed by racists, or whatever. That's in fact not what happens. What you find is that you have to tell the police about motive and you have to actually prove that the member of your family has been killed by racists. And you start to go through and find out in fact that, no, it's not just racism on the street, and it's not just one person has an asbestos-related disease—it's the whole State itself doing these things ... every arm of it is designed to aid and abet the perpetrators.

STUR: Can you tell us a little about your background, your work and trade union experience?

JK: I left school at fifteen and started as a message boy and apprentice compositor in the printing trade. My family emigrated when I was seventeen. There was nothing in SOGAT [Society of Graphical and Allied Trades] articles that would allow an apprentice to leave and emigrate with his or her family and resume the apprenticeship in another country, so you were basically expelled, and to get themselves out of it they called it "voluntary expulsion." I would say that was quite important for me because when I came back to this country, which was only a few months later, and I went back to the printer which was John Thomlinson's in Partick, they were very happy that I resumed as an apprentice compositor again—and the shop steward, my "father of the chapel," he had the horrible duty of having to tell me the firm would take me back but SOGAT wouldn't allow it. SOGAT said, "Oh no, we can't allow that, this guy is voluntary expelled, and we don't care, there is no way that we can allow him back in." So therefore I wasn't allowed back in.

So from that point on, in retrospect, I have a fairly kind of jaundiced attitude towards the full-time organisation of the trade union movement, because I had kind of bumped my head against it at that time. Another thing I remember when our family emigrated to the States, I remember going after a job at one point and finding this wee printer over in Pasadena and they said, "Oh yes, great, you can start work with us as soon as you are eighteen"—because you can't work in the States until you are eighteen—"you just wait another six months and you can start with us and meanwhile you can go and see the union man here." I saw the union guy there. And I remember being amused at that time, and surprised that the trade union guy in Pasadena had heard of the secretary of the SOGAT branch in Glasgow. I'm talking about '63, '64, that the guy knew of him. Back in Glasgow I remember I got a letter saying, "Are you coming back to work in the States, we've got this job for you." So if I had gone back to the States in [June] '64 I could have resumed my apprenticeship out in Pasadena, but here in Glasgow although the employers were willing, the SOGAT hierarchy would not allow it.

So from there then I began a kind of whole process of jobs at that time. I joined the line out in Shieldhall, the old Cooperative shoe factory. They used to make things like Beatle boots ... so I was a shoemaker for a time, I was given one of those horrible jobs on the line, you know, on the piecework line where you're worked twice as hard as the guy up from you but he's getting about twelve times as much as you do. Again, the sort of discrepancy amongst guys on the same assembly line also gives you a very jaundiced view of the trade union, what their priorities are. I stuck that for about four or five months. I did a lot of different types of jobs. What else did I do?—selling and various stuff like that, factories—and then I joined the buses. That was a liberation for me, becoming a bus conductor.

Then I left Scotland altogether when I was about nineteen and went to work in Manchester ... well, the irony there, I worked in Turner and Newall's in Trafford Park. I mixed for asbestos sheeting. My job was similar to what you do if you are a brickie's labourer except I mixed the cement with asbestos and water to make asbestos boards, with a wee mixer, kind of a third the size of a concrete mixer. I worked on that for quite a few months. It was a great job, you know, I mean, there was only immigrants that worked on this job, whether you were from Glasgow or whether you were Irish or whether you were from the Caribbean or occasionally from Pakistan or from Eastern Europe. There were a lot of immigrants from Eastern Europe, older guys from Hungary and Georgia and various parts of Russia and Poland. There was very few people from England worked in these jobs.

After that job I worked in a copper mill, another amazing kind of prehistoric type of operation. I mean the safety equipment in this job was just a joke, so there is a wee bit for a novel of mine where a character's toe touches the copper bar and his shoes burst into flames. That happened to a mate of mine who was an electrician but couldn't get a job as an electrician, so he came semi-skilling with me and discovered a whole new world! So when his shoe burst into flames he threw down his fucking tongs and just said, "That's me, I'm chucking it" and walked out. If he'd been a tradesman there he could do things like that but whereas if you're right at the bottom of the heap you know you can't do these sorts of things!

I stuck that job for quite a long while, these jobs always pay better money than ordinary labouring jobs. You could work things like twelve-hour shifts and that gave you plenty of money to buy your own safety equipment, you know, you could spend your money on safety shoes and things like that!

Anyway after that I went to London …

There is an important point in the way that trade unions are perceived I think, really, that hasn't, I don't think ever been stressed as much as it should be stressed—the difference between a trade union for an actual craft or a trade and how trade unions operate for labourers and semi-skilled people. As a boy in SOGAT I ran up against one of the strongest unions at that time and one of the most powerful unions in the business. And one of the ways it got strong, obviously, is also why I was expelled …

Now in all these other jobs, I experienced the exact opposite of that. I experienced trade unionism at its least powerful. I was either a labourer or I was semi-skilled and essentially trade unions don't exist for workers like that. All my experience in industrial disease and industrial accident and injury after that has always just established that safety is so far down the list for labourers and semi-skilled as to be non-existent. Labourers and semi-skilled people do some of the most hazardous jobs of all really, with the fewest safety precautions. In some of these jobs an ordinary part of your job maybe eight times an hour is avoiding serious injury or death, and that isn't an exaggeration. It is actually part of being skilled at your job and concentrating on your job that you don't lose fingers and ultimately you don't get killed. And it is very hard for people who have never worked in industry at this level or in the construction industry, they think that when people say what I'm saying just now that they are talking metaphors or something like that, and we are not—this is the literal truth, you know. Basically we have scars to prove it. You could actually point to something and go, "See that scar there, I remember getting that because I knew I had two winners up and I was waiting for another two, so I was thinking about how I was going to spend the money and bump I suddenly got hit in the eye ... "

The last ordinary job I did was in 1975 really, when I worked in McLellan's Rubber Works—and that was a case in question again. That was the Transport and General Workers. So many ordinary labour and semi-skilled jobs are covered by the T&G, it really is the general union for so many workers, but at that level it is basically non-existent really. So again I got a very jaundiced view of trade unionism, but from the opposite view. It was just so weak, I mean, it was actually an embarrassment to the labour movement. You couldn't even give it the benefit of the doubt and say it was corrupt, it was just so kind of weak and inefficient and timid and passive.

STUR: Recently you were involved in supporting RMT during the signal workers' dispute and put quite a bit of effort into that. But apart from that, what are your thoughts on the current state of the trade union movement, particularly in Scotland, and what do you think the STUC should be doing in the forthcoming period in the run-up to the general election?

JK: I think above all they should be listening to the members, and being aware of what actually the members feel themselves. They should be aware of things like the reality of democracy, they should be aware of the discrepancy between that and representative democracy and they shouldn't allow themselves to be sucked into the trap of being representatives, in the sense that they can make decisions on behalf of their members, often without recourse to what the membership actually think.

An awful lot of people are going to be very kind of sceptical about, for example, a Scottish parliament, so I don't think that the TUC leadership should try somehow to ignore the scepticism. I think they should be supportive of things like the Scottish parliament, or even the Labour Party, and allow their scepticism to be up front. In other words, I don't think they should align themselves with this kind of whole notion of representational politics.

I was talking about the internal elitism, the way all trade unions operate as a meritocracy. As soon as you talk about bonus, piecework, blah blah, everything like that, or issues like health and safety, you will find out that the higher up the scale you go the better the conditions. So that means for example if you are a joiner or if you are an electrician or a plumber then you are going to get much better access than for example a brickie's labourer, a chippie's labourer or a spark's labourer. The kind of practices that the tradesmen get, you won't get, you'll have to fight for them. So even at that level these kinds of discrepancies within the trade unions have to be looked at, I mean, these issues are absolutely fundamental. A lot of these things can actually be taken in hand by ordinary members themselves, they don't have to wait for the leaders to do it.

Take industrial disease for instance, I mean, anyone involved in the asbestos thing, you know, you become so cynical about the leadership of any union, because of what can be done and what cannot be done, that ultimately you feel that there is not much point talking to them at all, it is much better to try and get across or get access to ordinary members, what you might call the shop floor, and say, "Look, there are things that we can do just now." There are things that can be done and that will bring its own pressures on those who have greater power within the trade union movement.

Over the last fifteen or sixteen years, since the mid-'70s, before Thatcher came into power, the movement has become passive and one of the things ordinary members can do is embarrass and shame the leadership—not just the full-time officials but also other officials. To shame them and show this is how strong we are, there is this strength here and don't try and manage it. The problem of course is the leadership both full-time and otherwise fall into the role of being managers and they end up managing the activities of the membership on behalf of the employers. That is not what their role is, their role is to genuinely represent the views, beliefs and activities of the membership.

When I was on the buses there was no such thing as an official strike within the T&G, it was a long-standing joke. There only ever was one official strike. What happened in any strike was the very first people you took on was your own union, I mean, that was how it was, it probably still is. The first people who told you to go back to work was always the trade union hierarchy. The bosses always sent them, the first thing they did was get the full-timers down from Bath Street to your place of work to say, "Right lads, let's get back to work." That was just a standing joke.

That was how the trade union leadership was perceived and it's no different now.

If the TUC can do anything it is just not to be passive and not to be timid, not to be cowardly. Above all they have to have faith in the people and encourage open ideas, open discourse. A genuine democracy of thought really is what's very very important and not to be afraid of open debate.

11

2000

Interview by William Clark

This interview was recorded in late August 2000 and appeared in the Spring 2001 issue of *Variant*.

In September 1999 the first new play by James Kelman for five years was ready for production on a profit-share basis by a small Glasgow-based company; the actor Gary Lewis had already committed to it. At the time Kelman and Edwin Morgan were joint holders of the Scottish Writer of the Year award. Edinburgh's Traverse Theatre was the first venue approached, simply to stage his play as a profit-sharing touring production. The Traverse was Kelman's choice; during past years three of his own plays have been produced there, and his translation of a play by French playwright Enzo Corman. However, the Traverse requested that Kelman submit the play for consideration by the "literature committee." He reminded them that he only wanted to bring the play in on a profit-share, touring basis. The Traverse insisted and Kelman replied to the effect that he didn't do auditions these days. He withdrew the play and wrote to the Scottish Arts Council to express his feelings about the situation. No doubt somebody there read his letter. If so they kept it to themselves.

James Kelman: When I got involved in this thing last September [1999], almost a year ago, I thought of it as something personal and was wanting to keep it personal. I'd just come home from the States, I had been away about a year so things were kind of hectic and I didn't want to get too involved. I didn't have the time to get involved anyway, I had a lot of stuff to clear up; the new novel, get on with my essays, then the plays. But I thought about going public. There seemed to be a lot happened within the Arts Council in the last couple of years that was detrimental, and it should be taken on. The changes to do with the Book Trust for instance: as I understand it the Book Trust is now responsible for a lot of work the literature department used to do. Things that had been the case are no longer the case, such as money. Before, if you were ever taking part in a gig, doing a reading or whatever, where the audience were charged to get in, you'd always be paid a minimum wage. The writer would not take part in something where there was an admission fee and no payment and the Arts Council would not have supported such an event. There was always a basic payment for the writer. That was part of the way things used to operate so there's been a lot of changes, all these rip-off readings from places like Borders and Waterstones, writers never getting a paid a penny, why don't they boycott them. I remember a couple of years back the Edinburgh Book Festival broke the guidelines, they offered me a fee of fifty quid. I couldn't believe it. At that time the minimum Arts Council fee was £80, maybe £70. It was extraordinary they tried to get away with it. They were surprised when I said no! I don't know how it is at the Book Festival nowadays, I haven't been back since. Maybe it'll improve with Catherine Lockerbie in charge.

But no writer should ever take part in that kind of shit. The public getting charged money to get in as well, why don't they pay the writers a proper fee! The same with financial support to arts magazines: the main reason the Arts Council gave it was so the writers who wrote for them got a payment for the contribution. So there was that, then the way the education department has crept into the Arts Council reckoning as well.

Does that mean their criteria will start being used to deal with writers, censoring or suppressing the ones school inspectors don't want to be seen or heard in a classroom? So now writers who are in any way radical are going to stop getting readings? Is that what it means? It'll just be all the safe bastards who'll be earning the fees from school or university readings. Of course that is the way it is just now anyway when you look about, I'm talking generally, the ones getting the "Creative Writing" and residency jobs. You just have to look at the literary brochures and flyers coming at you, quite a cosy wee scene, and then there's the team doing their bit for the government with these British Council invitations—Burns Suppers in Turkey and Israel, Saudi Arabia, blah blah blah.

So a lot of different things, I felt there was a lot of questions needing to be addressed. Other writers must feel the same. And if I had got too involved in this thing of mine with the Arts Council I thought I would wind up having to get into it, these other issues, and I didn't want to, so I was being selfish, no time no energy. I tried to keep it at that personal level, just me moaning. Here was a situation pertaining to myself, one writer, a writer who has done this much work, x-amount. It doesn't have to be good, bad or indifferent work either, just that if this writer gets a new book out people will read it and if he puts on a new play audiences will want to go and see it. Good, bad or indifferent. Just because the writer has already done all that work in the past and the audience know it, and now here he's got a new work out, that's why the audience are going to be interested. They might go away and criticise it, condemn it, but they'll go and see it in the first place, because it's a particular writer they know: "Kelman's first play for five years, let's go and see it." The Traverse wouldn't have lost, it was just a profit-share, no wages, but we would've got some expenses. So these kind of arguments, basic arguments, I just wanted to let the Arts Council hear my side of it; I can't get my work on in this country unless I'm prepared to put up with these stupid insults. Not even for nothing! Submit your work for consideration! They're so fucking naive, they don't even know they're insulting you. Or do they? I felt part of the strength of my case was because it was one writer, it didn't matter who the hell you were, to the extent that even somebody who was joint holder of the Scottish Writer of the Year Award, Booker Prize blah blah blah, even a writer like that could not get a play on without auditioning, getting approval from some sort of literature committee, without meeting their criteria, whatever that might be, amazing crap. A profit-share, remember, we weren't looking for any commission-type payment from the theatre, just a percentage of the box-office, we were doing all our own rehearsals, finding our own space, in our time, every damn thing, props, the fucking lot, we were asking nothing from them at all except the space to perform the play for a week or two—well, a week, five or six days, they told us there was no chance of a fortnight—nobody gets a fortnight for a touring show, so they say. I thought the strength of the case lay in keeping it personal. A general case could come about but only as an effect of the personal thing. As well as that I felt it was something that could be put right if I explained the situation as clearly as I could: "I cannot get a play on at the Traverse Theatre for nothing, not even for no money," just something like that.

William Clark: You wrote to the Arts Council?

JK: Yeah.

WC: There's an expectation that they can do something. There's also an expectation—you were saying—you assumed that people were aware of your work or that people had made themselves aware of what's going on in Scotland. One makes these assumptions: that at a certain level the Arts Council are even aware of these things or aware of real problems within their organisation (or even aware of the outside world) and they're not. They're just completely oblivious. Somebody like me, who is deeply cynical, "Well, people in the Arts Council don't know anything about contemporary art"; you could almost live your life by that. It's obviously not the case, but you could be forgiven for thinking that it was.

JK: You're right to that extent, but it took me a while to realise that they didn't know my work. They maybe knew it by repute. And not always by the repute I would have chosen. I mean, what was coming across was that they didn't really know my work and some of the attitudes they had to it were the same kind of attitudes you would get from papers like the *Sunday Times* [not the Scottish edition].

WC: "It's not proper literature."

JK: Yeah, they regard me as a "primitive," "preculture"; writers like me are "savages." But it surprised me, even at this stage in your writing life how you still get the vaguely patronising, vaguely irritated attitude coming to you from the Scottish Arts Council. It's an Anglocentric thing, quite a common attitude to Scottish art from people in high Arts Council positions. So there are two points there, Billy, the first thing relating to what you scoffed at, the idea of the Arts Council being able to have some kind of influence on their own employees, I mean the staff at the Traverse Theatre. Of course they saw the Traverse employees as the ones they're in solidarity with. Whatever the employee says goes, and they'll back them up to the hilt. They see you as being the foreigner, the artist. The artist is the alien figure that they're in opposition to. They don't see themselves as people who are there in order to support and assist artists. They don't see themselves as that.

WC: Not at all.

JK: So the first point you made is dead right. Yeah, I wouldn't have illusions about that. Except I did have expectations! In relation to the Traverse you've got to remember that I'd already had a play produced there—two plays. In fact it's been four I've had over the years. One play was actually commissioned by them, and I had one translation commissioned from them as well, a play by a French writer, both about ten or twelve years ago. So what with that and my last play on—*One, Two—Hey* with the Blues Poets band—you felt, well, there's no question here, no economic question either, because *One, Two—Hey* sold out, there's going to be a proper box-office return, it's guaranteed. The Traverse'll know all that stuff already.

WC: They were aware of that?

JK: I don't know. I think I wrote to the director of the theatre in the first place just to make sure he was aware. If he hadn't been at that time then I was going to fill him in with the details. I was basically expecting that he was going to put a word in the ear of the Traverse admin staff: "Don't worry, it's James Kelman, he's a known writer here in Scotland and he's already got a track record, people'll go and see his stuff. It's just a profit-share touring thing anyway." Instead of that the director's position to me was, "Well, I'm backing up the decision already made by my staff and you're out of line expecting anything different. But don't worry, the committee are not going to actually *judge* your play, it's something else, they just want to see if it fits the Traverse bill." Something like that, just splitting hairs. "You've got to put your work in front of our literature committee the same as anybody else. Do you expect to be treated differently because you're a senior writer?" The Traverse director used that phrase, which grated on me, putting me in my place, "senior writer." Not because of the age thing, I don't dispute it, I'm in my fifties. But there was the implication that somebody like me expects to be beyond criticism just because I'm an old bastard, as if I'm saying younger writers should be criticised and judged but not me because I'm beyond it.

So that kind of shite. I felt it was important for me to address that. On the one hand I felt yeah, there's elements in what you're saying that are true. But I know my own response isn't just due to egocentricity or perversity or out-and-out vanity. There is some underlying critical point I want to get to. So I went into it, I tried to work out what the argument was.

Why is it that I expect to be treated differently from somebody else. Is that really what I was asking? Here's another way of saying it: Why does the fifty-three-year-old Kelman expect to be treated differently to the twenty-five- or thirty-year-old Kelman? It can't just be an ego thing. Or can it? So these kind of questions.

I was saying to them the burden of proof is not on me as a writer, that became the bottom line. Look, here is all the work I've produced, it's all out there, it's available, it can be criticised and looked at whenever. If you want to check out my stuff go to the fucking library. I don't have to prove to the Traverse literature committee or any other damn committee that I'm capable of doing this, that or the next thing. I've done all that, time and time again. Here is all my work, it's all out in the open. Just about everything I've ever written is still in print, including three of my plays. So why is it that you want to "consider" my work? What's the context or whatever that makes it valid for you to make that demand? Why do you feel that my work needs to be "considered" by you? Is it to establish that my play will be worthy of being staged at the Traverse? Is it just to see if it'll be "good"? What evidence do you have to suggest that I might give you in something that's "bad"? Away and check your records, go and see how my last three or four plays went, my last two plays sold out, you've got the figures, what the hell is it, what's going on here?

WC: So this is the Traverse Theatre literary department?

JK: Yeah, literature committee.

WC: Who is that?

JK: I hear it can be anybody in the Traverse who's around. They weren't going to say it was this individual or that individual. Just whoever was in that committee at that time. I don't know who it is. It wouldn't matter who it is. I wouldn't allow my work to be "considered" by any of the Arts Council bosses, never mind the literary committee at the Traverse. I'm one of the ones who would never apply for these £25,000 grants they're always on about, "Creative Scotland" awards! For me no one who is a serious artist, who has produced a real body of work, can ever apply for these grants. They're premised on certain attitudes or values in relation to art that very few real artists could support, not honestly, they would have just to kid on. There's a certain way of looking at art, or what equals the "end" of the art project, it can be seen in the brochure/application thing. It's a kind of end-means way of looking at art that I don't think artists themselves really share at all. Old-fashioned reactionary crap, it's nineteenth-century stuff. "How do you expect this work to be valued by the public?" That sort of stupid question Arts Council officers give to artists before handing them out money so they can go and do their fucking work. Naive shite. I would not allow my work to be put in front of any of these people, no, no longer. I might have when I was a young artist, because I had no body of work, fair enough, sometimes I did do that. But sometimes I didn't do it. When Polygon made that first contact with me for *Not Not While the Giro* back in 1981 I had already stopped sending my stuff out for "consideration." Even at that time I had stopped it. If they wanted my stuff, fine, I gave them it, if they didn't I didn't, I wasn't going to fucking audition. That was then never mind now. But if you have a substantial body of work there's no need anyway, I mean what the fuck do they want off you?

WC: So is it your concept of the artist that is alien to these people? You use the word *artist*, they use the word, but it's not the same.

JK: Yeah, not at all. It's weird to meet it head-on like that.

WC: For them an artist is some form of rent boy or something: you're rented; sometimes you don't even get the money.

JK: Yeah, that became quite clear, it becomes clear in the whole phraseology. I got another of the "Creative Scotland" awards information through the letter-box recently. It came through my agent believe it or not ...

WC: Ha!

JK: Yeah—"I thought I should make you aware of it." She's right but, of course she should make me aware of it, that's the sort of thing she gets paid for, she's a good agent. The first time I was sent it was in the middle of all the shenanigans, it was from the director of literature or maybe the overall Arts Council director. Probably an obscure form of put-down. You could only apply in a cynical way because like I said it's got certain attitudes towards art which one cannot share in the year 2000. To give the Arts Council the benefit of the doubt, these are very old-fashioned attitudes, not beyond first-year art theory or something. They make these assumptions about how "we" value art. It's like, What! In order to discover the merit of my work I've got to look at how the audience responds to it! I beg your pardon! The beholder's response to a work of art will define the value of the work of art! That sort of ludicrous shite. You expect it from first-year students, not from people experienced in art. But it's very convenient in relation to funding if you're representing a public body dishing out so-called public funds to so-called artists, you get seen as an efficient individual who is putting the wishes of the public totally to the fore. It's pure crap.

WC: It's just a bureaucratic expediency. They're now getting to the position whereby they prescribe the work: "We will fund a film like … " and then they name a filmmaker who they like. That makes their job easy, it makes administration rationing resources. That's all it is.

JK: There was a Scottish filmmaker based in New York, a young guy, he was wanting to do a film of my novel *The Busconductor Hines*, a few months ago. So I did the first-draft screenplay to get things moving, it was long, 250 to 300 pages, a full piece of work. Later on in the process the guy approached Scottish Screen. I didn't know he was doing that, but when he told me I went along with it. I thought there must be something in it, maybe a change in policy, maybe they were starting to support actual writers … then I was asked along to an interview with the Scottish Screen people. I liked the guy I met there and quite respected what he was saying at first. But then I realised that the only reason I was there was they were wanting to work out if I was worthy of being given a wee up-front sum of dough in order to complete a second draft, or maybe take it a stage further, get it finished, I can't quite remember. That was all it was, all that palaver, just to see if they would throw me a few quid to do more work on the screenplay, they wanted to see if it was merited or not. To give me the fucking money, I mean! I was supposed to submit the first draft of the screenplay to them so they could say whether or not I was worthy of getting this small up-front sum of dough.

I said, "No, you're not judging me at all, what are you talking about?" They were wanting to "consider" my first draft and chat about whether or not the project was merited or some such shite! I had already done all the work—the slogging stuff—for nothing, for no wages, that first draft like I said, I done a full job on it. Remember as well that this was a film based on my own adaptation of my own novel. So all this crap was just if they would deign to give me a wee sum of dough in order for me to go away and work on it some more. The public's dough! This is Scottish Screen, right. The guy who's interviewing me, he's got my entire first-draft screenplay in front of him.

It was to be a three-person committee. So who's to be involved in that? How are they going to do their judging? Are they going to read my novel and then read the first-draft screenplay, and if so then what, what does that tell them? And who's to do it anyway, who is there in Scottish film that's worth a fucking button, who is there to respect as an artist, is there anybody at all, maybe one or two. But really, it's hard to think of anybody in Scottish movies you could trust as an artist, they all compromise, they go for easy options, else they just sell out altogether, and now they're going to sit and "consider" my work! Fuck off. I just find that extraordinary, I'm talking about six months ago. At this stage in my life my work is going to be judged by people like that to get a couple of thousand quid to go away and work on the next stage of the screenplay. It is fucking unbelievable. This is public money for Christ sake it's for artists, to help them do their work, let us do our fucking work, it's just a wage, you'll get it back. What right do they have to stop us doing our work? That's what's happening. The same as happened to the play, that film project has finished, like every other film project I've ever been involved in, nothing.

WC: But all the public money in the administration of public money. You mentioned Scottish Screen. The guy who ran that [Alan Shiach?], an SMG person, gave himself a million pounds of Scottish Screen public money over and above his salary as an administrator for his own project. People are administering these things to get at the money first.

JK: Well, they're succeeding.

WC: The government policy may or may not be well-intentioned, but all they can ever produce is an opportunist's charter. Certain perennial problems of government exist. We're asked to believe that with prohibition in America they couldn't foresee the rise of ... well, look at the drug laws now: they actually think they're working. They can't admit that corruption will destroy any system.

JK: It was foolish of me to get involved. It was a misunderstanding. You see, I hadn't realised that the guy in New York who was going to get things moving had approached Scottish Screen at this trivial level. I thought there was a new approach going on and they were saying, "Right, Kelman is going to do an adaptation of one of his novels at long last and he's already done a full first-draft screenplay. The project's got x-amount of dough ready to come in from Canada and New York and wherever, once it's up and running, so if we give them such and such an amount that'll get the thing moving, once we stick in something the overseas money'll start coming in." That's the level I thought the discussion was going to be at. Then I found out no, it was the same old story, it was back to that old stage where I was going to have to audition my work for a committee of three just to see if I was worthy of the chance to develop my fucking screenplay. And not even to get proper dough, just a wee personal sum so I could revise the fucking script! There's a good boy, a pat on the head. I felt oh Christ I'll call this off immediately.

The way I see it, over the years Scottish Screen was always just a corrupt body, intellectually bankrupt, like the telly or something. All you have to do is see the people involved in writing the shoddy third-rate work that comes out. It never uses real writers. Why is that? Maybe once in a blue moon. It gives a lot of money to actors, directors and all these other people to do screenplays. How come they never pay real writers? The bottom line is they don't want real writers. It's like Hollywood in the '50s or something.

WC: But a lot of American writers did work for the movies, Faulkner …

JK: Yeah there was a good period. But the '50s was a time when they started to get rid of real writers, the McCarthy era. What you saw was how the directors became the main figures, real writers were too political. So Scottish Screen in that sense is just part of the usual Scottish Arts scene. All they want is working-class sentimental shite, a kitchen-sink fantasy land, fucking hopeless. What a waste of time, all the emotional energy. For me now it's finished, Scottish theatres like the Traverse as well, finished in a personal way. I should've known that a while back when the Traverse refused to let me, Tom Leonard and George Gallacher's blues band use their space to do a one-off night, they didn't think we could get an audience— for a one-off performance! Fucking hell, man. It was just to be a box-office split, that's all we were asking. That was just before I went to work in Texas. Of course theatre's been finished for a while now anyway and I should have realised that. I'm finishing this new book of essays of mine and there's a big diatribe I wrote back in 1987 or something, caused by the shit that went on trying to put on another play of mine, *In the Night*. So here I am just now fighting a battle I wouldn't have wasted my time fighting twelve or thirteen years ago. I wrote a bit about it in the introduction to that book of plays of mine, *Hardie and Baird*. Fucking waste of energy. It's shocking, but at the same time …

WC: Earlier on we were criticising the history of Scottish theatre and now there's no future. A lot of people, surely, would say there's been a lot of things: there's certain, some sort of reputations, but ultimately it's come through, a lot of theatres have come through "Thatcherite" arts council things whereby it's complete commercialisation and forget anything else, we're not dealing with anything else, these really commercial arguments. At the same time they're pushing this managerialism—you're swayed through that, which is presented as just purely administrative. Now it's all up in the air again: it's totally tied in with government policy, there's no two ways about that. The models for that: to get funding from the Arts Council you must follow and like the government policies and views or put up a believable impersonation of that. But what are we looking at there, Stalinist Russia? What're the models for that kind of thing? Who exactly is being helped along here? There's also the law of diminishing returns. How many plays that say the government's policies are fantastic would you want to go and watch in a year? That's where we'll end up. As far as—well, you mentioned it with Magnus Linklater—as far as he's concerned the arts are just … well, he's negotiated his salary straight from the word go and made sure he gets a lot of money and that's it, then just sit back. People that he knows will get money and those he doesn't probably won't.

JK: I suppose with myself when I wrote to Magnus Linklater at the Arts Council I also wanted things to be on record. So I don't really regret all the time I've spent, because I have this correspondence here and the idea of making it known like just now. Plus nobody can say I didn't try, like when I tell people in the States I can't get a play on and they look at me, well, here it is, I was stopped at this level and that level, this is me being stopped. I still can't get a play done at a place like the Traverse without doing a clown routine for the bastards, and I'm talking about for nothing, no wages.

WC: Maybe you didn't really see it but at the time of the Booker Prize a lot of the coverage—like the *Times* and so on—would say it's an insult to the Booker Prize, you get Waugh or Rabbi Julia Neuberger or somebody like that and their tirade of gibberish. But it must be quite effective. In some ways it colours some people's views of your work.

JK: Yeah … well, it did up here too, MPs obviously, they took the Neuberger line and supported the hostility against me. Brian Wilson and other ones, Donald Dewar, they attacked, every Labour MP who opened his mouth—apart from Gordon Brown, he was the only one I saw that came out in print without attacking me. Like the *Glasgow Herald* as well, after I won the thing just about the entire bunch that write for it came out and attacked, they all found their own wee way of doing it, it was like tossing cocoanuts, it was so bad the fucking editor was reduced to defending me, Arnold Kemp. What was interesting too was that bodies like the Saltire Society attacked. They just took the Neuberger line on language as having some truth in it. I remember the quote from the Saltire Society was something like "Oh yes, Scottish writers tend to shoot themselves in the foot." Something like that. So here you've got people who are directly associated with contemporary writing in Scotland just taking up that uncritical hostile position to a Scottish writer, basically on the word of an English tabloid, and you would have that hostility from a lot of the Scottish educational system, yeah, and people involved with the SNP of course, they came out and attacked the novel as well, Paul Scott …

WC: What, because everyone else was?

JK: Perhaps it was that. It was also because the conventional wisdom being peddled was that my work was "primitive writing" and they wanted to be seen as being on the side of "matters of the intellect" or something, the SNP, they didn't want to be seen as "parochial"! They were wanting to be seen as mature persons, they're big enough to attack a Scottish work written in a Scottish kind of working-class dialect blah blah blah ... it's part of that colonial mentality again, inferiorisation, plus the usual Anglocentric attitudes from the Scottish establishment. That would have been part of the crap that was going on from them, I don't know. One of the points that you were making earlier in relation to Thatcher and 1979, there certainly were shifts in the arts. One of the ways it happened during the next ten years was the way funding went, American-style corporatism ...

WC: The "if the private sector aren't funding you we're not funding you" routine ...

JK: ... the whole attitude of Ian MacGregor and the people who came in the '70s. Remember the title of MacGregor's autobiography? *The Enemies Within.* A typical Thatcher/Reagan Cold War line. But before the Thatcher government we were already being put into that way of thinking, so it's a mistake to say "Thatcherism." But between that and also as a way to control the arts—move it out of the public sector and into the private sector as a means to suppress or censor etc.—BP [British Petroleum] was one of the major sponsors of theatre, they had the Young Director of the Year awards and so on. So as soon as you have groups taking control like that, funding becomes a functional thing. There's obviously ways in which slowly but surely avant garde theatre—never mind left-wing, radical political stuff—will slowly but surely ...

WC: ... know they're not wanted.

JK: What's wanted is the Kings and Lyceum Theatre, the Citizens ... Shakespeare and P.G. Wodehouse, foreign writers and Noel Coward, pantomimes—and style as well, what's cool, can I join the gang, give us a fucking Nike stripe. But what I was going to say is it is an error to fall into that way of thinking that says how before 1979 things were okay. It's crap. What you're talking about, the 7:84 company, Wildcat, that sort of thing ... really, it was just what you would say Labour Party. And it was probably Manifesto Labour Party, it wasn't even Tribune. None of that stuff was left-wing at all, not if you step outside the Labour Party. In some ways it was really reactionary theatre. As far as they were concerned, political theatre ... as a musician friend of mine used to say ... "If you walked out, sang a song and said, 'Fuck the Queen,' then you'd get described as political theatre, and you'd get funding." That was what it was about at that period. Or so he said, I don't actually believe you could've said that. It was mainly shit though. Real radical art, genuine left-wing art, I don't think it was a possibility. There was nothing much going on then. Maybe not all shite. But as far as being at the cutting edge of literature, Christ, theatre's so old-fashioned, it was then and it is now, compared to straight prose fiction, give us a break ...

No. Whereas it might be nice to see maybe John Byrne's work, *The Slab Boys* or something, it's not ever going to be accused of being too radical. Or like John McGrath's work. It has a place and all that but it's surely not going to be regarded as radical theatre! Or is it, who knows. You had a lot of pseudo stuff then, as you still get, like Scottish movies it's full of pseudo left-wing stuff. It's "working class"—it gets sold as that anyway, so-called working class—and that gets equated with left-wing. But is it? A lot of it's just old-fashioned naturalism, and naturalism is only a sort of weird fantasy. In literature that kind of stuff was out of date in the early 1950s for Christ sake but this is what gets supported and funded in the year 2000 in the World of Drama, theatre and the movies, the telly. It's fucking hopeless, apart from one or two exceptions, okay.

WC: So you're saying you're never going to get a play in Scotland?

JK: The Tron Theatre didn't even reply to the letters we sent them. Maybe the Arches would have been interested, they did *One, Two—Hey*. But we just felt this particular play should go to particular places. Theatres are different, the spaces are different. I remember that play of mine *Hardie and Baird*, it would have been great to see it at the Tron. I couldn't imagine it at the Arches but who knows. It ran two weeks at the Traverse and it was selling out, and then that was that, it just finished, it never went anywhere else, it just died a death. I found that amazing. I know at that time in Glasgow ... I'm sure nobody in theatre wanted to be at loggerheads with the Labour Party and Glasgow District Council—a major funding body—and that would've been that, putting a play of mine on, because of the situation at that time. Myself and you and a few others were anathema in those days, Billy, Glasgow 1991 ...

WC: Not just at that time!

JK: Of course, and they've got longer memories than us. There's only been two plays of mine ever on in Glasgow, then the wee revival of *The Busker* a couple of years ago, the same company that were wanting to do this new one that's caused the bother. There would have been no chance of *Hardie and Baird* playing there in 1991. But maybe it wasn't a political decision at all, nobody's got a right to get a play on, including me. I've got three plays just now, new ones, the one we've been talking about plus another two. Where do I go with them? I don't blame people like the Tron or the Citizens for not trying to stage my work, because maybe they just don't want to stage it and they're entitled to that. After the Booker Prize the Citz wanted to do their own adaptation of my novel *How Late* .... I said, "No, why don't you commission me for a new play?" That was the last I heard from them. But I shouldn't moan about that, it was them gave us one of their wee studio spaces for *The Busker* revival. In relation to what you're saying, I could see them putting on *Hardie and Baird* after I'm dead.

WC: What, because it's historical?

JK: Yeah probably, that makes it safe. A couple of critics were amazed there was so much religion in it, they thought it was too much. But maybe that would make the Labour Party feel even more safe, if it was just religion, they would think there was no politics. I don't really know what's going on in Scottish theatre these days, I don't go very much. It's not just Scotland of course, it's elsewhere in the UK. A lot of things have happened. People down south are worried as well; it's not even politically radical or experimental theatre, sort of "mainstream radical" where they're just trying to put on a new play or something.

WC: Certainly there has been massive changes in theatre and I think a lot of this is due to notions of nationality. The Arts Council want to devolve power—and that's quite laudable in some respects—but all that comes down to is you cut touring companies because you don't have a national body to encourage that. If you're a national theatre, well, you can't be that anymore, you're going to have to fit into "devolved power sharing" mad bureaucracy. These moves come in the wake of the Audit report on all the big Lottery projects. It was really the Tories so you can't blame the present administration—well, you never can can you? It all centres on the Royal Opera House and the Arts Council have been castigated, although you could say that was incredible leniency on their part. A lot of people react against them but for fuck's sake they gave these people millions and when they needed more they gave them more. A lot of these things were obviously politically motivated, but people got the money and they did it through the usual ways. Even they are beginning to realise that if you build a theatre how then do people get the money to run it, how do people get the money to do the work. They'll cross that bridge when they come to it. But now they are less willing to give somebody money for a building. Important people had their chance first. They blew it and everyone else can fuck off. That's what happened. The big companies fucked things up for the wee ones. The entire drama committee just packed it in, which saved them getting rid of them. I don't understand these resignations. They should have stayed and said, "We're going to make life fucking difficult for you bastards," but they just resigned.

JK: Are they not part of the career structure themselves, part of that group? I'm resisting using the term "class."

WC: No. They're a committee to create the illusion of democratic decision-making. They have no power really. They realised that. That's the real reason why they resigned. Minutes were being withheld from them—the usual thing—decisions were taken behind people's backs.

JK: I always feel that these kind of committees are doing their bit for their own kind of class.

WC: That's certainly a motivation. It's all got to be seen as "We're all in it together."

JK: If you think about the dispensation of Arts Council money in terms of class, the artists in a sense tend to be treated as working class. One of the ways that operates is like—take the £25,000 "Creative Scotland" bursary, the best I've ever seen for Scotland—the money would be the equivalent of an excellent working-class wage, a top tradesman. Whereas the bureaucrats are getting a middle-class wage, an officer's wage, probably that *starts* from the £25,000 or just below. The arts administrators are the cultural officers, paid at the middle-class level, but the artists get a working-class wage, a hundred quid for a writer's fee, it's like an emergency call-out for a plumber, it's working-class dough, fair enough. Part of it gets carried through with entire groupings so Scottish Opera, or Scottish Ballet or big Scottish theatres maybe, they get treated in middle-class ways whereas other groups aren't, they'll be treated in a working-class kind of way where they'll get the crumbs and fight for scraps, "community art."

WC: TAG Theatre did commission an Edwin Morgan play, then the SAC cut TAG's money. There are divisions of labour, but even the notion of being an artist and a writer. You know, "Art critics should work for a nice responsible magazine," but I think there are tiers within tiers as well. Surely the lowest of the low are the poets and visual artists, you're treated as you're definitely scum …

JK: I don't think so. Well, it depends …

WC: In Scotland?

JK: Well, it's often assumed that if you're a poet you're an academic or you're making a good income anyway, Robert Crawford or Eddie Morgan, Douglas Dunn. An interesting thing to look at is the level of award that Tom Paulin got in England, to go away and write a poem or work at a poem, he got about seventy-five grand, something like that, to go away for a year's sabbatical. Because he is assumed to be on their upper-middle-class level. In some establishment quarters they see a poet as somebody who is a sort of dilettante—I hate that term, but to define it economically … these kind of poets have a great income anyway in terms of the day-to-day work they do, and they create art in their spare time … so not the lowest of the low, the opposite from scum.

WC: Well, I think there's something in what I'm saying.

JK: Yeah, I'm not generalising, most poets get treated badly.

WC: If I think about the visual arts, and I go into an art gallery, say the CCA [Centre for Contemporary Arts] in Glasgow. There's going to be a wee person sitting inside behind the desk, now I know that's an artist, that's somebody who's just left art school. And they're sitting there getting paid— what, a fiver?—for sitting there. And it's almost like they're on display, they're saying, "Look, this is what happens to you if you become an artist." Then there's the serious artist having an exhibition, but they're probably not really getting any money. Then there are all these people who are in the building, working away, maintaining the place: the people who hang the shows will be all similarly artists on the dole or back sitting at that desk and it's almost as if they are in the public stocks or the gallows at the tollbooth at the entrance to a city. That's repli-cated throughout all the major cities in Britain. Everybody's getting paid, the person who cleans etc., except for artists. In the visual arts that's the way it works. Until as you say, you get to a certain level where you cross some kind of class aspiration thing…

JK: Sometimes no, you think that's the case, but then it comes back and haunts you, as with this latest thing: you might get to a level but you never make that crossing, all the stuff you've done as an artist, as a writer, it's not opening these sorts of doors at all, you're still fighting all the time, I'm talking about just to do your work. So, you're back to—well … to introduce other people into that equation, I don't particularly want to but if I was thinking really off the top of my head it would be people like Alasdair [Gray], Tom [Leonard] and Agnes [Owens], Jeff Torrington, Janice Galloway, even Crichton Smith before he died, people who either have no money to get on with things or else still have to chase around. There's no harm in artists like them having to earn a living etc., of course not, but I don't see why at a certain stage they still have to be chasing around the country for paltry eighty quid here and a hundred quid there, people who have produced all that great work. I think that's a scandalous thing. Alasdair not being able to finish *The Book of Prefaces* because he didn't have the money, meanwhile the Arts Council are dishing out … I mean where the fuck are the … who's getting it? Where does all the money go when someone like Alasdair, he couldn't finish the *Prefaces* at that time because he didn't have enough money to get him through another year; he had to find private sponsoring, what's the fucking Arts Council for! These kind of questions which I don't really want to get into. Tom chasing up and down to England every week to survive, and Janice couldn't even do that, having a kid, and of course Jeff couldn't, and Freddie [Anderson] who's in his mid-seventies. That brings you into other areas.

WC: The funding culture, the Arts Council stuff: it's obviously a deeply bourgeoisie, middle-class, don't-rock-the-boat, status quo values … that's it.

JK: And also Billy, the rent boy thing, that point you made—for them ultimately there is no belief whatsoever in art, and somebody whether it's myself, as with the theatre carry-on, it's how they have absolutely no belief in what you do. They put no value in the art you create. They still think that if they were to give you a bursary, for example, it's just Kelman or Gray is getting £10,000 …

WC: You'd see the error of your ways …

JK: They would just … no, it's just how for them they're giving you ten thousand quid and somehow you're getting away with something, you're just getting the money, it's not for anything, it's not even old rope, it's just a game, a kind of scam, there's no value in what you do. There's no value in it, the Arts Council don't see it. Some people might talk about your work in a pub or something, yeah, the Arts Council officers know that, or maybe at least they'll see a book you've written on a shelf in a library, but they don't put any real value on the stuff you do, not in itself, they don't see it as art, not real art, there's no value in it.

WC: I don't think so. I don't think there is. If you look back to the original thinking with Keynes, it was Keynes that thought it up as an extenuation from ENSA [Entertainments National Service Association], you know to help the troops (which gave us Stanley Baxter and Kenneth Williams), that was for the lower orders, right. And CEMA [Council for the Encouragement of Music and the Arts] was this thing which basically was designed to fund the big opera houses. The financial methodology was loans. It was never ever intended to be, "Here's money on you go we will support you" …

JK: Yeah, that's a '70s thing.

WC: Exactly. The notion of continuing funding. Now they're attacking that again. Keynes's notions are taken from an article in the *Listener*. His notion of artists are pretty muddled actually. The analogy is that they are like butterflies in a jar, give them money and they have freedom. That's not actually what he said but it's quite a flowery, "poetic" … no-social-responsibility-whatsoever notion. If they do still believe that, they have also come to believe that if you let the butterfly out of the jar it'll go straight to the pub. That's what they think. If you give artists money they will spend it on their lives [*laughs*], they'll waste it, they'll pay bills with it. There is an anomaly there. I think at a very high level in the arts they have got to rediscover that the values of what we would call the "counter-culture," all these things that were wrongfully ditched by the establishment, the exact same process is happening right now. They refuse to deal with certain sets of issues because they call their own roles into question. Until they address these sorts of things and stop putting nutcases in charge because they're "good businessmen" I can't see anything changing, and remember they're doing themselves out of a job. Look at the BBC for instance. It's been commercialised. So it will compete with all these commercial imperatives. If that's what it's doing then why am I paying the licence? It will only do in the whole basis of the thing. You pay your licence fee so that it doesn't have to be ruled by commercial imperatives and it's the same with art. I can't see any real way in a "modern democracy" where they could say, "We're going to have this fund which will force people to go along with the government's hastily constructed views on culture." That just doesn't make any sense. I think there's a chance for them. If you look at the ACE's website it says we will try and challenge this historical bias: they're penitent. But they're right for the wrong reasons; they're just saying that because they're told to say it. They actually admit historical failure. But they're still not going to change things.

JK: You know, I fought that damn thing for nine months, nine months' wasted energy.

WC: Yeah, see there's the time scale of these things. The day in day out ...

JK: One of these letters I wrote took about five or six days' work—because I'm watching my back ... you have to be careful ... see, I knew the attitude was going to be, "Well, what does he expect, he acts like the theatre's his or something I mean

133

what right does he have to come walking in here!" That sort of attitude. These theatres are theirs, they belong to the admin officers, they've got nothing to do with us, the artists, that's the point. Well, we knew that anyway, that's just fucking banal. I landed myself in banalities for nine months. I got slapped down and put in my place. And how many times that has happened in the past for myself in this country, trying to get ... you know ... just get your work done.

WC: What is the root cause?

JK: What in other people's eyes?

WC: Well, if somebody as you say hasn't got a track record, well, they'll say maybe later. Somebody in the middle position who's getting treated like shit can themselves say, "Aye, maybe one day."

JK: When they're up there winning Scottish Writer of the Year Awards!

WC: Someone who is successful, a major writer, they're still getting treated this way: who is winning out here?

JK: No, but it is outrageous. So just to try and get it made public, that this is the reality here, this is what we're actually talking about, I can't get a play on for fucking nothing, this is what it is like to be a writer in Scotland. None of that is discussed. Meanwhile we get the usual crap from the *Herald* and the *Scotsman*, or *Scotland on Sunday*, attacking writers about this ... what's that one by Tom, their "feather bedded life of luxury ... "

WC: Yeah, "They're all getting funded and they're all moaning." But that's just sad wankers who haven't got a clue ...

JK: Well, they do have a clue ...

WC: What are you trying to tell me, that they're saying this to create a ...

JK: Well, some of the media are, yeah. And attacking people in a very underhand way. Just about every time you read a column about contemporary Scottish literature in the *Herald* we're getting attacked, in one way or another, not the

reactionary crap, it gets supported. But look how they attacked
Janice Galloway and Alasdair Gray in the *Scotsman!*—or was
it *Scotland on Sunday*? And when Janice and Alasdair replied
they didn't even publish the letter they sent but again they
attacked them, and they used bits of the letter for that purpose;
imagine it, cowardly bastards. This is the kind of thing they do
in Scotland. Imagine these little shits attacking writers like
Alasdair and Janice! Christ almighty. Magnus Linklater is a
former editor of the *Scotsman* anyway, but that's the Andrew
Neil team nowadays and Linklater is nowhere near as bad as
that, I don't think so, if he had been I wouldn't have written to
him in the first place. Who knows. He's an ordinary kind of
right-wing guy, I suppose, in a position of authority—another
one! But take people like ... what's her name ... writes for the
Herald and does stuff all over the place, for the BBC ... her that's
in the Labour Party, she's attacked me in the past because of
Workers City, her that always backed up Pat Lally and whoever,
the three stooges ...

WC: Oh what, Ruth Wishart!

JK: Yeah, people like Ruth Wishart, who have quite a
strong position within the arts ...

WC: She's the Labour Party hatchet. I can remember that
time she was really supporting Labour and ended up supporting the slave trade, the tobacco barons of the Merchant City in
Glasgow, saying they were misunderstood. The argument was
like saying you shouldn't judge the Third Reich on the first five
or six years—give it time. Her article in the *Herald* was from a
book funded by the Labour Party about cities as part of their
strategy of redevelopment. She gets away with absolute fucking murder. Completely politically biased writing. And she's
been let loose on the Arts Council because she's a pal of his ...

JK: Who?

WC: Linklater. Well, someone's getting her to write all
this policy ... it all seems very neat ... I don't really know if
they are real friends ... I have written against Ruth Wishart

in the editorial of the magazine. She's saying things like artists shouldn't be getting money from the Arts Council, this is all along the lines of turning it into a development agency, as if they were any use. So it's just less and less money for artists and more and more for Labour Party operations, propaganda operations really. There's no other way of describing it. There's wonderful things they're doing as part of the New Deal, where people are supposed to be forced to go working in an art gallery for an extra tenner. What they don't realise is that most artists are unemployed and they'd love to get paid an extra tenner to fuck about doing what they're already doing. I think a lot of government policies are folding back on themselves. But they're also linking up with a lot of non-governmental organisations. These things are sprouting up all over the place: consultancies and what have you, who are getting all the money. The results of which the Arts Council can either completely ignore or … they can't actually fund you but they can find £10,000 to find out whether you're viable or not … well, a lot of artists feel that is just taking the piss. They made a great show about how everything would be done in the open, except for the meeting where they decide who gets the money, which will be held in secret. They go to such great lengths to appear as a public accountable body and then whisper that some meetings will be secret. That's just an insult to people's intelligence, but it passes without comment, because where can this criticism exist.

JK: But these people really are the enemies in a sense, they try to hurt you and all that, and they succeed. I don't get so hurt because I'm maybe in a stronger position, I regard myself as quite strong, and yet for people who are less … in a worse economic position … they can get hurt really badly you know; they get stopped, they can't do their work. At least I know next year will not be as bad because I'll be in Texas, Texas half the time, England the other half.

12

2002

Interview by "Wayne" for Writing on the Wall

Writing on the Wall **is a writing and literature organisation based in Liverpool.**

Writing on the Wall: Do you feel you are part of a "movement" to document disenfranchised cultures?

James Kelman: I am a writer and I try to work from what is available to me. That really begins from the culture and community [including the linguistic] that I was born and raised within. This doesn't mean I am trapped by it. If this culture is disenfranchised or in some sense marginalised and, given I am not the only artist working from within it, then I suppose it is fair to say I am a part of a "movement"; whether or not I feel myself to be part of a movement is another question.

WoW: Do you believe that the written word has generally been used to constrain the language and therefore the imagination of the majority?

JK: I think there is a strong argument to be made in favour of that position.

WoW: Do you feel that history has been served well by popular culture, for example soul music, "generic" novels?

JK: I'm not sure what you mean by "history" here. The question seems to assume there is "the" history—the history of humankind perhaps—and that when we speak of "history" that that is not only what we mean by the term but that everybody sees it the same way. I'm not sure of what "popular culture" means here either.

WoW: Do you think that there is a definable "consciousness" of the majority, one that can be documented with words?

JK: I don't understand the question clearly enough to venture a response.

WoW: Can fiction be a reliable source of history? Are some kinds of fiction more "useful" as history than others?

JK: Fiction is one source for some histories.

WoW: How conspiratorial do you believe that the inaccessibility of literature has been? Is ever-increasing access to the media an unstoppable antidote to this?

JK: I won't attempt to define "conspiratorial" in this context and the whole nonsense about "conspiracy theories" leaves me cold. At the same time it looks to be necessary to do something along these lines in order to attempt a fuller answer here. I don't agree that there is "increasing access to the media" unless you are including under the heading "media" the general use the ordinary public can make of contemporary technologies, e.g., the web.

WoW: Your work often blurs the boundaries between "thought" and "speech." Is the use of "interior" dialogue a way of giving a voice to lives that are normally ignored?

JK: I think it is "interior monologue" that is meant here rather than "interior dialogue." Probably working with interior monologue, the thought process and so, helps writers create the inner lives of individuals. It is true to say that in the UK and other English-language-based societies many cultures and communities have been marginalised and excluded because of the way they use language. By making use of language as it used by people, writers are exploring areas that have been typically silent [or silenced] in Standard English literary terms.

WoW: Your latest work [*Translated Accounts*] is something of a departure in that it takes place in the future. Did you hope to demonstrate the "unknowability" of the future and (by implication) the impenetrability of the past?

JK: I don't see my latest novel as taking place in the future; perhaps it exists side by side with the present. If you were to ask me the same question in thirty years' time I think I could give you the same answer.

WoW: As with history, is the future determined by who controls the present?

JK: Surely there are different histories. Dispossessed people also have histories. Who does control the present? And whose present would that be?

13

2002

Interview by Fabio Vericat

This interview originally appeared in the *Barcelona Review*, issue 28, January–February 2002.

> See when you come to think about it he didnay really
> like Scotland. It was his country, okay, but that didnay
> mean ye had to like it.
>
> —*How Late It Was, How Late*

Besides his fiction Glasgow-born James Kelman has also produced critical essays such as "A Reading from Noam Chomsky and the Scottish Tradition in the Philosophy of Common Sense" (1988), as well as political writings such as his report on "The Freedom for Freedom of Expression Event" in 1997, published under the title "Em Hene!" (We exist!) in the *Kurdistan Report*, the Amnesty International journal, *Scottish Socialist Voice* and the *Scottish Trade Union Review*. He prefaces his latest novel, *Translated Accounts*, which was published last year: "These 'translated accounts' are by three, four or more individuals domiciled in an occupied territory or land where a form of martial law appears to be in operation." James Kelman is currently joint professor of Creative Writing at the University of Glasgow.

Fabio Vericat: Is the Scot naturally self-conscious culturally? Why do the Scots make a national sport of boasting about how "fucking shite" Scotland is? Is this a tactic of self-preservation, a form of linguistic resistance?

James Kelman: Scottish culture is pluralistic; there is no "the Scot." If there is a lack of confidence generally, a sense of inferiority, then the historical context is crucial. You have to remember that Scotland has existed as a sort of colony of England for the past three hundred years; its ruling class sold the country back in the early eighteenth century. Scottish children have been educated to recognise not only their own inferiority but the inferiority of their parents, community and wider culture, including language. It is a typical colonial position.

FV: Do you encourage the recapture of "high" culture as the legitimate realm of the people? Is the Scottish working class more likely to have a copy of a Penguin Classic popping out of their back pocket than pulp fiction, or is he/she a Billy Connolly with philosophical pretensions, as you yourself have been accused of being?

JK: People read one thing or another; "the Scottish working class" is composed of individual human beings, they have different tastes.

FV: Here in Spain there is a strong rivalry between Barcelona and Madrid, often expressed in football terms. What is your view on this, and how does it relate to the traditional Celtic/Rangers soccer enmity in Glasgow?

JK: People of my generation and older in Glasgow traditionally lean towards Real Madrid; this is because of the great team of the late 1950s and 1960s. The club match some argue was the greatest ever took place in Glasgow in 1961, when Real Madrid beat Eintracht Frankfurt 7–3. It sold out and tickets were hard to get. Approximately 130,000 people went to see it, including my father. That Real Madrid team had a tremendous impact on world football, similar to the influence of the great Brazilian team a little later. Boys of my age revered Di Stéfano, Puskás, Santa María, Gento and the others. As I understand it Real Madrid has had a neofascist element within its fanbase. I was not aware of that until fairly recently. Both Barcelona and Real Madrid are always good to watch in footballing terms but sometimes the politics can have an effect. I find it extremely difficult to watch the European tournament games when the crowds chant racist slogans. It is shameful, really. In Scotland there are only two big teams, both from Glasgow, divided on sectarian lines. Rangers attracts the harder, right-wing elements; Protestant Loyalist, pro-Unionist, pro-Monarchy etc. Celtic attracts the Roman Catholic population, is thought to be slightly more liberal than Rangers and is also popular in Ireland and in the US with the Scots/Irish diaspora; a Celtic supporters club rally was held in Las Vegas some years ago and attracted seventy thousand people. I do not give allegiance to either. As my father used to say, "I am not biased, I like any team who beats Celtic and Rangers." I would continue to play football if I could find a league for the over-fifties, composed only of players who were never any good in the first place.

FV: You have recently taken up a post at Glasgow University. You are also considered a working-class writer. Did you ever imagine that you would end up teaching at university? How would you describe and explain your work there, and in what way, if at all, has this environment affected your writing?

JK: The post is a three-way jobshare split between Alasdair Gray, Tom Leonard and myself. Therefore I have a third of a job with a third of a salary. But for an artist a third of a salary on a regular basis is always good. We have only been there since September. We assist in the teaching side of the Creative Writing Programme. This operates for postgraduate students who want to make a serious attempt at writing. It is too early to see how this will affect my own work, although obviously any form of outside employment means less time and energy available.

FV: In *How Late It Was, How Late* Sammy's only way out other than suicide is leaving Scotland. This is something of a recurrent theme in Scottish literature. To what extent did you, too, have to get away? How is that connected to your saying that your literary roots are in America and Europe?

JK: People have to leave Scotland to work. There is no link between that and my "literary roots." My own family emigrated to the US thirty-five years ago when I was in my teens. It didn't work out for my father and mother and we returned home, but one of my brothers remained there. Most Scottish families have relatives domiciled abroad, in the US, Canada, Australia or New Zealand. Traditionally Scotland's major export has been its working-class people. I left Scotland again at the age of nineteen to find work in England but returned home after I married. My wife was expecting our first child and we could not afford to live in London on one person's wage.

FV: In your article on Chomsky you say: "Reports of atrocities by refugees are difficult to cope with. We are not used to such testimonies; not unless, perhaps the refugees are in flight from the same ideological enemy as ourselves" (James Kelman, "A Reading from Noam Chomsky and the Scottish Tradition in the Philosophy of Common Sense," *Edinburgh Review* 84 [1990]). It seems to me that *Translated Accounts* was a long time coming. Why did you wait all these years to write it?

JK: I don't plan work in the manner suggested by your question. My stories develop as they go. I make them up as I go along. I don't wait to write something as opposed to writing something else. However, occasionally formal problems force a break in the writing of particular pieces.

FV: You seem to suggest that you don't rely on explicit theories when you write. Is that right? And how is it that "occasionally formal problems force a break in the writing of particular pieces"? Do not these problems demand a theoretical frame of sorts?

JK: No. I don't at all rely on "explicit theories when I write." I don't even know what that means, what it might mean. Formal problems will be resolved in the writing of the story, during the creation of the art. At least that is how it happens for myself; other artists may work differently.

FV: *Translated Accounts* could be seen as a wonderful access to a universal linguistic psyche that still retains political positioning. Do you have an explicit language theory deliberately applied in *Translated Accounts*? I am thinking of your article on Chomsky.

JK: I have no particular interest in linguistics as a study. I have no particular language theory, not in the way you suggest. There seems an "end/means" view of art implied in your question, a view that I reject.

FV: At times it seems that masculinity is only defined in your work by an emotional and/or sexual yearning for women who remain lost, far off or mysterious, with compensation being found in some kind of male bonding or homoerotics. Do you see a preoccupation with masculinity in your work?

JK: For most males, females are mysterious: the converse is also the case. It is true to say that the vast majority of my stories are written from a male perspective. I don't think there is a preoccupation with masculinity, except insofar as aspects of masculinity are a general preoccupation among males.

FV: The confessional nature of some of the accounts conveys a religious feeling that seems to be denied by other voices which hammer their atheism onto the page. Is there a therapeutic or religious side to your authorial stance, a way of keeping sane, which lets your characters do the talking and earn forgiveness for your sins?

JK: No. I don't accept the notion of art as catharsis, in fact I think it is nonsense. I am an atheist, and have been so since my early teens.

FV: One of the essential themes in *Translated Accounts* is oppression and power. What are your feelings about the current world situation, and not just the Kurds, for example, but Palestine, the September 11 attacks and the war in

Afghanistan? What about the moves to curtail civil liberties in Britain and the US? Are our societies becoming more repressive?

JK: This is very difficult. Who knows what "democracy" means? The concept is completely devalued. In Great Britain the little political control people did have through such vaguely liberal bodies as the Labour Party has now gone. In my own lifetime there has not been a more dangerous period. The Blair government is blatantly racist and more right-wing authoritarian than Thatcher's. Across Europe the movement towards fascism is in place and gaining momentum; it is humiliating to watch government authorities everywhere bowing and scraping before the US and its close allies. There is no question that European society has become far more repressive. It is worthwhile to look at the process since the late 1960s and the far-right realignment that has developed since that period. A certain level of domestic repression has always been the case in the US, perhaps disguised by its concentration on the non-European elements of society, e.g., Chicano, African American, Asian American, Native American.

FV: The reviews of *Translated Accounts* have been somewhat mixed. Some reviewers (e.g., Sally Mapstone in the *LRB* [*London Review of Books*]) seem to have found the different voices difficult to come to terms with. Why, do you think?

JK: I suppose it has to do with the lack of familiarity. There has been a fair amount of hostility to the novel. But really, it is not a question I can answer.

FV: Are you working on anything at the moment? What are your plans? Will you go back to the kind of non-Scottish voice that figures in *Translated Accounts*?

JK: I have a new collection of essays published in London in April 2002, entitled *And the Judges Said*. It is a while since there has been time to concentrate on my own fiction. I always have different projects in process, and in my fiction there are always different voices.

FV: One last thought: As a fellow smoker, I cannot help noticing through all the documents I have been reading the number of times you have tried to give up and failed. Is it worth the bother? Is there a relationship between smoking and writing, do you think?

JK: I suspect I'll be giving up smoking until the day I die. There is no relationship between it and writing that I can figure out except that, as with writing, smoking can be an enjoyable solitary pursuit.

14

2003

Interview by Michael Gardiner

This interview originally appeared in the Spring 2004 issue of *Scottish Studies Review*.

Michael Gardiner: Why write *Translated Accounts* instead of something safer and more apparently naturalistic, like a *How Late It Was, How Late* Part 2?

James Kelman: Well, I don't think that *How Late It Was* is naturalistic. Whenever you try to use "indigenous" language, to put it that way, it gives the impression that it's supposed to be naturalism. But I don't think that's the case at all. However, *Translated Accounts* came about really I suppose through working with short stories that appeared to be related in a certain way. This meant that I kept them back from the very ordinary collection of short stories [*The Good Times*]. Some of them didn't seem to fit into an ordinary short story collection. Gradually the stories were coming about that time, and I kind of left them there while finishing *The Good Times*. I kept them aside and then worked on them.

MG: I suspected you might object to the word "naturalistic." I suppose I'm thinking of a certain use of the word in contradistinction to realism—I'd never describe your work as "realistic"—naturalism as, at best, a method of artifice with a certain commitment to describing specificities. Naturalism isn't the word but it's hard to think of an alternative word to describe the aesthetic.

JK: Well, one of the things about this is that once you start to use language like language that's used by people then it gives the impression of naturalism.

MG: And a knee-jerk journalistic response is to say, he's trying to write exactly the way people talk—

JK: Yeah—

MG: And this allows people to ignore any craftsmanship that goes into it.

JK: Sure.

MG: I wonder if *Translated Accounts* is a kind of "revenge"— since for Scots to engage in English literature is always an act of translation. Structurally, *Translated Accounts* looks very much like earlier stories, the sentences assume the same kind of shape, yet are lexically and grammatically dislocated. Here I'm also thinking of W.N. Herbert's comments on Edwin Morgan's "The First Men on Mercury," that the Mercurian language sounds uncannily like Glaswegian speech. Similarly in *Translated Accounts*, there is that odd sense of familiarity. Is this change of tack a way of making the scenery more "real" by making it more strange?

JK: Yes, I can pick up what you're saying, in the sense that it came out as a form of revenge, and again actually what you mentioned about working as a naturalist. "Naturalism" suggests using a less formal technique, a writing with less attention to form and craft. So I think in a way it's impossible to approach or get into *Translated Accounts* without being aware of formal necessities—it makes it impossible to assume that the stuff is done without any attention to form.

MG: I kept noticing how often in *Translated Accounts* where you'll get a word which in Standard English would be seen as inappropriate, yet its meaning is obvious—this struck me as a pointed relocation of the linguistic integrity of using non-standard words, *ken* for "know," and so on. And you could make a similar point about the orthography itself. So structurally the book felt not that removed from previous work.

JK: Yeah.

MG: Back to the specificity; in a recent *Edinburgh Review* dedicated to your work Alan Freeman questions your politics of apparent total libertarianism in the essays of *And the Judges Said*. Freeman points to a disjunction between the committed naturalist presentation of detail in the stories and novels and the advocacy of a universal freedom in the essays. Universal statements are very dangerous, and you carefully avoid them in the novels. Why not in the essays?

JK: Well, the thing about working in fiction or working in creating art I think is that there isn't any intentional thing behind it, there isn't anything aside from creating the work. I mean obviously if you have a political sensibility, then that cannot be submerged completely in your work. Now there's nothing really that's being brought in intentionally—it's not possible in the way I work anyway. In that sense, quite a few of the essays in *And the Judges Said* only came about as papers for talks, so there was always a knowledge of where I was going before I began. That's not the case at all in fiction—there's never any notion of getting to a certain point in the writing. It doesn't happen. I mean you might have quite a clear political view, but it's not going to get into the fiction, apart from the fact that it's going to flavour it or colour it in some way. In a way as well, you've got to look at a writer's or an artist's body of work to be really sure. It's only valid retrospectively, in a sense. And a lot of the stuff that had been written about my work before *Translated Accounts*, or even before *How Late It Was*, a lot of stuff that I see occasionally about my work, really doesn't know the body of work at all, it makes judgments—condemnations—without knowing the short stories for example, or having any idea of the other novels, or the plays, and doesn't want to know anything.

MG: Do you feel happy with *And the Judges Said* and *Some Recent Attacks* [books of essays]?

JK: Yeah, you know, they were both things it was time to do. It would probably have been good if two or three essays in *Some Recent Attacks* had gone into *And the Judges Said*—retrospectively, that might have been an idea. But it was hell of a big as it was. So yeah, it's just part of my work as a writer. But again you get kind of irritated on occasion by some of the attacks in the press, the critics and so on.

MG: So you do read the reviews then.

JK: Well, I don't get sent as much now, because my publisher doesn't use the same clippings service. So for example I don't get them sent from the States any longer. There might be some quotation from the *LA Times* or the *Herald Tribune* and, you know, I've never seen it. So I don't really get the chance to see these now, whereas about ten years ago, everything would have come. Round about *How Late It Was*, all the reviews would have come, but they stopped just after that. When they come you tend to kind of scan them, even good reviews, it's difficult to read them.

MG: Especially around the time of *How Late It Was*.

JK: Yeah, so I don't read all the reviews. Occasionally I do, it depends whose it is, if it's somebody I know, if it's somebody I know is going to attack. If it's Scottish people I know who are on the attack, it can be useful to see what they're saying, you know, for future reference. Lies are difficult, though. And I sometimes wonder whether it's because they know I can't respond, I can't get a reply into the *Guardian*, for example, I can't reply to the *Glasgow Herald*—I can't reply. You know, so unless I start to think about defamation—there's no libel in Scotland—defamation is about the only response I can make to them. I don't know how you can respond to them.

MG: On the other hand, you know how many novels you sell, you know how many readers you've got.

JK: Oh yeah, well certainly in respect to your question about reading good reviews and bad reviews and what's written about you, I'm just saying that the kind of ones I'd be likely to scan would be those of people whose names I knew.

MG: This is almost a restatement of the question on universal values versus specific details; in the essays it sometimes sounds like you want everyone to write and get published, you know, you say there are countless great stories written by truck drivers and cleaners and the rest of it, and anyone should be able to write and get published. But if you take this to its logical conclusion, it means the deprofessionalisation of writing, since if everyone got published, no one would really get paid properly. This seems to sit uneasily with a comment you made to some schoolkids in Texas [reproduced in *And the Judges Said*], that you were "lucky" to be a writer. In fact it doesn't seem like luck, it seems like a long struggle to maintain integrity while dealing with a very standardising publishing industry. Now, not everyone can have that sort of "luck"; most remain truck drivers and cleaners.

JK: I'm not sure how specific I was being with that comment, but I might have been talking about Mary Gray Hughes, who I happened to meet when I was twenty-five and who showed my work to a publisher over in the States. That may be what I was talking about, and in that sense it is lucky, it's a kind of fluke, you know, most writers, generally, are not published as young as that. It's never a worry if you're not published at twenty-five in writing, whereas if you're involved in music you might worry about it more. It just takes a longer time to be doing, so I think twenty-six is, I still feel, retrospectively and in view of everything, kind of young in a way. So that was a fluke, and it's good for young writers to know that. I mean, you could go to "writers' pubs" forever in Scotland, and just get drunk, and never meet anyone useful, or just mean-spirited writers. There seem to be periods in Creative Writing, or in a community's culture, when there can be generosity, and other periods when the generosity is not as it was. So if you look at the period when [Sorley] MacLean and people were around, [Norman] MacCaig and [Hugh] MacDiarmid and others, you know, there was a feeling of generosity amongst writers, and solidarity, as there was for myself and writers around the '70s and the very early '80s. I'm not sure how much of that there is—certainly there's been some kind of thing around the Clocktower Press, and around the *Edinburgh Review*. I don't know how much of that was genuine as it filtered down through Rebel Inc. [Irvine Welsh's first publisher], I'm not quite sure if that's still around at all. So what you're saying, it may not exist. And again the proliferation of Creative Writing courses—I think some of the generosity goes, with the older organic ways of developing contact with other artists. The point that everyone can write, I don't mean that merit's out the window or something, you know. What gets shown depends on different kinds of text, and the web, and there is a kind of democratisation in one sense, with everyone using it. But I don't see what else that will do other than just oblige people to make their writing better, because there'll be so much of it.

MG: It's a kind of meritocracy then?

JK: Well, in writing, certainly the better writing will eventually go somewhere—to improve your chance of being read you pay attention to what you're doing. I mean it's more to do with the idea that there's some kind of a priori going on, because of class or something—that you cannot be a writer if you're like, you know … [working class].

MG: Yes, but given the proportion of people that write in some capacity, most of those people who are driving buses or clearing floors are going to have to keep doing so. Sometimes in the essays it sounds like you're almost believing that we can all become writers.

JK: Well, we can all become writers. Put it this way—I could easily have said that we could all become musicians, or all become composers, or sculptors. That's really the kind of context I'm saying it in. So when I talk about writing I mean as a literary art, so what's brought to bear in any art, you have to bring to bear in creative fiction.

MG: To go back to luck, the way I read your idea of "luck," in stories like "My Eldest," is that luck represents a hegemonic space waiting to be filled with recognition or action. We feel that your hopes for your characters is not simply to wait around, but to convert luck into action. Is that a reasonable reading, do you think?

JK: I think it is a reasonable reading—and that element of the way you're speaking about luck is an underlying thing with my work.

MG: There's something about *The Good Times* that isn't like the earlier stories, where, for example, at one point you describe pubs as "waiting rooms."

JK: That's *How Late It Was*.

MG: Right. But *The Good Times* feels very different; it feels like the old waiting for a change of luck is being gradually converted to action. The characters are audibly asking themselves, why is there all this empty space we call luck, and what can we do to fill it with social action?

JK: You know, I actually see that very much in all my work, and I see it as central within the first three novels too before *How Late It Was*. *How Late It Was* is different in a sense, because the character in that I think is a much more positive person, a character who's used to action, and is used to having to fend for himself and fight his way out of difficulties. In the other three novels I think characters are in a situation where, it's a kind of anti-existential thing in a way, it's almost like, when will action be pre-determined—and it's not going to happen. I think the guy who's closest to that awareness would be in *The Busconductor Hines*, who's more aware of what's involved, but again part of the conflict within him is that he's just in an ordinary kind of life, and a job that is dehumanising in some ways, but only in the ways that other jobs are. He's married with a young kid and the house is gonny get pulled down, there's always all these things that are pressing in on him, and it looks as though something like that may force change, or force action, but that's not the case. Actions can't be forced onto anyone; people are going to have to act for themselves.

MG: That's also very true of *A Disaffection*, except that the stakes are raised because he [Patrick Doyle] is educated, he's a schoolteacher, alienating him from his family and giving him an obsessive interest in his own situation. We see him walking back and forth in his head between action and inaction, driving half-way to England. It's quite a terrifying book at times.

JK: Yeah.

MG: But now, since you've talked about that alienation, in your essays you've often fairly candidly set yourself against academics generally assumed to be middle class; yet you now find yourself in this academic position, sharing a university chair with another two figures of very similar standing. Where do you draw the line between the institution and the person in the institution?

JK: Yeah, I mean I'm not sure. It's a complex thing just now, especially in the way the so-called Creative Writing courses are programmed. So it's not simply to do with class; the results are a very fundamental thing in having artists within the institution. This is quite a radical change, and I think that difficulties are arising because of those who have been brought in, like Alasdair [Gray] and Tom [Leonard] and those in other university departments. I think the situation is unfortunately that you're having to conform to academic criteria—not so much standards as the bureaucratic criteria for what it is to be employed within a university. For academics, that's part and parcel of their career; it's integral to what they do. For artists, it's not at all, and I think the university has to cope with working artists, and it really takes an effort to radicalise working practices, and stuff like that.

MG: Is that another way of saying it takes up too much of your time?

JK: Well, it's not another way of saying that, but certainly that's one of the effects of it. Yes, that is the case: the time for creation gets cut—and that's where the contradiction comes in. You can't be here as a lapsed artist, it's not like you take a year's sabbatical every five years to write a book. So you have to have a genuine part-time sort of thing.

MG: So the universities have to adapt to working artists' practices if they want working artists. But universities don't always want to adapt.

JK: Who knows. Because again—and this goes back to what you were saying about the line between the institution and the individual—that's a kind of fundamental question across the board. It's become fundamental because of corporatism—it's almost like every decision is not a real decision at all, it's just a kind of logical inference, and no discretionary practices are really allowed. Every time you make a decision, there's always pressure on you. That is the way things have gone, but that's not to say things must always be like that, because there's no such thing as just a machine that rules—there has to be an individual somewhere. And it's like being involved with the DSS or something—if you're doing any advocacy for people, you have to try and find, where is there any discretionary judgment allowed, and go for it. It's exactly the same in a university. Working simply for ease and so-called efficiency, where do you go? But yeah, individuals are going to have to make a change to things. And people at the top are not necessarily opposed to that, you know, sometimes people who get higher up in a university, it's not simply because they play the game—though they might play some aspects of the game—but also because they can take account of an unusual step, you know, they are capable of making a decision. That's one way to get to the top—it's not necessarily because they're fucking cowards or something. So also it doesn't mean that people in my situation won't be supported by people at the top. You can be, but you have to find, how can you do it? How can things be altered without bureaucracy? These pressures go across the board, but it's interesting because of the existence of artists, or genuine artists, in other words those who always do it. I mean I'm up at maybe five o'clock every fucking day to get in three or four hours before I come in, 'cause if you don't, I mean I'm practiced and I know I'm gonny get set back. It doesn't mean I can't take two or three weeks off, but it's going to be difficult to do it, to get back into a project. So the best thing is to be doing it all the time. So these are things the university system or the institution is not geared towards; they don't really have an understanding of that.

MG: Why do you stress in the essays that you don't have to go to university and study English literature to become a writer, even though that was exactly what you did as soon as you started getting published?

JK: Well, I was a writer, I'd been published three years ago—

MG: Yes, but why did you go?

JK: Purely economics, you know, I had two kids at that time, and I really was becoming unemployable. I was no longer able to drive a bus; I'd been in the buses too often, so I was basically barred out of the three bus companies at that time— Alexander's, SMT, and the Corporation of Glasgow. So the only job I had was working in a factory. It was a really difficult job, you know, and there was no other way of surviving. At that time a mature student had an earnings-related grant, and it wasn't means-tested. So my wife was working part-time, and at that time it was just quite straightforward, it was the only alternative I had to working in a factory—and I was working night-shift and it was a physically dangerous job. But even then I'd written a great deal, and in my second year I wrote a lot of *The Busconductor Hines*. So I was constantly just really playing a game—well, not playing a game, but it was a means. I was only there to conform to the criteria necessary for them not to take away my grant. If I could conform to that, I could do my own work. That was basically what I did. And I was working on *The Busconductor Hines*—never mind *A Chancer*, which was of course before that.

MG: Family certainly has a lot to do with it; yet a lot of your characters have lazily been associated with drinking and alcoholism, even though only Sammy Samuels [in *How Late It Was, How Late*] and the odd early character drink to excess.

JK: Yeah, I mean much of that is simply the usual stereo-type about Glasgow working-class males. Working from the old stereotype. So that's the kind of thing I get accused of—it's just assumed that that's the way I would be too.

MG: The history of the whole process of the Booker judg-ment would make an interesting book, the collected journalism and so on.

JK: Yes, it is an interesting one. Both the attacks during the short-listing and after it. I mean it was difficult for me to read the papers. Up here it became so bad in the *Herald*'s attacks on me, the editor at that time was Arnold Kemp, and he actually came out with a kind of defence, saying, well, some of his work can't be all that bad, or there must be a couple of good points somewhere. It was like that, like being an Aunt Sally, you know, all the time, it was just consistent. It didn't matter whether it was the music critic or whatever, it was just all the time.

MG: As you know, I've been looking into getting a publisher willing to let me cotranslate *How Late It Was* [into Japanese]. This has proved remarkably tough despite the fact that including yours there have only been two, I think, Booker Prize winners of the last couple of decades which haven't been instantly translated into Japanese on winning. The official reason for reservations about the translation seems to be that the book didn't sell well enough in England, but you can sense also the journalistic shenanigans rubbing off—though I'm not sure how much Japanese publishers know about that—a sense of the book being somehow risky, and therefore probably better not touched.

JK: Yeah, because I don't think the argument about figures is sustainable, certainly looking at the figures for a period of fifteen to twenty years.

MG: Do you feel angry about the whole thing?

JK: Well at the time, occasionally, yeah, it was a surprise, because one of the worst critics was the director of Dillons, and at that time they were competing with Waterstones, so here I had this guy, this director of Dillons attacking me publicly, saying this book shouldn't be stocked, and if you've got to have this book it shouldn't be in our bookshop. Now the very interesting thing is that my publisher at that time was Reed, and Reed and Dillons were supposed to be working in a synergetic kind of way. So it was like, hang on a second, this is my publisher, you're supposed to be working with my publisher to sell these books. That was a throwback for me to *The Busconductor Hines*, when they said, "Take the book out the shop window." So the anger or the disappointment of it was that it hurts your publisher, and it hurts them in such a way that the marketing team then start to lose confidence, so that becomes a consolidation of fears of some sections of marketing. You don't get any space: there's no longer any marketing goes on. And when you look at the editions [*passes over a couple of the now-familiar two-tone-covered editions*], they really are horrible, horrible paper, and you can't even read the titles. It's the cheapest kind of quality you can get. But if you look at the American version of *Translated Accounts* [*shows book*], they're still trying to sell the damn thing.

MG: Right.

JK: But obviously these decisions are taken at high level, and when there's a drop in quality then the booksellers start to lose confidence in it as well, 'cause the thing's not getting sold, you know.

MG: It's interesting, because I appreciate these publishing worries, but from another perspective, you've just had an *Edinburgh Review* dedicated to your work, and you have very persuasive expositors like Cairns Craig, who really under-stand your method, and in those circles you couldn't be doing better. It's slightly sad you have to feel annoyed about the pres-entation of books.

JK: Yeah, well, like it or leave it. Eventually you just get fed up with it, you get sickened by it. That's really how you get hurt, it's actually by default. That kind of stuff causes disarray concerning the marketing people and those who sell the books, the distributors. They're the ones who start not to lead with it. "You don't need this kind of person in bookshops"—I mean what's all that about? And around the time of the Booker Prize, the government launched a "good English" campaign—

MG: Ha. "Good English" is a phrase which goes back to Adam Smith and other pro-British Enlightenment Scots.

JK: Yes. He was the man, I suppose.

MG: Okay, so back to the question of action. R.D. Laing said of Kafka—someone you've written about—that his only form of positive participation was in his own anxiety at the unreality of the world around him. There seems to be a parallel in the way your characters are constantly rushing into doing nothing, are centred in trying to escape from inactivity. The story "It happened to me once," for example, is a perfect exam-ple of the prevalence of what Laing called a "false-self system," taking over the conversation of a narrator waiting in a dole queue and really wanting to connect to the guy in front. In this story you neatly remove the chance of recognition to leave a game of evasion played out by false selves. Yet in other stories in *The Good Times*, like "Strength" and "The Norwest Reaches," mutual recognition is there in abundance. Is *The Good Times* a turning point?

JK: I'm not sure, but you know, a couple of stories had been written earlier, and sometimes it's just good to look at the way other artists function, the way a musician builds an album, or an artist holds an exhibition. Usually it means they want to mark a different period, something different, but you see during that you're kind of working on a kind of version of what you'll show. I'd already started some of the stuff in *Translated Accounts*, so you start working on other things. You have to shelve them eventually, because there are other works nearing completion that you've been working on before that. So in a sense you might say the change—yes, there could be a certain change, I've always wanted to explore certain things in stories like *The Good Times*. And in *The Good Times*, yeah, there was a range of situations, males from ages fourteen to seventy-four; there's one story based in New York, one story in London, one travelling around in England somewhere, but apart from that I think they're all based in Glasgow.

MG: A story like "The Norwest Reaches"—with its almost blissful sense of recognition and community—I can't think of anything as positive before that.

JK: [*Laughs*]

MG: Before that, you get scattered points of recognition, but not the prolonged content of "The Norwest Reaches."

JK: Yeah. When you mention that, I mean in that sense of when people look for positive things in some of Kafka's stories, and you think, for fuck's sake. [*Laughs*] But they are, in a sense. The elements of this story concern the relationship of this guy who seems to be quite settled emotionally or something, or maybe the other way, who knows. Yeah, but that's valid I suppose. Some of the stories of *The Good Times*, like what's the [second] last story, "Constellation," a story about a boy with his girlfriend who seems to be moving away, you know, it's a positive story—but it's actually quite a hard story. Obviously it has a class thing, and has a lot to do with forms of elitism. I think it's a kind of positive story, but you know, it's tough.

MG: I think it's also "tough" in a philosophical sense—in *The Good Times* you have this combination of some people completely failing to talk to each other, and others talking in blissful abundance.

JK: Yes.

MG: In your account of the stones on the beach in "My Eldest," did MacDiarmid's poem "On a Raised Beach" cross your mind at all? In the MacDiarmid poem, there is a kind of ontology locked into the stones, a wishful end to the separation of the subject from the object-world. The narrator can't quite get at it, he remains alone, but his determination to open up this ontology seems to wish at a dialectical method of writing. Your story offers a very similar scenario, plus hints that the narrator, or perhaps the narrator's son, really has become part of his surroundings.

JK: Well, I don't know MacDiarmid's "On a Raised Beach" that well, but that makes sense, it raises a lot of things. But then who knows; the character himself is aware of other members of his family apart from his son, yet I think he's more aware of a certain understanding between him and his son, and perhaps a rejection of that. You know, the story in a sense is to do with suicide, and I think in some odd way that's intuited by his son, and the son rejects it.

MG: What makes it very interesting is where you set it [on the beaches of a nuclear base], and that fact that "chance" in relationships is explored within a location marked by radioactive dangers, a form of chance via which the narrator views his son as his own genes warped in some way, the extent of which dangers are in a sense decided by the government yet unknown to him, since he can't measure radioactive damage.

JK: Yeah. Right. It's a complicated story. When I used to read from *The Good Times* I used to read that one. I once stopped half-way through it, because somebody laughed at the wrong place. They were very apologetic, but I just stopped. [*Laughs*] I didn't stop the whole reading, I just stopped reading that story. It was nobody's fault, you know, it wasn't deliberate, and I wasn't even angry. I just couldn't read it, so I did something else.

MG: The issue of nuclear bases was a very national one. Why do you go to such lengths to avoid nationalism in the essays, when so many modern liberation struggles have been nationalist in character?

JK: Well, I'm not involved with any parties, you know, the idea that this guy's an anarchist is a bit of a laugh in some ways. But again I think that libertarian socialism is definitely more important as far as that goes. So I don't have any leaning towards party-type politics. Actually I find it even hard to appear on a platform, whereas a few years ago I'd usually go to any worthwhile platform. But now, the kind of debates, for example, are just horrendous, shocking. I mean, like the Scottish Parliament, I think we'd need Frantz Fanon to talk about the kind of organisations we have here, but Jack McConnell, I mean, it's almost like he's crawling to TV interviewers, never mind English politicians; it's a really weird circumstance. It's like a school bully or something, but the other aspect of it is that he's a school prefect, and that carries further in the media—

MG: Frantz Fanon is exactly the sort of figure I have in mind. He is careful not to speak of nationalism, but a revolutionary politics which functions strictly at a national level without being nationalist in the classic sense. And I'm thinking about what seems a majority view amongst the Scottish people—not necessarily amongst MSPs [Members of the Scottish Parliament], but amongst people—that they want national determination because they want more democracy, not because they want to vent some kind of ethnic pride.

JK: Yeah, you know, that situation has been going for some time, and I don't think it can stop now, so "nationalist" is the conventional terminology, but that has to be quickly qualified by saying that any country should determine its own existence, so I'm in favour of the self-determination of Scotland. But I think it's good to look at examples around the time of the First World War; the CP was being formed and the anarchists were quite big up here, and it was quite valid to have these theoretical discussions about "ways forward." And that was certainly where James Connolly and [John] Maclean went, and that is where a lot of socialists have gone, that idea of the workers' republic. And I kind of go along with that. I think there is a basic, healthy socialism in Scotland, I think it's a gut thing here, and I don't think the Scottish Parliament's going to destroy that or kill it. But I think they're trying, that's the point, and will try for many years to come.

MG: One of the ironic things about living outside Scotland is people coming up to you and saying, "Well done, you've achieved freedom now."

JK: It's shocking, the disinformation, you know.

MG: You've struggled for an integrity of local language in your work, despite people complaining that Glaswegians don't swear all the time. Yet one thing that's noticeable about your fiction, and again someone pointed this out in the *Edinburgh Review*, is that your women hardly ever swear. Why is this?

JK: Again, it's about these false notions of writers representing the people, you know, the idea that the artist stands for his community. I don't see that at all. I really don't represent Glasgow people at all. I don't know, it depends, sometimes in many cultures the men will not use that kind of language in front of women, they try to cool their language. That's just some of the cultures that some of the characters inhabit, I think. The premises of that sort of stuff, I just don't go along with. What was it Ian Rankin said—"My father says people don't speak that way in Glasgow"—I mean, Christ, it's such a shocking comment. But again, the elites, people who are supposedly critics, lose all their critical values in prejudice. I mean, some of the most basic notions that you'd try to instill in a first-year student about distinguishing between character and author and all this, all that goes by the board, so that the characters are all read as being like me. You'd never say this about any of these ordinary literary-type writers like Julian Barnes or Graham Swift or Ian McEwan or Martin Amis—that kind of stuff would never be said. This again is a very formal thing to do with language which is up-front, in a way that's local to West Central Scotland, I suppose. And it's given fewer concessions to literary form, because it's already taken away from "the literary" or something. But people are not even given the benefit of that kind of critique. I mean, for example, Douglas [Dunn], one of his claims was that "Kelman expects us to believe that Sammy wouldn't be given his taxi fare [by the police]." They never think about, why would one writer say that about another writer, when the situations are fictitious and specific to that text. It's not much better than the pure prejudice itself. So the second point is, why the hell am I being so upset about this, why is this guy's comment hurting me in this way. Somehow I've fallen into these prejudices I thought I'd got rid of.

MG: On the other hand, this so-called controversy; if you look at the impact your work will be seen to have had in twenty years' time—

JK: Yeah, well, *Translated Accounts* has already started in Russian; the French one was abandoned because it was said to be untranslatable, and the Croatians are looking at it and seeing if it is possible to translate. So it's up to us. My work, and Alasdair [Gray]'s too, and others, we've kind of bypassed Scottish views for, like, twenty-five years, because of bad reviews, right. Now that's not to say it's always water off a duck's back, but you're always having to aim at a wider role, and that's the case for getting into Europe these days, or even the States: you're seen as a real writer. Especially now in Europe there's more translations being done. Again, it's too late in Scotland for those who are attacking, as it has been for twenty-odd years now. People know that, and when you go outside the country people ask you questions in a generous capacity about Scottish writers, while the Scottish critics are trying to exclude you from the debate, and show somehow that you're inconsequential, figures of fun. They have done that with the likes of Janice [Galloway] and Alasdair [Gray], to try and ridicule them, you know, which is an extraordinary situation, but fortunately there's a much better response from outside, even England, parts of England, you know.

MG: As you've already said, you've written as, and about, many different kinds of males, from many perspectives. Have you ever thought of seriously adopting the voice of a woman?

JK: Well, yeah, a couple of stories are from women's perspectives; there's no reason at all, I just feel like I'd be writing like someone from Venus or something—

MG: Well, we're told that women are from Venus—

JK: I mean there's no reason. That kind of question of what you represent, one interesting thing is that some of my biggest advocates, those who don't attack my work, are often women. They're more happy about the way I approach women in my work, you know.

MG: I was thinking, because the presentation of men-women relationships works well in stories like "The Norwest Reaches," why not take it a step further and take up the female voice more?

JK: I'd love to do that, I really would, you know. Also the thing about age groups, it would be great to write as certain age groups, or certain types of male, it'd be good to operate within different types of psyches, but part of this comes back to time. If I look back on the last twelve years, how much time have I actually had for writing? Now, *How Late It Was* was not a bad earner, yes, I made maybe a hundred grand or something, but spread it over the years, I'd already spent eighty thousand of that by the time the book came out, break it down into annual earnings, so from something like 1991 to 1996 I lived on that. And I spent two years of that time working as a volunteer—unpaid in other words—at the asbestos campaign, so I didn't do much writing then. So since 1995 I started having to worry about what was going to happen for the next phase, or should I rely on the wife to bail us out, which is usually the situation. So it was slow, very slow advances of twenty grand or something, and that was to keep me going for a certain period, but it couldn't. So I had to go to Texas in '98 five years ago, and I worked there for a year. And then I came back and started working in London in the autumn, as I still do, only part-time, right, 'cause I don't have enough dough. Then I went back to Texas for six months, and now I'm here for the last eighteen months. So yeah, it's just working conditions—I've never actually had the time to be a writer. It's always buying time. So it would be great to have the time to do it [write in other types of voice], and explore—I'd love to do more plays, and again there's different ways in which I'd like to be able to handle things, certain relationships. But part of the problem of, you might say, the formal aspect of where my work has gone is that transition from imparting the narrative of the inner psyche, the most natural place, and 98 percent of that time is in the male psyche, because I am a male. So maybe it would be more natural for a writer like me to be in drama; if I had the time and the opportunity to be involved in drama, I'd love to. But I can't even get a damn play on here, never mind get commissioned or something, or never mind being able to work with a director and a repertory company, you know, there is absolutely no opportunity for that, even when I'm working somewhere else to try and pay for it. The real pressing thing for me has been the prose, and this is where the urgency goes in my work. So it's like any other artist—if you're a musician who works acoustically, sure it would be nice to work with an electric blues band, but there's never been time for it. I would love to have the space to do it all, and if I had the time and the space, I would.

MG: Right. Thanks very much.

15

2003

Interview by Andrej Skubic

A collection of Kelman's stories was chosen and translated by the Slovenian writer Andrej Skubic, from four short story collections. It was published in Slovenia as *Preživljanje, preživljanje* (Making a living, making a living).

Andrej Skubic: I remember how surprised (or should I say amused) I was a few years ago when I saw a *Scotland on Sunday* article on the SAC [Scottish Arts Council] initiative to donate modern Scottish books to Scottish schools, when a critic described the current situation as the "dark age of Scottish letters." Is such reception of "the language of the gutter" not a thing of the past? Do you still receive such reviews?

James Kelman: Yes, occasionally, but only in Scotland and the rare time in England. It is simply another method of marginalising the work of a writer.

AS: In spite of your public image (in England) as a fierce Scottish revolutionary, Janice Galloway once said the she, paradoxically, never thought of you as a markedly Scottish writer. When I first came across your writing, I found your mixture of social activism and raw power very familiar—closer to the Central European tradition than to what was going in the British literature of the '70s and '80s. But this anger, with which you were prepared to submerge in the world and language of "the least of men," this refusal of any kind of censorship,

seemed very refreshing even in comparison with this tradition—it was exactly what the world anticipating the "end of
history" and arrival of some sort of consumer heaven needed.
Do you, in hindsight, feel that your message of social prejudice
really "came through" with readers and critics? What is your
feeling on publications such as the *Edinburgh Review* issue
dedicated to you?

JK: Well, I don't have "a message" as such; I see art operating in a different way. My own views are fairly traditional. I
make stories as best I can; the only "discussion" is between me
and the page. I do the stories properly and the politics takes
care of itself. Questions relating to "social prejudice" and so
on may be implicit in my work. These aspects of my work have
"come through" to some readers and critics, but not to others.
About the *Edinburgh Review* issue: there is nothing a writer
can do about a matter of this nature so it is better not to worry
about it. Praise and condemnation both function to the detri-
ment of a writer's concentration.

AS: On skimming through *Translated Accounts*, my first
reaction was that perhaps your intention was to finally give
the academics what they had always wanted—an enigmatic,
inaccessible book practically devoid of living language, without tangible emotion, without "bad language."

JK: I was aware of that argument, and its ironies, during
the writing. But the writing was so damn difficult all such
external thought vanished. I disagree with your use of the
phrase "practically devoid of living language," although I
think I understand what you mean. I don't know about "without tangible emotion"; I would be disappointed if it lacked
emotional strength but accept that it might be described as
"intangible."

AS: Having (almost) finished the book, I see it as your dark-
est work so far. Until now, your characters always retained a
possibility (or illusion) of defence or retreat in the face of the
hostile social circumstances—if nothing else, at least fantasy,

the experience of a bright morning, of change or departure. But *Translated Accounts* is a story about the loss of language, which is in a way a loss of humanity. The reader feels a wall between himself and the world in the novel—a wall that he cannot cross. But is this wall really there, or are we on the other side already? The Empire rules by war, and its president and administration are illiterate. Language is no longer a medium of negotiation on values. What can we write about in such a world? In what language? Is this also a book on your personal disaffection?

JK: I accept some of your reading of the novel but I don't think it is a work of "personal disaffection." Like other artists I occasionally try to struggle through difficult areas; the "struggle" is almost always formal. I disagree that "language is no longer a medium of negotiation on values"; perhaps some of what is going on in contemporary literature is an aid to my position rather than yours. And I am thinking here in particular—because it is my own language—of how writers from non-English-speaking cultures are obliged to work in English, and engage in the attempt to transform that English, making use of the rhythms, cadences and so on, of their own indigenous languages.

AS: I hear that you currently share the chair of professor of Creative Writing at Glasgow University with Tom Leonard and Alasdair Gray. In comparison to other Glasgow universities like Strathclyde and Caledonian, this one is supposed to raise Glaswegian cultural aristocracy. How does a writer of your reputation—or one of Tom Leonard for that matter—communicate with these students? Is this a time when those who oppose elitism in principle have to choose between cultural elitism and material elitism of the more market-oriented universities?

JK: I'm unsure about your question on "cultural elitism and material elitism of the more market-oriented universities." In my own case it is a straight economic deal. I have only survived as a writer in the way that I have because my wife worked full-time. The University of Texas employed me for three semesters which was crucial and helped us through a fix. There was no work in Scotland at that time. The vacancy at the University of Glasgow later arose. The writers Alasdair Gray, Tom Leonard and myself are friends. The three of us agreed that we could work together. Although neither of us felt we could do the professor's job on a full-time basis we could manage it as a three-way jobshare, leaving us the time and space to get on with our own work. I still haven't worked out about the "communication with the students" part of the equation; that is probably better directed at the students to answer.

AS: Do you believe in the critical activities of writers' organisations (these have always been very respected in central and eastern Europe)? Or is it just about screaming abuse out of an ivory tower? What is your experience with such organisations?

JK: I am not really involved in any at present. I have always been in favour of writers operating in solidarity. Difficulties always arise in organisations. Writers have to write.

2008

Interview by Darran Anderson

This interview was originally published as "The War against Silence" by *3:AM Magazine.*

Darran Anderson: *Kieron Smith, boy* is both a continuation of themes that have run through much of your writing (giving voice to the alienated, exploring grammar and syntax) and a departure away from the adult world. What inspired the work?

James Kelman: There is no inspiration in that sense. If you are a writer you do better to write, and keep on writing. Some pieces develop more quickly than others. This novel developed from a few pieces I was working on over a lengthy period, especially one short story which did not stop. Eventually this story was not part of the novel. It concerns the boy as a thirteen- or fourteen-year-old, whereas the novel ends a year or so earlier.

DA: In keeping with life, your books have a meandering feel. Do you approach them with a plot mapped out or do you find yourself getting swept along as the book progresses?

JK: I'm unsure about "meandering." Kieron's life seems packed full of incident and trauma. I certainly don't use plots, but nor do I get "swept along." This is a working process. Creativity is not passive, I don't see the creation of art as passive.

DA: You've said previously that books are the last truly free art form left. In what sense?

JK: I think I said something along these lines but not that, not precisely. The beauty of prose fiction that I see is simply that in order to create something you need only pay attention to personal exigency. If you work in drama there are all these other constraints; I enjoy working in drama—stage, radio, television, film—but it very rarely happens; all these other people come between yourself and the piece. And I'm not talking about actors here, but the sorts of pressure that gets applied to directors, producers and theatres. The work gets squeezed to the point where it hurts to continue. The most obvious example is language itself, if you want to work in drama, and create it from your own experience, if that experience happens to be male working-class culture around West Central Scotland. Be prepared to censor and suppress your characters, or write only from tiny corners of that experience. In prose fiction the freedom to work honestly exists, although you may have to fight for it. In those other areas of literature, I mean drama, there is only silence. That sort of aesthetic integrity does not exist in radio and television, and seldom on film.

DA: There's a sense in your books that language is a battleground, that pride at the richness of language comes as a form of resistance against establishment-speak and that by denying the language of a people the authorities deny the very existence of the speakers. It's evident in Sammy's encounters with representatives of the State in *How Late It Was, How Late*, the isolation of Patrick Doyle in *A Disaffection* and in the attempts to mould Kieron Smith "to speak proper." Do you still see this as a battle still raging and have you seen any change between your first book and now?

JK: The distinction between battles and wars: people mistake battles for wars. Questions around language and imperialism have been to the fore for hundreds of years. My work still suffers in this respect, the new novel notwithstanding. The forces of reaction are what they are, they don't go away.

DA: Do you ever tire of the controversy that your books inevitably stir up in some quarters or do you enjoy fighting the good fight?

JK: It is not a good fight. The crucial factor is the ability to earn a living, this is what is taken from writers who work on/ from the margins. Your question suggests it is a fair go, an even fight, or some such nonsense. It isn't. One side has power and authority and the other doesn't. One has the power to stop the other from earning a living. It is better to be acknowledged as a writer than have to continue proving it all the time.

DA: You've said your method of writing is to keep several projects on the go at once. Are there any that have gotten away or that you plan to come back to one day?

JK: A couple have got away; I thought I would have written at least one earlier novel but I could never devote adequate time to it. I was having to work in ordinary jobs at the time and eventually it did "get away." However, I wrote many short stories from the wreckage. But maybe it would never have worked as a novel anyway, not at that time. Occasionally in art we take on work that we are not quite ready for technically; we need to work our way through other stuff before we can get it finished. It happened to me with my first novel, *A Chancer*. In order to finish it I had to write *The Busconductor Hines*. No doubt to finish *Kieron Smith, boy* I had to finish *Translated Accounts*.

DA: There's been an institutionalised view of Scottish history and culture that it ended with the Jacobites or the "tartan-and-heather kind of bollocks" of Walter Scott, an outlook that's been shattered by yourself and colleagues like Tom Leonard, Alasdair Gray, Liz Lochhead and the sadly departed Jeff Torrington. Do you feel part of a new cultural era in Scotland or even the continuation of a forgotten buried one?

JK: A new cultural era in Scotland … ? There is so much dishonesty around, so much humbug. Your "forgotten, buried one" is more interesting. Wouldn't it be nice to see the radical tradition acknowledged within our education system. Imagine our college, university and secondary school students knowing about Alexander Wilson, Thomas Muir, Andrew Hardie, James Wilson and John Baird, about Hugh Miller, Helen McFarlane, Keir Hardie, Cunninghame Graham, Jane Rae, John Murdoch and Willie Nairn, Agnes Dollan, Helen Crawfurd, Arthur McManus, George Yates and James Connolly; John Maclean, Guy Aldred, John Wheatley etc.

DA: For all its evocations of a turbulent childhood, *Kieron Smith, boy* seems arguably your most optimistic book. Do you find there is cause for hope or is the light at the end of the tunnel just an oncoming train?

JK: I don't know what you mean by "optimistic" in this context. The novel concludes towards the end of the boy's first year at senior secondary school. I don't know what that signifies. I don't think it signifies anything. Already he has started dogging it, i.e., truanting. Who knows if he even makes it to the end of first year. He has already said "fuck" in the classroom, maybe he'll fuck off altogether.

DA: What's next for your writing?

JK: The usual: short stories, long stories, plays and essays.

17

2008

Interview by Jesse Wichterman

This interview was originally published by the *Velvet*.

Jesse Wichterman: Your first book, *An Old Pub Near the Angel*, was initially published in America. Was there a specific reason why it was not released in the UK? Was this common or is it now common for an author to find publication abroad?

James Kelman: It was a small press, in that literary tradition more normally associated with poetry, basically a one-woman operation; and the woman was Constance Hunting, based in Orono, Maine. I never met her but corresponded with her, irregularly it has to be said, up until her death only a couple of years ago. She was a hero. The stories in this collection were my earliest, written between the ages of twenty-two and twenty-five. No publisher in Scotland or England showed interest until about one year ago, thirty-five years later, when Polygon Books of Edinburgh, Scotland, published a new edition, with a sixty-page afterword of my own, which I enjoyed doing, setting a context, giving a much fuller answer to your question.

JW: You had written and had published short story collections before your first novel, *Busconductor Hines*, was published. Was this novel the first one that you wrote? How was the transition, for you, from short story to novel?

JK: My first novel was *A Chancer*, which was only published after *The Busconductor Hines*. Neither has been published in

USA. *A Chancer* was difficult to write; I needed to work my way through *The Busconductor Hines* before being able to finish it. There was also another novel but I never managed to finish it at all: I never had adequate time. I was working in ordinary jobs, driving buses, working in factories and so on, and a couple of kids. I made many short stories from the embers. It is possible it just wasn't working, maybe it never would have. Sometimes we have to give up on stories because we are not quite ready for them technically. What happens is we need to work our way through other stories, we need to develop technically to get them finished. The transition from short story to novel was straightforward; my method was more or less the same, to create stories, some will be long and some will be short. One of the trickiest things is to recognise that a story is finished.

JW: Many of your books are short story collections. Is there any method to balancing the writing of one over the other? Do you continue writing short stories while in the process of writing a novel?

JK: I work on many different things, like other artists. In my own case, besides the short and long stories, I also enjoy work on drama—stage, radio, screenplay—and essaying. Prose fiction takes precedence though. I'm working on many many short stories. Gradually this pares down to half a dozen, then to a couple of pieces, then I bring one to a conclusion, then another. I do work on short stories while working on a novel. It depends. Sometimes you need a break, you get scunnered working on one thing, over and over and over, the process of revision; I incline towards overworking, it is a mistake. Sometimes I need to regain enthusiasm for the process, batter into unfinished stories, see what I can do with them.

JW: Have any of your novels started out as short stories?

JK: My stories—long or short—just start out as stories. It is rare for me to see one as a novel when I've just begun. I don't plan anything, remember. No design, no painting by numbers, I leave that to religionists.

JW: When you hit upon an idea, are there specific indicators that it will be a short story or a novel?

JK: I rarely have ideas. I sit down and make it up as I go along. Inspiration, talent, genius, it is all crap and can be lumped in with ideas. If you have them or get them you still have to sit down and do the work. They might bring you to the desk, but that is all. There is no other way but work, not that I can see.

JW: You have a couple books of essays, *Some Recent Attacks* and *And the Judges Said*. Are these pieces that you were approached to write for a specific outlet or are they more in the line of something you felt a need to express in written form? What is the publication process like for essays compared to fictional stories?

JK: Almost without fail the political essays and nonfiction I have written have come about through being approached by someone. I used to involve myself in campaigning politics; some of those essays didn't begin as essays at all, I wrote them to deliver as talks. A couple began as reviews, like the one on Rushdie's *Satanic Verses*, or else they just got longer and longer, like the one on Noam Chomsky and the Scottish philosophical tradition. The essay on Kafka's three novels began years earlier as a paper I wrote while a student. I left school at fifteen years of age but later on, at the age of twenty-nine—a published writer and father of two—I went to university. The essays on racism, industrial disease, the plight of Kurdish people, began either as talks or commissioned pieces.

JW: Many of your essays are political. What are your thoughts on the current political state of the world?

JK: We enter unknown territory but certain factors remain constant: the lack of information, the lack of analysis, the propagation and imposition of ignorance, the cult of celebrity, the shameful wealth of the few, the way society makes heroes from cowards and bullies, and rewards dishonesty, not to mention the fifth rate in art and so on—the usual …

JW: Besides short stories, novels, and essays, you also write plays. Three of these have been published in *Hardie and Baird & Other Plays*. How did these come about? How many plays have you written? How did you get involved with the Edinburgh Fringe Festival? Have any other than those three been published?

JK: Only these three plays have been published. I have written a dozen or so and had staged, or produced on radio, maybe seven or eight but it has never been satisfactory, and never showed a profit financially, far less allowed the chance of earning a living. You are forced to be a dilletante. When you work in drama you enter areas of censorship and suppression that do not exist in prose fiction. This makes it tough to survive. Theatre, film, radio and television prefer to aspire to the third rate in art; anything stronger than that demands integrity, honesty—even originality is frowned upon. I enjoy drama and always had a need to work in it. But I learned not to take it seriously. I was talking with a good young director last week, who has recently been awarded two awards for a movie he directed. He is also a good stage director and directed a play of mine twelve years ago that I wrote for a blues band [*One, Two—Hey!*]. We were discussing a new play of mine that he would love to direct. During our conversation it dawned on me that we were assuming it might not be possible because the language was too "strong." For fuck sake, man!

JW: Recently, Polygon has reprinted some of your books. How or why were these specific titles chosen? Are there any additions or subtractions to the material in the reprinted books?

JK: The only addition was the afterword I wrote for *An Old Pub Near the Angel*, my first collection of stories. I was really pleased that Polygon Books decided to reprint these titles, otherwise they would have gone out of print. Polygon is a Scottish publisher. In Scotland I have a reputation, in England it is not something I take for granted. Unfortunately USA is overly influenced by what happens in England—and England means Greater London. I don't see much difference between the literary establishments of Greater London and Greater New York City. The *New Yorker* wouldn't publish my stories in the mid-1970s. Thirty years later and they still won't. I suppose I should take it as a compliment. I was disappointed when teaching in Texas and California to find so many academics in thrall to Standard English Literary Form. Too much cowardice around, a failure to recognise the value of indigenous forms; inherent racism and elitism, people unwilling to stand up for what is great in US history—and I mean the radical tradition, both in art and politics.

JW: You've had work published by numerous publishers. What have your experiences been like? What are your thoughts on the state of the publishing industry?

JK: Your questions are taking longer and longer to answer. Another book for this one. Literary fiction makes publishers nervous. People have lost their nerve. Writers have to stay strong and take strength from their own tradition. Art is not a career. We have to draw courage from people like Tillie Olsen, June Jordan, Tom Kromer, Meridel Le Sueur, Ralph Ellison, Upton Sinclair, Mark Twain, Sherwood Anderson, Zora Hurston, Gertrude Stein, Kate Porter, Flannery O'Connor. Writers have to forget about the crap and get on with their work. If good art is being rewarded by society then artists have to question what it is they are doing.

JW: It is well known that your winning of the Booker Prize for *How Late It Was, How Late* created a stir. In the UK, your work, for being about real people for real people, has been harshly criticised. Your work is not judged or perceived that way elsewhere. Is this something typical of the UK, at least amongst critics and people with a public voice? Is it that, in creative endeavours, they don't wish to see the reality of their culture and lives represented?

JK: You have to remember the hierarchical nature of society in the UK. There is a monarchy for fuck sake. In the

UK, and many other parts of the world, there are hordes of people who accept the divine right of kings. Here we are in the twenty-first century and there is a monarchy, an aristocracy. Can you believe it? But I wouldn't be too smug here in USA. My language is perceived as "working class" and working-class language is presumed an inferior and shoddy thing, incapable of producing literary art. Many writers believe this too; they seek to perfect their Standard English Literary Form, the voice of assimilation. People get jobs and careers via assimilation, this includes literature. There are many academics and critics who refuse to accept that writers like myself are "real writers," they see us as kind of Alan Lomax figures, walking about recording the lower orders. I blame Henry James.

JW: Do you feel awards such as the Booker serve a purpose?

JK: I think that question is better put to the publishing industry. For the writer it is a double-edged sword. Generally it is a positive thing; it wasn't for myself. I believe my work was damaged because of it, but maybe other writers would say the same.

JW: I wouldn't consider your fiction experimental. However, your novel *Translated Accounts* is a bit of a departure in style from your other novels. What led to the writing of this novel and to the style in which it is presented?

JK: I think "style" is a confusing term. What I do comes about through necessity, so "style" or what I understand by "style" really has nothing to do with it. People use different grammars, that is the source of my work. Mainstream literature advocates one grammar, higher English.

JW: Your latest novel, *Kieron Smith, boy*, is about a period in a young boy's life. I believe this is the first time a child has been the protagonist in one of your stories. Was the writing of this story now influenced by having children of your own and seeing them grow up?

JK: I have written stories before with young folk—boys— as the central characters. I doubt if I was ready before now to do something as sustained as *Kieron Smith, boy*. The novel makes use of a first-person narrative, and moves through the boy's life from age four through twelve going on thirteen, so issues around grammar are primary. I had to work my way through *Translated Accounts* in order to write *Kieron Smith, boy*.

JW: Something about *Kieron Smith, boy*: the cuss words are not entirely spelled out, are accompanied by stars for the missing letters. Was this planned from the beginning?

JK: It was not planned. Like most working-class boys Kieron censors and suppresses himself as soon as he starts using English. His family, community and society at large impress upon him that his own language is an inferior thing and should be stamped upon quickly. Like the rest of us he is encouraged to aspire to the language of power, the language of authority, which takes us back to the hegemony of Standard English Literary Form. It is strange for me to listen to US students talk; they all try to sound the same, and most seem to have succeeded—European Americans, that is, African American, Asian American, South American American, all differ—or do they? Not always.

JW: Also, his mother is constantly correcting his speech. Why the emphasis on this?

JK: It is not my emphasis. Censorship begins in the home. Family life is probably the greatest tool of tyranny, after the education system, probably before it, certainly prior to religion.

JW: In terms of writing, what's next for you?

JK: A gaol diary.

JW: James Kelman, thank you.

18

2009

Interview by Paul Shanks

This public interview took place at the University of Aberdeen; further details about the event are noted in the introduction below.

One of the highlights of the Migrating Minds conference in May 2009 was undoubtedly the public interview with James Kelman which took place at King's College on the evening before the WORD Festival (May 14). The main purpose in inviting Kelman to speak was not only due to his standing as an author of world stature but also because of the experiences he had recently written about concerning his migration to the USA as a young man. The Kelman family moved from Glasgow to California when he was seventeen but were forced to return within less than a year. As Kelman remarked, the experience served to split the family; two of his brothers remained in the States (one settling there permanently) and, shortly after the return to Glasgow, James moved southwards in order to find employment. In recent years, he has returned to the US and has spent some time living and working there as a teacher of Creative Writing (including a substantial tenure at Austin, Texas). These experiences were reason enough for arranging the event. However, it is equally pertinent that the idea of migration often filters into Kelman's fiction and sometimes serves as a central plot device. The characters in the novels and short stories frequently have aspirations towards leaving the UK for the English-speaking provinces of the New World: Australia, Canada, New Zealand and, of course, the US. Such desires often manifest themselves in the form of daydreams, as Kelman's protagonists rarely have the economic means to hold even a chance of following through their inclinations. Given the downtrodden predicament of many of these protagonists, it is unsurprising that the one novel that Kelman chose to set in America (*You have to be Careful in the Land of the Free*, 2004) centres upon a "failed emigrant" who has plans to return to Glasgow.

Over the course of the interview, Kelman offered a number of illuminating insights into his life and work; he also spoke about his sense of being part of a radical tradition that is simultaneously political, philosophical, cultural and literary; which spans from the eighteenth century to the present; and which includes figures as diverse as James Hogg, Noam Chomsky, Helen Crawfurd and Amos Tutuola. At the time of the event, he had just been short-listed for the International Booker Prize and would subsequently receive a Scottish Arts Council Award for the novel *Kieron Smith, boy* (2008). After an introduction from Cairns Craig, the evening began with a brief reading from the latter text:

James Kelman: The issues of immigration and emigration are fairly strong themes within all of my work ... although it's not often picked up, and I mean by that the Irish connection with Scotland. Cairns mentioned *A Disaffection* (1989), you know, but the central character is a Protestant atheist by the name of Paddy Doyle. This boy is on his way to becoming a Protestant atheist whose name is Kieron Smith. The central character in *How Late It Was, How Late* (1994), his name is "Sammy" Samuels, which when I was growing up—there was a Jewish boy in my class, Samuels is a Jewish name. For me the naming of characters has always been crucial but the irony is very rarely touched on. Another strong character in *How Late It Was* is Ally. Now it's always assumed, and assumed by the central character, that this is Alasdair. But if you look, if you read the text in fact, this strong peripheral figure is Ally but should it be spelled Ali? Sammy is blind and can't see, remember, and all he hears is the Glasgow speaking voice of this guy and he's dealing with issues around race and immigration, apart from when he's supporting a guy like Sammy. These are the issues that he deals with, and it's quite overt within the text. In Scotland, or rather in Glasgow, I always assumed that everybody would be saying, who is this Protestant called Paddy Doyle? Nobody ever says that. I'm the only one that ever says that! [*Laughter*] Anyway, I'm going to read a little bit of this novel and it's a bit where some of these kinds of issues as they affect childhood come to the fore …

[*Reads extract from* Kieron Smith, boy]

Paul Shanks: Great stuff! I found when you were reading that passage that there was a simultaneous impression of overhearing the character's thoughts but also that it's a story being told in the past tense. There's also this sense that the boy in the story is really trying to figure things out for himself. What was it initially that made you decide to turn to childhood in this latest novel? I mean, the idea of the ambiguous name and that sense of a missing piece of information comes across strongly in quite a bit of your fiction, but why was it you chose to focus on that aspect of the boy's experience?

JK: Well, it's not really the way I work in a way. I just work all the time really—and it depends on how stories are going. Some stories move on more readily than others, and I just kind of go with them. This *Kieron Smith* novel is quite tricky in terms of the grammar, the syntax. It's written in a … it's a peculiar thing in a way because it gives the impression of being written in Standard English, and it's not. It's Standard English in a sense, it seems to suggest Standard English Literary Form, and it's not that at all. It's using grammar also as users use it, as we use it as speakers. So it's the way people use language as speakers, how we think etc., so the grammar operates differently from literary form.

In terms of how we speak, especially in communication with people, it includes a lot of non-verbal communication and various things; and what we as writers, many writers have been doing for many, many years has been trying to find ways of … eh … it's almost like transcribing the oral form onto the page. There's really a tremendous tradition in this, and it's not only a Scottish tradition. There are obvious figures going back: James Hogg, and further than Hogg, and it's quite obvious now that we think of what he was doing in the *Justified Sinner*, which is a really complex, technically a very complex work, and he's using language that's really … I don't know of anyone who was using it at that time; language as complicated, as rich as he uses in the *Justified Sinner*. But even then, there was that tradition that he would be aware of as a poet; so right into the eighteenth century, the politics of language and culture at that time, and what was going on from people like David Hume and the whole anti-indigenous Scottish thing linguistically, which in a way I'd regard it as … I feel strongly now, more than I ever did … that it has been a bad thing really. It's been a bad thing for our culture, because what is involved in that becomes the denial of a culture, or denial of central parts of the culture, that I think have been really not good at all—and they still pertain just now—to do with assimilation towards the authority of the imperial power, which then and now continues to be this High English form, which has really been very destructive in various cultures throughout the world. Writers have often attempted to fight back and defend against this, and I regard my own work as being part of that tradition.

In contemporary literature over this last forty years or so, if we think of what was happening amongst writers within parts of Africa and parts of the West Indies and the Indian subcontinent, places where the English imperial voice had been forced on the people, and writers ultimately trying to

make sense of this with their own voices being denied them …
I'm sure I've spoken about this before in Aberdeen, but I'll refer
again to it: the best example for me would be contemporary
Nigerian literature really, in terms of prose fiction, and I'm
thinking of Amos Tutuola and Ken Saro-Wiwa. These writers
and the type of debates that went on in Nigeria during the '60s,
'70s and '80s; really powerful ideas to do with decolonization
rather than postcolonization, and trying to make sense of your
culture, your own culture, and give it a value. I would rather
just say the freedom to be a writer with whatever means are
at your disposal.

I know in Nigeria, without getting bogged down in it,
somebody like Chinua Achebe for example would have an axe
to grind with some other writers from Nigeria because he was
brought up in an English-speaking household and demanded
the right to write in English, whereas other writers were trying
to find a more radical way in that sense. And these struggles, I
find that they're just part of precisely the same as what we're
doing. They're never given, even just now in this contemporary
period, they're still not given credit, it's still devalued, and I find
this makes the whole of English literature, the world of English
literature … I'm only hesitating about using the term "corrupt."
[*Laughter*] Why is it I daren't say fucking "corrupt"; because
it's debilitating, let's put it that way. Whereas the verve and
the excitement of literature is English language literature, but
the problem and the reason why sometimes I think "corrupt" is
right, although maybe it's better to go with Chomsky and talk
about the myopia of the intelligentsia or something, because
it means because of what they've done they fail to see what's
under their nose, and they've failed to see maybe the beauty
of what Emily Brontë's doing in *Wuthering Heights*; and they
actually fail to see the beauty of some of the stuff that even
Dickens does; Dickens in his later work, where he's actually …
you think, Christ, he's actually involved in trying to find a way
into voice here; how people use language as speakers, and not

just as the standard grammar in the page, which to some extent was a nineteenth-century issue in terms of language, not only in our culture, in English language culture. It was an issue. An obvious place would be within Yiddish literature, well, the thing that became Yiddish literature in the mid-nineteenth century, because they had that same struggle, fighting against, almost the fascism of the language owned by the main elite in society, and that same struggle took place in places like Italy, in parts of Yugoslavia.

So it's kind of a nineteenth-century struggle in a way, as part of that nationalist stuff maybe. However, where was I? [*Laughter*]

PS: Well, actually you've covered a lot of the material that I was going to ask you about [*more laughter*] at the end of the question session, where I was going to ask a little bit about language hierarchies and English language literature. But could we just do a little scale-back to the beginning; go from the end to the beginning? I suppose the interest of today's event is really finding out more about not only the experiences you've had of migration but also the different connections given your rootedness in Glasgow, and the other cultural influences that you've had over your life, and maybe the way that's filtered into your work.

First of all, in the recent afterword to *An Old Pub Near the Angel*, you talk about your family connections with Aberdeen, and I believe your grandfather is buried on St Peter's Cemetery in King Street.

JK: And great-grandfather too, yes.

PS: Yes, and you professed an early interest in Aberdeen Football Club, but I think you might be a little bit more ambivalent about that now. [*Laughter*] I wondered whether these strong affinities with Aberdeen have ever affected your work in any way.

JK: Well, it was through my grandfather, the paternal grandfather. Kelman is a very northeast name, as people who are local to here will know. It's the kind of name from MacDuff, around that area. So yes, in that sense of immigration, or not quite being from Glasgow, because my grandmother was Catriona Mackenzie from Keose in the Parish of Lochs, Lewis, and she was a Gaelic speaker of course, and that was on my paternal side, and then the other side, my maternal grandfather, his dad was from Gateshead. They came to Vale of Leven for the shipbuilding around about 1880 or something like that. And the maternal grandmother, my other grandmother, her people came from around Dumfries and that area, South Ayrshire, and Ireland. So, on the one hand you'll say, well, that's just a standard Glaswegian boyhood. I don't know about Alan for instance, Alan Spence is here [in the audience], but we have a kind of shared boyhood in a way. Both of us are from Govan. It's funny how the writers of Glasgow all come from Govan, or a great many of us and, in a sense, we have very much an ordinary Glasgow background where immigration, you have such a strong sense of that, and even I would say that there's the sensibility that that brings about, has been to the fore politically; the radical political core that has been in Glasgow politics right from the eighteenth century since the Calton weavers were murdered by the British State, which would've been around about the 1780s, '90s, at the time of Thomas Muir, and that whole period around that time; from there through to the Scottish Insurrection: that period, 1819 from 1780, right through that period, and you had, well, a guy from here in Aberdeen who was very crucial intellectually, Thomas Reid, and you had this tremendous melting pot in Glasgow, and the great Francis Hutcheson, who came from Dublin. I would think probably the central figure in the Scottish Enlightenment as a teacher was Francis Hutcheson—of course his father was of the Scottish clergy, and I think that family came from this northeast area. But you saw the whole thing as you get in any culture where you have all these different influences, intellectual influences, coming in. You get a very strong culture in ways that often become quite radical politically. If there are minorities that are still being treated badly, sometimes shockingly badly, as has happened in Glasgow over two-hundred-odd years and more years, then there is this sense of an intellectual excitement that grows politically.

Well, I find that to the fore right the way throughout our politics really, in Glasgow, but it's that immigrant thing that's given it strength. The thing that I've come to be aware of so much, which I used to put it down to, as most of us would do here, as the suppression of radical politics and the true Scottish history is a radical history. For example, Hardie and Baird: I've written somewhere that I didn't know anything about Hardie and Baird or such a thing as a Scottish Insurrection, or that people were murdered by the British State at that period, and all the papers have been taken out, you know. You can't get hold of anything to do with them properly. I knew nothing about that until I was in my late twenties, and I wrote a play about it [*Hardie and Baird*, broadcast by the BBC in 1978], and I became aware from that period, very much about … which seems a cliché, the suppression of radical history.

Over the years or latterly, maybe since I started to teach in the States, some of my own experiences as a teenager returned, and you meet Scottish people in the States and Irish people, and it made me think more that part of the thing that's going on is not only a suppression of radical history, that part of the suppression is that of the Irish voice, or the right of Irish immigrants eventually to be known as Scottish without reservations. I found that by the time I'd finished working through *Kieron Smith* and other things that that to me is almost like one of the missing links. Certainly when you look at radical history in Central Scotland, not only West Central Scotland but also in Edinburgh, around Leith, you start to see the importance of it, and you think: why does no one talk about James Connolly as being central to the Scottish radical tradition when he was the first full-time paid member of the Scottish Labour Party?

Why do we have to go and dig through books on republicanism or on early Sinn Fein and the Easter Rising? If we don't look at that, how can we explain James Connolly's response to the death of Keir Hardie? How can we explain the response of the radicals around in Glasgow at that period to the death of James Connolly? How do we explain Jim Larkin; what he was doing around at the docks, in the yards, and that radical political situation then? How can we explain the republicanism of John Maclean and his friendship with Jim Larkin's family?

These things stop us from making our own history, and even the denial that John Maclean was essentially murdered by the British State; we don't take these things onboard. It's this denial that in a sense—and those of you who know Frantz Fanon's work and, you think, Fanon is really absolutely right when he talks about inferiorisation—that to me is the essence of contemporary Scotland, inferiorisation, and I don't see much of a change. I still see boys like James McCarthy or Aidan McGeady following Ray Houghton and others, choosing to play not for Scotland but for the Republic of Ireland, and you think that wee boy [Kieron Smith] in my novel would've chosen that too simply because of the victimisation that goes on; it's just such a part of the culture. People will deny—adults will deny—it is still such a part of the culture; it's been a part of the culture for nearly three hundred years: nobody will take it on. Well, people do take it on, but it means that those things are denied, and it also means that some of the people whom we should regard as heroes, we don't even know they're heroes. Nobody even knows about them. We have something like Helen Crawfurd's autobiography lying as a manuscript in an English institution. How the hell can we have something like that; the woman who invited Paul Robeson to fucking Dunoon—as far as I know. A tremendous figure, a powerful figure right through the women's suffragette movement, right the way through the 1930s and into the '40s, who was with Sylvia Pankhurst when they met with Lenin in 1920; how do we not know these damn things?

INTERVIEW BY PAUL SHANKS

PS: Yes, that radical inheritance certainly seems to be a presence in your work and also in your writing and essays. And of course there's the more recent novel you wrote, *Translated Accounts* (2001), where you have these voices striving to be heard through this translatorese. I'd love to talk about that, but I think we need to home in to this US experience. I wondered if you could just start off by recounting some of your experiences of living in California as a teenager. I mean, you've written about this quite extensively in the afterword to *An Old Pub Near the Angel* (2007). If you could just recount to the audience about some of those experiences?

JK: I should put in a word for Polygon Books here by the way, who are republishing about seven books of mine in new editions. They did a new one of *An Old Pub Near the Angel*, which is great really, because it had never been published in the UK before. It was published in the States in 1973, and it's now available here, and they allowed me in fact to write an afterword too, which I finished in California, where I was teaching at the time. It was a coincidence, not an irony really, that it was the first time I'd spent any length of time there. I'd been through California quite a few times but I'd never ever worked there or been there any length of time since I was seventeen. And it was while I was there that I started to get into doing the afterword, or I said to Polygon, okay, I'll take on this afterword, because it was quite meaningful for me to be in California all those years later. Well, you don't like to sentimentalise yourself, which is very easy to do, because most of us do. It's really good if you're on your own, and my wife was back in Glasgow, and I could go out and drink as much as I wanted, and look at myself in the mirror and think, I've had some life, and then cry myself to sleep. [*Laughter*]

Anyway, sorry, so I was actually doing that one night, and there was a great radio station; the last of the independent radio stations based in San Jose, San Francisco, and, as I say, a truly independent one, and I was listening to the radio, and on came a

191

pal of mine, George Gallacher, he was a member of the Poets—a great Sixties band. They did some really fine music at that time, and John Lennon was fond of it. Anyway, I'm sitting here in San Jose, only two years ago, and on came George Gallacher from 1965, with this great fan base in California, and that was one of the things that took me back into writing this "afterword" essay.

It was a tricky period for me personally when we emigrated to LA, because I'd left school when I was fifteen and I was working. I was serving my time as a compositor in Glasgow. When I went to California I was seventeen and I'd been working more than two years. But in California you can't work at seventeen unless you know the local ins and outs of the economy. You can't work, although I had a green card and all that, you're just too young. So I used to just walk around all the time in LA. I was living in Pasadena at that time; it was eleven miles from central LA and I just used to walk in to save money to buy twenty Camel because my old man was skint. My elder brother was working but I didn't like to borrow money all the time because he was very good, he would give me money, but I didn't want to take his money for twenty fags. So I used to do a lot of walking to save money and go looking for a job. I didn't give up but it was a very long walk in and I got into doing quite a lot of walking in Los Angeles.

We moved from there into a district called Hawthorne, which is just on Watts. Some of you will have heard of Watts. That was where the riots began in 1965; that was that horrible time. Well, as a young guy from Glasgow, it was just at that time Malcolm X was doing great work up in New York and the East Coast and the whole civil rights movement was coming to the fore … what had happened in Montgomery and places, and there was a lot of horrible stuff. It was surprising to know in LA at that time also that African Americans still had to sit at the back of the bus. Now, as a young smoker, when I got on the bus, we always smoked at the back of the bus, so I used to go and I used to wear a sharp Italian suit. It got me into a lot of trouble in other places. [*Laughs*] However, it looked very weird, sitting at the back of the bus, and I used to get some very strange looks; but at that time, I wasn't aware that that kind of apartheid existed in the public transport then. It was really quite shocking, and being back in Glasgow later, when the Watts thing happened, it really just made sense in a way because of the pressures and the tensions that were around in that period.

But it did have a big effect on my life, the immigration, in a sense. It split our family, and my elder brother stayed in the States because there wasn't enough money to come home; it was a very typical immigrant's experience. My father, who was involved in a family business, he was a very good skilled tradesman. He was a picture-restorer and gilder and frame-maker and he was having to do very basic work in LA that eventually didn't suit him and he decided to cut his losses and go home. I've got four brothers. He couldn't afford to take everybody so one of my younger brothers had to stay with my elder brother. I had go back to Glasgow and help out with the family economy. So a very typical immigrant scene really. I could come back to Scotland and get a job, in the cooperative shoe factory in Govan, and earn a man's wage when I was seventeen. My younger brother came home in six months or thereabouts but my elder brother had to stay, and eventually he went into the American army. I would've been called up obviously too; that was a period when you could volunteer. You weren't conscripted, conscription didn't happen until just a little bit later, but my elder brother eventually had to join, effectively for economic reasons. So it did have a big effect; and I was realising recently, talking with my cousins in Aberdeen today, when we came back, even to Glasgow, it was just such a typical scene as an immigrant experience. There wasn't enough room; we had to live in two rooms. I stayed elsewhere with my grandmother, and just visited, all that kind of stuff. A few months later, I just was off really, went down to England to work. When I was doing that afterword to *An Old Pub* ... I realised how typical an immigrant's experience it was, and in that personal way, because it meant I became that rootless type of character, you know? Manchester, working in Manchester and London and the Channel Islands and places like that. That was my life until I met Marie in London. She was twenty, I was twenty-two.

PS: One of the things we've been talking about in the conference today, some of the papers we've had, are documents of this experience, of passing from one culture to another, and the almost traumatic effect it has, and it does lead to a sense of uncertainty and rootlessness. Would you say that your experience of the US—the immigrant experience—led directly or inadvertently to that feeling of rootlessness which is so much a presence in your work as well, in your writing? And actually, the whole immigrant experience; I only noticed this after you'd written your recent work, but every four pages or so, there's mention of migration to New Zealand, "the greater Englishes"; they are often daydreams but they are also real aspirations. So there's a constant presence of the idea of migration in your work.

JK: Well, yes, but the thing is, immigration was part of my life in Glasgow anyway, whether or not I had gone to the States, simply because of the work situation. For me, I was a compositor, that was my trade, but because I'd gone to the States I was forced out the trade. It was regarded as "voluntary expulsion" so I couldn't go back and serve my time. I was forced into being an ordinary labourer; a semi-skilled worker. Now, in Glasgow at that time, in the '60s, there was very, very little work around, and I did some of it, mainly on the buses and then factory work. So Manchester, London, Liverpool and the Channel Islands were four places that people in Glasgow knew intimately. If you went to Jersey and you were picking potatoes ... I picked most things until I got robbed once. [*Laughs*] It's an anecdote, but once I was away picking potatoes with people from Brittany, they came from Saint Malo, farm labourers and I was working beside them. And it was quite good, but it was twelve-hour shifts you worked, and I was living in a wee tent. The weather was good, and I was away picking potatoes, it was that nice time, it must've been May, and I was wearing a pair of flip-flops bought out of Woolworths; ten and six they cost [53 pence]. I've still got them, and a pair of jeans, and I have to confess, without underwear, except a T-shirt—I was on my own and nineteen, laundry hardly came into it! So that was all. [*Laughter*]

When I got back from the field everything was gone, everything had been stolen, and so I had actually nothing except that pair of jeans, one T-shirt and a pair of rubber flip-flops. I had to send to a friend in London for the boat fare back; that was how I left the Channel Islands. So it was a really difficult time, but wherever you went like, in the next field there would've been people from Glasgow (oh, look, there's Billy so-and-so from Drumchapel!), and the same in Manchester when I worked there. I mean, if you went to the Twisted Wheel Club just off Piccadilly, it was all Glasgow people there. I was in Rowntree's Bar one night, a dance place off Piccadilly in Manchester, and there was a pal I used to play football with, a wee spark I knew, Colin Hendry, a great wee player, reminded you of Bobby Collins. "How you doing?" A pint of lager, and then we just started talking, about anything, something daft. It wouldn't matter if you hadn't seen him for a year, it didn't really matter. He would start complaining about somebody he'd met in Glasgow three weeks ago. To some extent it was the same in London. I used to live around the King's Cross area a lot, and in Kentish Town and worked in various places around there. But the thing about it, as a lot of guys who have worked in London will be aware, if you're in a pub in London and you hear somebody with a Glasgow voice, you tend to shut up and move away.

PS: I like those tales of living in the tent in the Channel Islands. It's like the itinerant stories where you've got a lot of these narratives about being reduced to fundamentals and being rather wry about the body and clothing, and things like that. And I suppose what you also have with the narrators of those stories, these itinerant stories, especially the ones that you collected earlier in *Lean Tales*, is that they're always nameless. You've got the rootlessness of the characters, the short sketches, and they always seem to be nameless. Is this the same narrator, or is it several different voices?

JK: Yes, but originally that should've been a novel. I think if I had been in an economically advantageous position, it would've been a novel. It would probably have been my second novel, but at that time I was married, we had two kids, and I was on the buses, and it was difficult to have time, as I've said previously, to do the work properly. You just could not do the work properly, and a novel, as people know, it's very hard to sustain it over a period of time, and you do really need to be working every day and it's difficult to do. So that should've been a novel really.

However, I didn't manage to finish it as a novel and there's also that sense some writers here will be aware of, that a shift takes place in the narrative point of view within a story, and you realise that maybe, especially if it is not quite working, that it's not quite working because that shift—or shade in the narrative—is almost making it become another character, and that also happened. But I also wanted to have the central character being anonymous for different reasons, and I wanted that kind of enigmatic quality too. Some of it, I reckon, was a political position of my own; it was my own disenchantment with the English literary tradition that thrust voices like mine into dialogue at best. Otherwise it was off the page altogether, where people who use language as in my culture, from within my community, were not allowed a proper voice in English literature so in these stories I was writing, these "suppressed" voices were to the fore, right in the central narrative, whereas usually voices like mine were treated in an elitist and racist manner within this Standard English literary tradition entrenched too in these ideas of canon. That is really what I would argue. My own literary heroes at that time and as a teenager would've been from Russian literature, some German, some French, and some American. There was absolutely nobody in English literature. I mean that literally, not that I knew although it is true I didn't know as much obviously, at that age, because leaving school at fifteen I didn't go through higher education. So I followed my nose and I just stopped reading stuff, because every time I saw a Glasgow character he was being scorned in one way or another. As a young writer, it was virtually impossible to write a story about my grandfather that did not condescend to him, and I found that throughout my adult life as a shocking thing. But that is the reality, I mean, that extraordinary elitism and racism at the core of English literature.

I find that's such a destructive thing, so part of what I was trying to do, and also finding the first person, these stories that we are talking about, they're mainly first-person because in the first person you have that freedom for your character really to be anything. It doesn't matter whether it's a minor aristocracy in Moscow or if it's somebody working on the buses in Partick or having a tent burnt down in the Channel Islands or working in a copper mill or asbestos factory in Salford or something like that. It doesn't matter; in the first person you have that possibility, because the inner psyche will be central to the story. I had to find a way to work through, and try and make the third-party narrative; it's what I was always after. I wanted to steal that from the ruling class. I succeeded with *Busconductor Hines* (1984), fuck them. Right, has that been recorded?

PS: Yeah, I'm glad.

At the end of the interview the floor was opened for questions from the audience. Given the interest in the interviewee, time inevitably ran over. The event was eventually cut short because a university-based Conservative Party Society had scheduled a meeting at the same venue for the subsequent hour. *Irony* is perhaps too slight a word.

19

2009

Interview by Roxy Harris

Roxy Harris came to Glasgow for the Self-Determination and Power event in 1990, along with Gus John, John La Rose and Iain Macdonald. He and Kelman have been friends since the late 1980s, during the time of the International Book Fair of Radical Black and Third World Books. This interview originally appeared in the June 2009 issue of *Wasafiri: International Contemporary Writing*.

James Kelman is one of Britain's best contemporary writers and has radicalised the conventional narrative of the novel form. One of his comrades was the late John La Rose, a political and cultural activist in the Caribbean and the UK, founder of Britain's first black publishers and bookshop, New Beacon Books, poet, writer and publisher (1927–2006).

As a measure of his affection for La Rose, Kelman asked New Beacon Books, and its sister organisation the George Padmore Institute, to host an exclusive event around the publication of his 2008 novel, *Kieron Smith, boy*. James Kelman's long association with the International Book Fair of Radical Black and Third World Books (1982–95), which was initiated by John La Rose and others, led to the founding of the Scottish Book Fair of Radical Black and Third World Books in 1993, where Kelman played a pivotal role.

James Kelman was born in Glasgow. During the 1970s he published his first collection of short stories. Since then he has published numerous novels, short stories, plays and political essays. These include *How Late It Was, How Late*, which won the Booker Prize, *A Disaffection* and *You have to be Careful in the Land of the Free*. James Kelman is in conversation here with Roxy Harris, a Trustee of the George Padmore Institute and another long-standing comrade of John La Rose.

Roxy Harris: I can't remember when we first met, but I'm pretty sure it had something to do with John La Rose. Over the years we've met often, including when you participated in the book fair. Those of us associated with the International Book Fair have also visited Scotland for the events that Jim's put on there. One I remember was the Self-Determination and Power conference in 1990, was it?

James Kelman: 1990, that's right.

RH: The conversation we're going to have is going to be about Jim's new book, *Kieron Smith, boy*, followed by a wider discussion about Jim's life as a writer. I've no claims whatsoever to being a literary critic but I am confident that this will become a classic work about childhood. I think it's universal in a layered kind of way. Anybody who's interested in childhood will find something significant in it. If you're somebody born and brought up in the UK in the 1950s and '60s, you'll find it compelling. If you're a male, born and brought up in that period, you'll find it even more compelling. If you're a working-class male brought up in that period it will be more compelling still, and if you're a Scottish working-class male brought up in that period it will hit you right between the eyes. The first thing that strikes me about the book is that it's about childhood, which looks to me like a major move on your part. I wondered what motivated you to take on a book about childhood at this stage in your writing life.

JK: The question, and it's been a similar question for me the whole way through my writing life, has been to find a way to use language that would allow me to get within the psyche or the psychology of the character. It's trying to find a way through the value of some part of Standard English Literary Form; it's like trying to revalue everything and not be forced into a certain corner, just because you happen to use this kind of narrative form. I don't want to be forced into using an RP [received pronunciation] voice and have all the values associated with that. Now, for me the issue of trying to write has always concerned that, and in this book it's been to try and get involved in the language as it's used by a child. The central character of this novel is a boy between the ages of four and twelve. It's a first-person narrative, not a reflective third person. If there is a reflective voice, it's a boy of twelve discussing his life from the age of four, it's not an adult's reflection at all. And that means that there is the political involvement of narrative itself but there's also the fact that, at that age, you don't really use literary forms all the time.

I mean, part of the grammatical structures you use as a kid are oral structures. As a writer you're using grammatical structures that are involved in the oral and in the literary. You're finding a way of marrying these two things and coming out with something else. For me that took a lot. I mean, it's a simple tale in a way, but the use of language is quite sophisticated. I'm now approaching sixty-two, but I feel that I could only have written like this now, after all those earlier, seemingly more sophisticated novels in terms of the formal things going on in them. But they were measures in order for me to try to get to this kind of first-person voice of the boy, engaged in life as it is lived. In other words, it is not a reflective narrative, it's not a description of past events; it is the life as it continues right at this moment.

RH: One of the themes the book explores is of a certain kind of social change that happened in Scotland concerning housing—that is, people being moved from what was regarded as bad housing into new housing in housing schemes. What was the significance of that?

JK: This would have been in the late 1940s and early 1950s, a time after the Second World War when they started to build a lot of council houses for returning soldiers. I suppose this happens often after wars, in case the soldiers keep their guns and use them. So what they try to do instead is to give them something. What they gave in Scotland was housing estates or housing schemes. Generally they were away on the outskirts of town, on land that was fairly worthless as far as property goes, and way out of the city centre. It was a process which destroyed communities. When my grandparents lived close by it was a very tightly structured community—without waxing lyrical or sentimental about it—but it was a community in which, say, people would know that there was an old lady living by herself, so they would watch out for her. If she wasn't seen, people would be aware and sometimes you were conscripted with messages to go up the shops to buy her stuff. It was that kind of community, and that was destroyed through this, besides the fact that everybody was uprooted and had to go away to these townships miles away. The other thing about it was that it was an environment we'd never seen before, like seeing apple trees and, "What was that?" "That's a cow!" We were from a district called Govan, which was regarded as quite a hairy place. There were no gardens in these new housing estates, so the men went out to a very posh area called Bearsden and actually stole grass. All the fathers came by with their old cars—I'm talking about the early to mid-1950s—laden down with turf and they came out and laid the whole back. Meanwhile us kids were away robbing apple trees and strawberry patches. We had these great experiences discovering frogspawn and tadpoles and catching rabbits. Because we had come from Govan, which was the centre of shipbuilding—that's where the QE2 and all that was built in the days when that was allowed in Scotland, there's no longer any apart from military stuff—but the old place was a difficult place. The novel is not autobiographical, but the experiences of this boy, the cultural experience, is shared by me and that generation.

RH: There was a film called *Ratcatcher* by Lynne Ramsay which evoked part of what you've just described. But on a wider theme, one of the big things about your book is the Catholic-Protestant division which runs throughout. Could you expand on this and what it meant at that time?

JK: It's difficult. I'm not sure what the situation would have been in London around the docks. I don't know if there was ever that sectarianism. People in Manchester or Liverpool would probably have some inkling of what it is, and in Swansea. But certainly in Scotland it would have been at its height in Glasgow, parts of Edinburgh, right through parts of central Scotland. It basically links to the Irish diaspora since the early eighteenth century and the manipulation between Catholic and Protestant. That goes right back to the turn of the eighteenth century, when both the Catholic and Protestant working class were made use of and exploited, in Ireland and Scotland, united Irishmen, united Scotsmen.

The background of the boy in the novel is Scottish Protestant, which equates with the kind of politics that give rise to the Ulster Defence Association and the Loyalist organisations in Northern Ireland. One of the ironies during the Troubles there was that, for both the Republicans and the Loyalists, much of their funding and arms would come through Glasgow. I don't think you should underestimate the importance of this Protestant working class which, in a way, has a richness about it and a power that is often ignored simply because of the downside. The downside is major by the way! Because it has given rise to things like the Ku Klux Klan in the States. I mean, for example, you read about the Hillbillies, well, the Hillbillies are like the Billyboys of Glasgow. The link is with King William of Orange. In football, the two teams in Glasgow are Celtic, which is the Irish Republican team, and

Glasgow Rangers, a Scottish team, who fly the English flag and bow to the Queen, who is of course the Head of the Protestant Church so they would see the Queen or the English royal family in opposition to the Papacy. It stems from Henry VIII.

But I'm only paraphrasing because I'm an atheist, a long-standing one, so I'm not quite sure of church history.

Sorry, Roxy, it is such an important thing because that sectarianism still exists. There are still Protestant schools and Catholic schools in Scotland. Not all over but certainly in Glasgow, Lanarkshire and around the central belt. In the novel the boy has both Catholic and Protestant pals, but as soon as they hit that age of five and go to school, those friendships drop off. The Protestant boys maybe go to the Life Boys and Boys' Brigade, and the Catholic boys to the Boys' Guild. So that separation exists all the way through. And people outside may not understand how shocking it is and of course the English flag is because of the Unionists, which you can see has been of such importance within Irish struggles.

Part of the extraordinary thing is the marginalisation of Irish politics in relation to Scottish radical history. I would say that you cannot get an understanding of radical politics, probably throughout the UK, but certainly in Scotland, without understanding the significance of Irish politics as well. Take James Connolly for example. About twenty years ago when a young refugee, Ahmed Shekh, a boy of twenty-one, was murdered in a racist attack and a protest march was organised, police said it couldn't take place.* The reason why was because one of the groups marching in solidarity was the EIS, the teachers' union. It was the local branch, which carried on their banners a portrait of James Connolly, the Irish Republican martyr who was murdered by the British government in 1916. The extraordinary thing about all of this

---

* The murdered man's name is Axmed Abuukar Sheekh. During the campaign to recognise his murder his name was spelled Ahmed Shekh.

was that James Connolly was actually an Edinburgh man, he's Scottish. He didn't go to Ireland until his early twenties. His father was Irish, but he was born less than a mile from where we were about to march. You know, there are a lot of ironies; a lot of Scottish-Irish people, because of the indoctrination and propaganda, don't even know that James Connolly was Scottish. I'm talking about guys who are maybe seventy-five years of age who are Scottish Catholics. They're not necessarily Republican because the whole thing's a kind of mish-mash. But when I speak to them about James Connolly they will know that type of background and until that kind of background is known by everyone, there will never be a real understanding of radical politics in this country. These areas are still marginalised or suppressed.

RH: One of the things that's really amusing in the book is that poor Kieron is a Protestant but in his social life people keep saying, "Are you a Pape, because you're called Kieron?" He keeps going, "No I'm not," and they're replying, "Yes you are." It's really difficult from the point of view of a boy.

JK: Kieron is a Catholic name. All you had to say was, "What's your name, son?" and that name, Kieron, would be enough to do him in. You can disguise certain things and get by, but there is a point where you don't quite know what to say, and it becomes difficult. It's not like being black or white. One of the subtleties was how you were taught Latin as a Protestant and as a Catholic differed for example, how you'd pronounce Latin words. If you said a soft *c*, it could suggest that you went to a Catholic school. Also, in my street in Govan, if somebody worked in the shipyards you could immediately tell what job their father might have. It wouldn't be a dirty trade, because Catholics did that. It would be a clean trade, if it was a trade at all, because, if they were Catholics, they would probably be labouring, they would have the brush. Whereas the Protestant tradesman would have a shirt and tie. That was my experience; it was similar to Kieron. The subtleties, they're extraordinary.

RH: This is part of Kieron's landscape. He's having to learn all this stuff, to work out when you're walking along who the guys are walking towards you. Which group are they? And what will they do if they think you're a member of the other group? Was that a common kind of experience?

JK: Yes, I think it was. Certainly that was part of my own upbringing. It much depends on what your parents are. The novel is not autobiographical, so Kieron's family is not my family. I had four brothers whereas Kieron only has one. And my family also was a family where there were books. It was a working-class family, but one with books. There were other working-class families where there might not be books. And, coming from this background, there were also the allied forms of prejudice and racism. You would have noticed somebody who was not racist, somebody who was not prejudiced in this direction, because that would not be the norm. The norm would be racism or sectarianism or whatever.

RH: There's a strong sense in what you say which suggests the Scottish experience was a kind of colonial experience, but that seems very hard to articulate in the United Kingdom and certainly in England. To say it's colonial doesn't mean it's colonial in the same way as people's experience in the Caribbean or Africa, but there's a kind of colonial experience going on and one of the areas is in the area of language. One of the struggles throughout your career has been trying to be a writer who uses the language of the people in his work. In the UK, the main critics don't accept the legitimacy of Scottish people speaking Scots language and thinking in Scots in their head. So how have you handled that issue in relation to this book?

JK: In a sense, that is a struggle that's not allowed. These links are not really allowed by the establishment. Interestingly, there was a good review of the novel in the *Irish Times* about a week ago. The person who did the review praised the work, but she made a really interesting comment at the end saying I was shifting the bar of language, so it was a real praiseworthy thing, but she went on to say—and I'm paraphrasing here—that only an Indian or an African can go where this bar in language is being shifted now through writing. To me it was quite a perceptive observation that you really don't get within the UK literary establishment because they will not allow these links.

In an essay I wrote as a tribute to John La Rose a few years ago, I said that some of the writers and books I've felt a kinship to have been either published or distributed by New Beacon. That would include, for example, *The Lonely Londoners* by Sam Selvon. And also once, when I published a collection of stories, I was reviewed in the same space as Amos Tutuola, the great Nigerian writer. I'd been reading Tutuola and I'm not alone in this—Tom Leonard, the poet, and others had read him too. We were interested in what was going on with writers who are operating against the imperial voice. You're a writer, okay, that decision has already been made, but how do you do your best writing? This is a really interesting thing. And I always found the struggles going on in Nigeria really interesting in a writer like Chinua Achebe, for example, who's brought up speaking English in a Baptist family. On the other hand, what was going on when Amos Tutuola was writing? I have always felt that with Tutuola, when you read some of that extraordinary prose in his fiction, what's going on within that English, is the rhythms and the syntax of the suppressed indigenous languages. If you were to do a proper linguistic study of Tutuola and all those other writers, that's the kind of thing that might come through.

I thought that that was what was going on with Scottish writers too. My grandmother's language was Gaelic, which was also a suppressed language at one period. So what was going on in this kind of speaking voice were perhaps the rhythms, the phrasing and the syntax of Gaelic and other languages. But we are brought up to inferiorise our own languages and to look on the imperial voice as being the voice to mimic and adhere to. We are brought up, as this boy is, to assimilate at all costs to the voice of authority, which is Standard English Literary Form. So writers who were operating against that, writers who were not assimilating, that for me was really crucial. Black writers had been doing that for a while, but not only black writers. It had been happening with Scottish writers since the eighteenth century. This was an Enlightenment struggle among Scottish writers, from the time of David Hume, in the mid to late eighteenth century.

RH: I remember when you took radical steps to make links with people such as John La Rose and others of us who were part of the struggle for racial equality and social justice. It was the night you won the Booker Prize in 1994. After you won, you left the ceremony immediately to come to meet us in a pub in Liverpool Road in Islington for a celebration drink.

JK: In relation to the Booker Prize, I was actually thinking about the Stephen Lawrence campaign. Stephen was murdered in April 1993. Now, the actual launch of *How Late It Was* was in Southall, and it was part of the Stephen Lawrence family campaign, through Suresh Grover and Bali Gill and others. The Lawrence family were there and spoke. A bus of supporters came down from Scotland that night. Various writers—Linton Kwesi Johnson, myself, Tom Leonard and others—were also there that night and it was a really powerful event. We sent out the publicity for that book launch event as part of the Lawrence campaign six months before the Booker Prize. All of the media had information on this, but not one of them did anything. Even after the Booker Prize result, when links could have been made, nothing happened. It was an example of the marginalisation and suppression of a kind of genuine political event that had made connections of solidarity, but when it's not in the interest of the establishment for that area of solidarity to exist, then they find a way of ignoring it.

RH: Some of your critics have complained about too much swearing in your work, so one of the funny things about this book is it has no swearing at all. Whenever there's a word that could possibly be a swear word or could possibly have a sexual connotation, you've put asterisks in. One of the joys of reading the novel is trying to work out what these words are, which made me laugh. Why did you do this?

JK: Well, the book is written from the perspective of the central character, who's a boy. He's a boy who's brought up within what is called an ordinary Christian upbringing in Scotland, and it could be either Protestant or Catholic. One of the aspects of this upbringing would be repression, self-censorship, because, as a working-class kid, you're supposed to try and assimilate to middle-class values in order to get ahead in the world. There's nothing really wrong with that; your parents are doing their best for you. You therefore have to cut out these forms of language and you learn to do it yourself. I mean, you could never swear in your house. When you're a kid you know not to use "bad" language and you can distinguish between "bad" language, "dirty" words and "swear" words. Amongst your friends you could actually have ethical debates about it! So this boy, he gets trapped into not swearing amongst his pals, which is a kind of horrible thing, and then he's got to come out as though it's a considered decision. He also has to justify why he can't say "bum," but has to say "b*m" and he can't say "nude." I mean, is "nude" a swear word? Is it a dirty word? And there are about four or five different words for excrement, all of them bar one not allowed. I think the only one that's allowed in English is "jobby," but every other word has to have asterisks. And some of those are very old Scots or Norse. But because of the elitism that goes on in the UK, there can't be any serious proper linguistic studies of language as it's spoken in central Scotland because it's assumed to be an inferior form of English, so proper studies of these different traditions and the linguistic heritage are not allowed.

RH: Kieron's mum is a kind of conscience of Keiron's voice, checking his language use. The duel between them is about his use of working-class Scots language, and his mum's different social aspirations, feeling that they should be more respectable and upwardly mobile people. So she checks his words all the time, just in ordinary everyday life. How big a role does language play in the life of somebody who wants to move up in Scottish society?

JK: It's really crucial. I usually think of V.S. Naipaul and people like that in relation to this, particularly in his early stories, where there's such a tremendous "voice." But I think, "What the hell happened to you?" Naipaul had such a great ear, such great rhythm in his early stories, which seems to have disappeared in his work. It probably doesn't matter what kind of ethnic background you came from, but once you were part of the empire, you would bring your kids up to assimilate to Standard English and you would iron out their voice, so they would all end up speaking like Trevor McDonald and Kirsty Wark. That's the Caribbean and Scotland, for fuck sake, and they all sound like the Queen! I mean, what's going on here? But these forms of assimilation are never quite spoken about in politicised terms. I mean, there is talk about assimilation now, but people forget what's actually happened in language. About two or three months before I won the Booker Prize, a working-class boy of eighteen was in court in Stirling in central Scotland, and was admonished but allowed to go free, and the judge said to him, "So do you understand that?" He said, "Aye," and the judge said, "I don't know what you mean by 'aye,' but if you intend what I think you mean, it's 'yes,' do you understand?" and the boy went, "Aye." The third time he did it—and this is actually true—he was jailed for contempt. Now, that happened about two months before I was awarded the Booker Prize, and I was having to defend myself against all these spurious questions about language. It's so difficult not to get angry. I was being asked all these questions, but they've just jailed a fucking eighteen-year-old boy! You know, never mind the word "fuck," he just said "aye"! This attitude even applied to my own kids at school. They'd be saying "doon" and told they should be saying "down." They say "doon" one minute then "down" the next minute, and you never quite know what to say except you never say it within the hearing of any authority, because you might be punished. Our kids would be punished for that, they actually would be punished if they heard you saying it. You couldn't say "aye," it had to be "yes." And you couldn't say "nay," it had to be "no."

RH: Let's shift away from the book. Where do you get your compulsion to write? The late comedian Peter Cook had a joke about going to a dinner party and meeting someone who said, "I'm writing a novel," and Peter Cook's reply was, "Neither am I!" So I wonder, where did this compulsion to write come from?

JK: I didn't actually start writing until after I met my wife, Marie. I started when I was twenty-two. Beginning at twenty-two is not young. I left school at fifteen but I knew from an early age that I wanted to be involved in the arts. I really did like what went on in that world. It wasn't the *Lives of the Saints* that I read, it was the *Lives of the Artists*, and I used to read biographies probably, I would say, from the age of fifteen, especially about painters from the impressionist and post-impressionist period. I really liked the way they lived their lives. There was something about the integrity of their lives that I really approved of and could get quite sentimental about. I read about Cézanne, Van Gogh, Gauguin and Modigliani, they were my favourites at that time. I liked their degrees of honesty and passion, particularly Cézanne and Zola. Van Gogh to me was a kind of exemplar, his letters are just extraordinary. I had this whole idea of becoming an artist around about twenty-seven or twenty-eight like he does, and having that kind of life, trying to find a way through religious and political feelings and then moving into art and eventually taking that seriously. I remember being in London when I was twenty-two. I had just stopped working at the Barbican on the building site. I became unemployed and went over Theobalds Road to Holborn Library and also discovered Regent Polytechnic and its great library. I was reading certain writers and really enjoyed them, even then knowing I preferred Baldwin. Then I went out and, though I had no money, I bought a notebook and pen, because it was a serious commitment. Before, I'd thought I would be a painter, but in fact I was not going to be a painter.

RH: So you didn't have to make a transition to writing and then call yourself a writer? You had that feeling from the start, that you were a writer?

JK: I felt it was important to say that. I thought that was a big political thing to do in terms of class. My friends were just ordinary working-class guys so it was important to give them the problem of having to introduce me to their friends and having to say, "He's Jim and he's a writer." I didn't find that difficult to say, but you've got to find a way you can accommodate that as a political position as well. If you're a working-class person, whether you're an artist or a writer, it doesn't matter. You are a writer. It's not like as soon as you're a writer you have to become middle class or something. And if you're a reader, why call yourself working class? You're a reader! I always hated that position, even amongst the left, an orthodox or a Marxist left, because they wanted to hand art to the right wing. What does that mean? That Plato was a capitalist or something? That you cannot be moved by Dante? It's saying that, in order to be moved by Dante, you have to have gone through higher education. That's not the way I operate.

RH: How did you manage to produce writing about class, racism and bigotry, which are all deeply embedded in your fiction, as well as your nonfiction, which is directly political?

JK: Well, that depends. A lot of the nonfiction began from being involved in campaigning, so it's different. It was basically trying to ask people to be involved in political campaigns. I can remember doing a review of that great Caribbean Artists' Movement (CAM) book by Anne Walmsley and saying to John La Rose and Sarah White how great it would be to develop CAM's idea of having a kind of self-sufficiency. Okay, we're being excluded and marginalised here, so what do we do? Well, we just do every damn thing! You know, we're going to sell the books, we're going to distribute the books, we'll publish the books, we'll write the books, we'll talk about the books and we'll buy the books. So in that sense it becomes a really self-contained culture. For me that was very important, just that basic thing that was happening around the New Beacon community from the 1960s; some of the power of that has been dissipated. Sometimes when we're discussing things, you think, "People were already discussing this in 1930." I was talking with some students last year and I began thinking of African American writing, about the issues that were being discussed by Richard Wright, Ralph Ellison and the great Zora Neale Hurston and the kinds of issues that they were involved in to do with language. I just want the right to be an artist, whether I'm black or Scottish or working class. I want to be able to write about these issues. I just actually want to be an artist. I want to be able to create art as art should be created, as I should do it. I've always felt comfortable with these issues. But the problem is that, within UK white society, these are not issues that people have access to generally. As soon as you start to talk that way you don't normally get asked onto BBC programmes.

RH: You've made another difficult transition because you've also been involved in working in universities, as well as being an artist and a creative writer. How have you dealt with this?

JK: I'd been tutoring in Creative Writing and the arts since the 1970s, so it's not really a jump for me to go and be a university tutor, or to give students the benefit of my experience. I have quite strong views on tutoring on art and how Creative Writing or art might be taught. I kind of like the idea of being able to just to teach the subject. As an artist, why should we be not allowed to teach our subject? Why should the subject of being a literary artist be taught by academics who have never created any piece of literary art in their life? A professor at the University of Texas at Austin—she's an African American woman who had made certain links with my work—began teaching *How Late It Was* and then constructed a course to do with Virginia Woolf and James Kelman.* These links and this course would have been unthinkable or seen as absurd in the UK. It often takes someone from outside the culture to see that there are things that can be shared, that can be talked about.

---

* Professor Mia Carter.

20

2010

Interview by Viola Fort

This interview originally appeared in the *Drawbridge*.

Viola Fort: Do you feel political? If so, how do you think this affects your writing?

   James Kelman: It isn't that "I feel political," I just go about my business and others perceive this as political. There again, the intrinsically elitist and class-biased nature of the British socio-monarchical system is at variance not only with the existential core of my created beings but of me myself.

   VF: Do you think writers have a responsibility to make social or political comment? To reflect in some way what is going on in life? If so, do you think writers are succeeding at this or ducking behind more traditional narrative models?

   JK: Responsibility to whom? In the UK people are encouraged to enter into the Band Aid–BBC School of Politics, Let's Put on a Red Nose and Sing a Song for Haiti. It applies to writers and artists generally; their primary responsibility is to the system itself, which rewards obedience and allows their "career" to blossom. Good art does not reflect life except in trivial ways. "Traditional narrative models" are at the heart of the mediocrity known as Contemporary English Literature.

   VF: For example, there has been an increase in "credit crunch" literature and books approaching environmental issues. Do you think such novels can work, and last?

JK: Any novel can work. It depends solely on its creation. There are no a prioris other than singularity of vision. Be yerself. Use yer own language. Anything and everything is possible; just write it properly.

VF: Are you optimistic about contemporary culture, literature in particular? Do you think an encroaching "reality" into culture is to be encouraged? Has anything been lost?

JK: This is a difficult time. There has been a dehumanising process in line with globalisation and the freedom of movement allowed capital. Young people are now having to be convinced that it is wrong to torture and torment those weaker than themselves. It isn't what they see roundabout. People are inured to abuse; physical, sexual and psychological. Most businesses, whether in the public or private sector, operate by a process of harassment and bullying which is a fair reflection of the interaction between countries. It is institutionalised; we have departments whose employees are paid to torment their colleagues. This department is known as "Human Resources." Elsewhere the public are encouraged to snoop on their neighbours and report unconventional or unusual persons to the authorities. Ordinary citizens are guilty until proving otherwise. The conditions for fascism have been in place for a while. Some might argue that it is already here.

VF: You write about marginalised characters on the edges of society who have to navigate official agencies for help and assistance. These agencies are both gently, comically inefficient and vast, unwieldy organs that alienate their wards with bureaucracy. There are shades of Orwell here. Do you think this is a reality today? Have things improved or declined?

JK: Improved or declined for whom? How can you generalise like that? The elite always find a way. Most of what the old labour movement fought and died for has been clawed back, the common good, welfare and education.

VF: Do you feel class is still a relevant subject?

JK: What an extraordinary question. It reveals the depth of indoctrination that has taken place within our society.

VF: Much of your writing is in the vernacular. Can you say something about why you decided to write in this way? It's something that seems more accepted in European and world literature, but the British seem to take a dim view when it's closer to home. Why do you think this is?

JK: What do you mean by "vernacular"? Do you mean my language, the language of my community? Is this what you mean by "vernacular"? Why should I use someone else's language. I begin from myself. I am a Glasgow man. I didn't decide to be a Glasgow man. The stories I write are my stories. They wouldn't exist in somebody else's language. [The value or function of translation is another matter altogether.] I don't think people in Scotland, Wales or Ireland use "British" in the same way people do in England, not as a general rule. "Britain" is synonymous with "Greater England," where everybody knows their place and thank ee kindly master.

VF: The use of phonetic accent, idiom and free approach to spelling and grammar gives your writing a very distinctive style, but has also riled your detractors. How do you react to such criticism?

JK: I don't see it as criticism at all. It is a simple prejudice and like all prejudice it begins and ends in ignorance.

VF: How did winning the Booker Prize change things for you?

JK: It gave rise to expectations that were never realised.

VF: Do you feel that such prizes are useful? Do they help celebrate literary culture, or distort it? (Or both?)

JK: Most prizes are useful in one way or another. But for whom? People tend to forget that books are sold.

VF: How did you come to meet Philip Hobsbaum, Tom Leonard, Alasdair Gray and Liz Lochhead? I understand the five of you had a writers' group. How did that come about and what affect did it have on your writing and your approach to literature?

JK: I signed on to a Creative Writing class tutored by Philip Hobsbaum and showed the people there several stories I was working on. The class itself had little or no effect. None of the other writers you mention attended it. Philip and his then partner, the poet Anne Stevenson, organised an informal writers' group in their flat. This ran for a year or so. Tom Leonard never attended any of these meetings. Liz Lochhead went on about two occasions. Alasdair Gray went along on a more regular basis, as I did. I was on shiftwork driving buses at that time, had two small children, so it wasn't as regular as I would have liked. I enjoyed meeting other writers, being able to talk about related matters. After a year or so I stopped going. I have been friends with Alasdair, Tom and Liz for more than thirty years. Philip died a couple of years ago. He was a good fellow.

VF: How do you feel about being described as a Scottish writer? Do you appreciate such distinctions or feel them to be unhelpful?

JK: Well, I am Scottish, and I am a writer.

VF: Are there any writers you feel a close kinship with, or particularly admire? Why?

JK: I do feel kinship with writers whose work is part of the struggle against the forces of colonialism and imperialism. We see this in how they use language, impressing within it their values and value systems. The mainstream Anglo-American elite describe these languages as "vernacular."

VF: Are there any particular things you want to achieve or are still striving for?

JK: A winner on the first day of the Spring meeting at Cheltenham races.

VF: How would you describe yourself; your writing?

JK: I'm a grandfather and act like one; accident-prone, grumpy, and a compulsive writer.

VF: How do you live?
JK: I'm not sure of the question.
VF: What next?
JK: Bejasus.

21

2012

Interview by Rosemary Goring

This interview originally appeared in the *Scottish Review of Books*.

Rosemary Goring: *Mo said she was quirky* is a fantastic novel. I'm really moved by it.

James Kelman: That's good, I'm glad.

RG: What was the inspiration?

JK: Initially there wasn't any inspiration. The gist of it began about twenty years ago when I wrote a very short screenplay. I was quite happy with the short film, but I wanted to do it properly, and do it as a story—as I thought a short story. But it was quite complex, so much so that it never kind of worked. I realised I would have to spend time on it, more than I had thought. So I shelved the project, but I looked at it every now and again over the years, but it was never right as a short story and eventually I realised I would have to allow it to kind of breathe properly. And that eventually became a novel.

It never stopped being complex or complicated, because you know, when you're doing it as a film you don't have to operate within the psyche of the character in the writing itself; when you're doing a film you can convey an interiority, if that's the term, but once you're working in prose it becomes trickier.

In the novel I kept the opening the same, so the point of the drama begins with the young woman coming home from work, in a quite innocuous way for a casino worker, just sharing a cab with her friends who are fellow workers. And the opening, that fleeting moment when the taxi has to stop, and she is in her own world anyway, not quite part of the conversation with her two friends, she sees this guy walking with his pal, he bears a resemblance to her brother but she's not quite certain, she hasn't seen him for a few years. It just seemed better to be situated in London itself.

RG: Because of its size?

JK: No, not so much to do with size. It was the feel. There were different levels. One of them would be that the guy she thinks may be her brother, it was not his home either, he was displaced.

That's how it began. It was a difficult novel to write. Not because it was from a woman's perspective, that wasn't the trickiest part of it. But operating within that inner dynamic is always difficult, when you're working within a normal third-party narrative but you move from there, that transition to the inner being of the central character. Which I was working on elsewhere anyway around that period; the other two novels from then were *A Disaffection* and *How Late It Was*.

RG: The interior voice that all of us have in our heads can't be translated onto the page really, because it is inchoate and sometimes almost wordless. So I wonder how you create art out of an idea.

JK: There is a point where thought itself, as you say, it's not even to do with transcribing. The inner musing of a human being is composed of more than language. Language will also be a part of it, but there's other things—whether that's images or sounds, very loose associations. So it is difficult, but ultimately as a writer you only have language to work in, so how do you use language to convey other forms of thought that are not just linguistically based?

RG: Yes, that's what I'm meaning.

JK: Well, the thing with a third-party narrative is it allows you to be external to the character too. So at that point when you can talk about her lifting a cup and moving within that to a subjective view of what's entailed by lifting a cup—I see that now, I've come to see it, as being quite in the Scottish intellectual tradition. I had written an essay at that point, twenty-five years ago, trying to connect the Common Sense tradition with Noam Chomsky's work. The more into the Scottish philosophical tradition you go, well, there is a point where you reach the conflict between David Hume and Thomas Reid, to do with apprehension. I find I'm moving between the external world and the subjective perception of it. So in a way, I think the intellectual context is already there, within the Scottish Common Sense tradition, as it would be within the French or continental tradition. I can see that kind of coherence, or consistency.

RG: Do you think it was something you were already attuned to by being brought up in Scotland and studying philosophy as you had? And also, is there anybody in Europe doing something similar at the moment?

JK: Technically I had already been involved in attempting these things in my earlier work, even from *The Busconductor Hines*, that movement of the outer world and how a human being operates within it, and how a character is seen operating within it. I think in some ways, even Hogg's *Justified Sinner* is operating on that level when you have these different ways of looking at Gilmartin, Hogg's central character.

But I don't see it as a Scottish thing only. I didn't see it then like that either. But I do think it's one way of seeing it, it's a context for people in Scotland. At that time I would have equated it more with the existentialist tradition and seen it more in relation to the writers and artists I really responded to as a young artist/writer. Thirty years ago I would have been inclined more to speak about Dostoevsky, *Notes from the Underground* or *The Devils*. And I would have seen Kafka, the way Kafka worked in *The Castle*, very much part of this. Although the finished novel is a third-party novel, at the same time during his working processes he operated in the first person. Probably for me as a young artist I would have prefaced that by "of course," because I thought that's what Kafka would have been after, drawing together the two worlds, external and internal, that's how I would have tried to argue it then, he wanted to put forward the one thing.

RG: You sometimes need that distance from your younger self to see quite what you were doing, or where it fits in.

JK: Yeah, that's right. But I would have seen it more through language at that point, and formerly would have seen the use of Standard Literary Form in a sense as the objective world, the external world, and when you move into the phrases and rhythms of the ordinary language-user—ordinary human beings, they use language that's not standard in that sense—it is a reflection of the internal world of the human being. Third-party narrative as the external world, and the thought processes or maybe dialogue as the internal, the subjective, belonging to human beings, how we use language, perceiving the world around us. So you have the two distinctive worlds there, as the outer and the inner.

RG: And the friction between them.

JK: Yes. So for me, the formal issue as a young writer too, was how to marry these two, and how to get from the one to the other. These issues are to do with theory of mind, I would say, or philosophy of mind, but are part also of literary tradition.

RG: The closeness of the writing in this novel is fiendish really, the achievement of making it look as easy as if I feel I could sit down and write this—well, I don't, but you know, the reader will feel this is so readable, and won't actually see the mechanics of it. So how much do you sweat over it? Is it painful?

JK: Well, it really is. That's why maybe it took so long to do it properly. But you don't want the mechanics or the nuts and bolts to be obvious to everyone. A writer friend of mine, Mary

Gray Hughes, said many years ago to me, that is part of what we do. These are things for writers to enjoy or appreciate in the work of other writers, but it is like a craftsman looking at the work of another craftsman, and you do respect the way they manage to put a shelf up using only one nail! So if other people are looking at a good piece of furniture, another carpenter might whisper to you, "Do you know the guy that made this never used any nails?" You'll go, "What do you mean?" "Well, he joined it so well that there are no nails. He only used one in the whole thing, then when he finished the joining he took the nail back out." It doesn't stop you as a layperson enjoying the furniture, but your appreciation is slightly different from the joiner who was talking to you, that is, the great craft but not for everybody to see.

RG: It's not the intention.

JK: It's that sense that it's to be seamless, it's to be the great illusionist. Others might know how you're doing it, but when the thing is presented nobody should see any of that kind of thing.

RG: Interesting that you mention Dostoevsky there. I was going to ask you a very fundamental question about the way you write—to what extent the novel is mapped out in advance, how you choose tenses and so on. And also, I think he drafted *The Idiot* something like eight times. Can you tell me a bit about your writing process?

JK: Ordinarily I just begin, I work it out on the page. There's never any plot, or anything like that, I never know what's going to happen. I can only intuit something is maybe longer than a short story the more I get into it. And sometimes even after the third or fourth sentence I think, "This is going to be quite long."

RG: As quickly as that?

JK: It can be. Because I know that once I begin to unpack those sentences, that paragraph—nowadays the analogy would be that once you double-click on it, you find out that it's a suitcase folder rather than just a folder of documents. And you can kind of intuit that, but not always.

So, there's not any plot. I would have been quite happy in this particular novel if the ending had happened quite soon, and I'd had to continue beyond that. It wouldn't have been unthinkable, and certainly wouldn't have worried me.

RG: So if the very last page had happened a third of the way through?

JK: Yeah. And continuing on, it would just have been different. But the more into it I got, I realised that the ending would probably be as I suspected it was going to be, but I was prepared for something else.

RG: I like that. You just trust your—is it your unconscious?

JK: No, not unconscious. No, when you're talking in these terms there's major issues around creativity, around how we create art. I don't have anything against using the term "the unconscious" or "the subconscious," but I think it's more to do with how we order things as human beings. When you get into talking about it this way very quickly it takes you into things like creationism, and why it is there's a need to have a belief in god—or God, a god, the God—and what do we mean by providence or fate, or is it a purely existential kind of process.

It takes you into issues around determinism. But if you look on it a different way, it is a bit easier, in terms of "how do we create art." I think that the problem with writing is that because we use language, it seems to suggest—how can you say it—a kind of Platonic thing, that you are putting words to an idea that already exists. And that is a mistake. If you look at visual arts, and how you compose visual arts, or even music, how a composer would operate—I mean, if you take a piece of music, and it doesn't have to be Beethoven's Seventh Symphony, and it doesn't have to be Miles Davis or a piece of jazz, it can be a good piece of rock music. Once you talk in these other Platonic sort of ways you have to be careful, well, you very quickly move into absurdity. It's like, how did Cézanne know that this painting would end in that way rather than this? It takes you into something like painting by numbers. Because the painting alters with every brushstroke. As soon as Cézanne puts in a certain colour, or moves his brush in a certain way at one end of the canvas, that will alter what he does at the other end of the canvas, and it becomes a process of pure composition. I think it's best to think in these ways of story writing too, as a composition. So, when you get to maybe chapter 8 in a novel, that allows you to go back and develop chapter 3. It's why a writer like Chekhov might say, if you're having trouble with a story, destroy the first paragraph. What's come out of it is the composition, and the thinking that's begun it, seen in the earliest sentences, might be hindering the finished thing out. If you worry too much about these early ideas, you'll put too many restrictions on yourself, you'll stop the story breathing.

RG: That's also great advice for aspiring writers. I'm slightly embarrassed by using the terms "unconscious" and "subconscious," as you talk there, because it makes it sound as if it's beyond yourself.

JK: It does give rise to that Platonic sense, you know, the idea that an idea exists, the ghost of the idea, and your words on the page will fulfil, or represent thoroughly, the idea that already exists.

RG: You're the conduit.

JK: Yes. And obviously many writers and artists believe that's the case, or have thought that's the case. When they appeal to the Muse or to the hand of God, whatever it is, they believe they're fulfilling something that already exists.

RG: Does that not make it harder, in a way, because then it allows something like writer's block to come into it, because you could feel there's something between you and something other?

JK: Yeah, I think it does. It also stops the drama. It's better when the drama keeps you going, you the writer, and you don't know what will happen. When you open the door you don't know who's behind the door. It's tricky, if you always know who's behind the door, if you're involved in that kind of plot, you'll run into difficulties in the writing of it, because you'll probably bore yourself.

RG: You once said that for most men women are a mystery, and the same works the other way round. I wondered if the fascination with the unknown was part of the challenge of writing this new novel?

JK: What's interesting is some of the male responses, them not knowing what's natural. Do women act in this way? Do they feel this way? Is this how women react? These levels of anxiety? Is that how women are? So when males ask these things, implicit in that is their acceptance of unknowability. Whether or not I personally go along with that, it's evident to me that they begin from that, because those are the questions they ask.

I don't see anything wrong with that, it's just that some of these things are gender-based. That's a generalisation. In some of these obvious ways, a woman is, generally speaking, in a more vulnerable position than a male, because she has to trust him. And she has to trust a male in situations where— and it's not only in a sexual relationship, but that's the most obvious—you have to give yourself, and you have to have faith in the man you're entering into this relationship with, because he's more physically powerful. And Helen has to do that not only for herself but for her daughter. She has to put her six-year-old daughter into situations with a male who is not even her husband. Some of her friends might say, "You've left your daughter with this guy for how many hours? And he's to dress her and put her to bed and to bathe her?" So there's these instances where women are more vulnerable than men, and a single mother even more vulnerable than other women, because of her kids.

RG: You talk about how children are patted and pawed, and patronised, and it's absolutely right. I'm pretty sure I'm guilty of that myself. They're like little animals—you forget they are adults in very small form.

JK: Yes, they're beings, human beings.

RG: They're not someone you can encroach on.

JK: Yeah, that's right, they have their space, and if you do, that's what you're doing, encroaching.

RG: In this novel, it's a household of very vulnerable people. With Sophie and Helen, and Mo, and Mo saying Glasgow and London are the only cities he could work and live in, despite the fact he faces racism.

JK: Yes. Her anxiety also goes to that, because she's very sensitive to the idea of going down the wrong street with her boyfriend. He's Muslim, from a British Asian background, so she's already prepared to meet racism. And he treats it occasionally in too cavalier a fashion for her.

RG: He's a very likeable character.

JK: I hope I haven't sentimentalised him. I think he is a likeable character, but I also want an unknowability about him, because the trust from her to him has to be true. She can't know him 100 percent.

RG: I began to wonder, when you talk about Helen's brother Brian's relationship to his father, and Helen's with her mum, if you feel a lot of the problems that we face in society start in the family?

JK: I suppose as a generalisation, yes. And often you might say an unjust system has unfortunately been propagated by its victims. I mean by that, an ordinary kind of working-class father will have great problems with a son who says this system is shit. A father might not want to hear it from a son, and will enter into great battles over something like that. This is probably a theme in my work, from earlier novels and stories of mine, the relationship between father and son, parents and young people.

RG: It's maybe too personal a question, but what was your relationship like with your father?

JK: In many ways it was a good relationship. It was a good relationship with me being a young artist, because he was used to young artists, he was used to old artists too, because that was part of his work—he was a picture-restorer, frame-maker and gilder. A lot of his clients were artists, so he was used to them, J.D. Fergusson, people like that, they were people he knew— Tom Honeyman—friends of my grandfather. Of course my father worked in here for the last eleven years of his life. So that side of it was not an issue for him, being a skint young writer, or wanting to be a writer, or rather an artist. He didn't have a problem with that at all.

But the other side of it, he was an Eighth Army man and he'd been through all the Eighth Army battles, fought their way up through the African desert, through Italy. Then I would be a teenager, and older, talking from an anti-war position. So that became a struggle for myself and my father. Politics was an issue. As my wife remembers well, even before we got married, it used to cause us great problems.

RG: The casino in this novel stands in my mind as a reminder of chance and what a gamble life is. Was it a reminder to people that life can change on the flick of a card, or am I being fanciful?

JK: No, I don't think you are. That's what Helen has to deal with in a day-to-day way. Also, people working in casinos have to deal with the fact that they are on an ordinary working-class wage, they don't earn bourgeois salaries, and they're in touch with—acquainted with—people who are wealthy enough to lose large sums of money without worrying about it at all. They're in a world of alienation. They have to deal with that. That world is obviously a world I knew about as a teenager, because I used to gamble too much, as a young guy. The experiences of *A Chancer*, that early novel of mine, a lot of those are semi-autobiographical. So I would have been used to that myself, but not from a working point of view.

RG: Yes, on the more painful end of it even, if you're not lucky.

JK: Yes, it's not too much to say that!

RG: When you've sent a novel off to an agent, or publisher, how much advice are you willing to take from them?

JK: I am kind of happy for any response. I don't send off much nowadays. In the past occasionally I would send an early work or a work in progress, or even a finished thing to a few people, in the early days Mary Gray Hughes but then Tom Leonard and Alasdair Gray, Liz Lochhead, they've been good friends for thirty-five years. Also Jeff Torrington, and Peter Kravitz—Peter is another reader I trusted. It's good to get some kind of response, because sometimes you're not sure. You don't even need a response, really. It's almost like gauging the silence!

I've got a good agent, Gill Coleridge. She's been my agent for about ten years. I feel the same with her as a reader. And my recent editors too, I think I've been lucky. Not because any of them would come out and say something is not working, but the level of response is enough for me to make an inference that leads me somewhere, that will confirm something in myself, that really this is not working as well as I thought it was.

And that can happen, because sometimes my work's on the edge, not always, but often it's on the edge and even with people I trust, ultimately I have to make a decision myself.

RG: Do you look ahead to the e-book revolution as being to your advantage, because it's simply all text, or to your disadvantage, because you're so careful about the way the page is laid out?

JK: It's not something I'm fearful about. In terms of storytelling I think it's probably quite exciting. For somebody who tweets or does a blog, they have to make it interesting. It's the same as being a good journalist, or a good feature writer or story writer: ultimately you have to make it as dramatic as you can, distinguish it from other pieces of writing, so someone will read it, otherwise they won't.

RG: Denise Mina said that with e-books, she thinks it will mean more working-class writers might get into print.

JK: It'll be interesting to see where it goes. It means there are repercussions for publishing, and for writers engaged in so-called literary fiction. I was in WH Smith a couple of days ago, and there are no Scottish writers apart from genre, there is not one. You don't find any. Even in the old days when Scottish fiction was a genre in WH Smith—pigeonholed in our own country—at least we were there in the shop.

I had a Polish publisher, but they've just gone bankrupt, they've been liquidated, all their staff made redundant. Things are in a process of real deep-rooted change, and many writers of non-genre, we don't quite know the way things are going. It doesn't mean writers won't go on writing. And there's an exciting element to it. We should worry when art isn't alternative.

RG: You've won so many prizes, and yet you've retained the mystery of the writer, you've not been sucked into the establishment as maybe you might have been in other countries. There's a strong sense of you remaining on the edge.

JK: Do you mean in Scotland rather than the UK?

RG: Yes, I do.

JK: In England, there's been no prize for about twenty years, since the Booker Prize. In terms of Scotland, I think roughly speaking, Scottish writers are still marginalised in the UK. I don't have any problem in stating that. The issue is across the board in the arts: sometimes it's best to look on Scotland as a colonized culture. The people who are in control don't really know Scottish culture, although they do control it. It happens in the visual arts, as well as in literature. Not so much the old Arts Council. Individuals maybe within the old Arts Council knew something of Scottish traditions in art. I don't think that's applicable now.

So in a way you're always on the periphery, Scottish writers, whether it's Alasdair Gray, Agnes Owens or Tom Leonard. They have places, but not like it would be in other countries, where there might be an excitement seeing your own artists.

You're never bothered by people saying, "Oh, there's such and such," you very rarely get that here.

RG: Would you like that?

JK: I don't know. It depends on the setting, I suppose. It's nice to be able to walk around, of course it is, but there is a—not a knock-on effect—a kind of corollary, it's how does a country value its art? In Scotland it's not really valued in that way, not generally. Scottish literature in itself I don't think really is known. But that goes across the board. Scottish people don't know much about their own history at all, I don't think.

RG: That comes back to the old colonial thing of not being taught your own traditions, or being told they are secondary.

JK: Well, there is that. There's also the fact that to some extent Scottish history is a radical history, it's a history in opposition to the mainstream. And radical history is marginalised, and not necessarily taught. Heroes who are radical heroes, like John Maclean, John Murdoch and Donald MacRae, James Connolly or Arthur McManus, Helen Crawfurd, Agnes Dollan, they're not really known. In other countries they would be heroes, but they're not known in their own country, they're radical figures politically. In other countries everybody would know who Wilson, Baird and Hardie were, Thomas Muir—or Thomas Reid, or Ferrier, or Clerk Maxwell, Hugh Miller. In Scotland they don't know these things. They don't know about George Buchanan, they don't know about these great Reformation and post-Reformation figures, they don't know about the Scottish Latin tradition. They just seem to know these silly things, fantasies about royalty and religion, Gaelic super-heroes. It's really shocking, in a way; pathetic is a better word.

I would very much like to have known Gaelic. My grandmother never passed on Gaelic to her sons, never mind her grandsons. For the usual reasons. This side of my family suffered the effects of the Clearances, from the parish of Lochs in Lewis; Keose village, where the Napier Commission was held in the 1880s. MacKenzies and MacLennans. They went to America mainly, my grannie came to Glasgow. I've got a typical Glaswegian family, immigrant to the core, about 85 percent Scottish, a wee drop Irish, maybe East Europe too, and a great-grandfather from Gateshead. I don't know how many clans I'm associated with—Camerons and MacNicolls. MacArthurs and Macleods are there too. Hebridean, Argyll, and the northeast. The Kelmans are from the Cabrach traditionally, west of Rhynie, along the poitín trail. So both shades of Gaelic—P and Q.

RG: Do you think the Gaelic strain has any bearing on your literary temperament?

JK: It's always interested me. I've always liked that side. I've been reading *Tales of the West Highlands* for forty years. The great work John Francis Campbell did, people like John Dewar, it is of fundamental importance to the Scottish and wider Gaelic traditions, tremendous collections of the old stories and tales. I suppose at an early stage reading them I was interested in the actual form the storytelling took. I liked the use of the verb, and used to relate it to Damon Runyon's first-person present-tense narratives. That for me was, yeah, this is you telling me a story. That is the foundational structure of that form. That's me sitting down at a ceilidh at the fireside, telling a story. So when someone begins, "I am walking down the road"—once I grasped the subtlety of that, the use of the oral form, it begins in the present tense, but is of the past, that for me has been very important.

RG: Who are you reading now?

JK: I read for different reasons. I don't read as much fiction as I would like to. I've been interested in trying to get to grips with the Scottish intellectual tradition, and how movements in thought maybe give rise to movements physically...

Scottish history is not nice history. It's the history of subjection. We are so used to tipping the hat to our superiors. And that's still the way things are, unfortunately. How many other countries do we know, how many cultures in the world do we know where there's a debate about "Should we determine our own existence or not?" Such inferiority, it's shocking. Independence is not an economic decision, it is a decision to do with self-respect. How we determine our own existence, this is what we do as adults for goodness' sake, it's our culture, ultimately it concerns survival. And we'll see it literally, if the independence movement is set back again, emigration as usual, for those able to do it, spiritual demoralisation for others.

RG: I'm hoping that they start to put some intellectual weight into it.

JK: I think it's up to us, up to the public, that discourse should go that way. I'm not saying it's being deliberately manipulated, but the way the discourse is at present, it's almost like, how many people in Scotland even know that those in favour of independence are not necessarily nationalists? Of course more so in England. It's said of me that I'm a nationalist. I'm continually having to deny that I am a nationalist but at the same time I am 100 percent in favour of independence. They don't get it.

I was thinking there about the Edinburgh International Book Festival. I was doing a reading there this year but eventually I felt nauseous about the Writers' Conference, fifty years after the 1962 thing and commemorating that.* I've withdrawn from it. Not the book festival itself. I don't have a problem there. I don't really see it as a Scottish literary festival, I see it as an international book festival that takes place in North Britain. What I really object to is the British Council and its involvement as co-organisers of the Writers' Conference, I can't stomach it.

RG: Because of what they stand for?

---

* See Alison Flood, "Edinburgh Festival to Recreate Books World-Changing Event of 1962," *Guardian*, March 9, 2012, https://www.theguardian.com/books/2012/mar/09/edinburgh-festival-books-world-changing-1962.

JK: The British Council is the British State. I stopped being involved with them years ago. It means I don't get many invitations abroad, because they do most of the foreign funding. It turns my stomach to see them listed as co-organisers. I don't think it bears scrutiny for long. It reminds me of 1979, when people were pushed into Scotland to take on positions of power, as in the BBC, preparing for the independence referendum, in case the Thatcher government failed to stem the tide. It reminds you of the old Russian aristocracy towards the end of the nineteenth century, pushing family members into positions of power with the radicals in case the revolution succeeds, or the defence industry and major financiers during times of war, backing both sides.

RG: You still feel this is not an open country.

JK: The British Council is not some autonomous, free-thinking arts body. It is sponsored by and accountable to the Foreign and Commonwealth Office. It's the FCO's cultural wing, that's what they are, and fair enough, they're quite clear about their remit in terms of pushing English culture and English language—although of course their charitable status has allowed them to outsource English jobs to India to save money. These are the people who are co-organising these writer debates. The 1962 thing was important in Scotland, without overrating the thing that happened with MacDiarmid and Trocchi, but it has its place in a contemporary context, not a thing we should all think was great, because it certainly wasn't and we shouldn't glamorise it. I don't think either MacDiarmid or Trocchi came out of it particularly well, to be honest about it, but there was more to it than that.* There is definitely room for a healthy debate about these issues, what it is to be a writer in Scotland, to create within an inferiorised culture, the dangers

---

* At the Writers' Conference of the 1962 Edinburgh International Book Festival, a public quarrel took place between Alex Trocchi and Hugh MacDiarmid in the company of many other writers, including William S. Burroughs.

of nationalism. Here's an interesting thing. Alan Warner and Louise Welsh, Alasdair Gray, Keith Dickson and myself were on a panel in Montpelier in the South of France two or three months ago. Each one of us favours independence, and not one of us is a Scottish nationalist, not as far as I know. Each of us has a different position, yet each of us favours independence.

There are all these different areas up for discussion, among people who share a basic feeling or sensibility, writers who have entirely different political positions from me, people on the right, unionists—who cares, just to see things debated properly, as an autonomous thing, where we know at the outset that it's not being hijacked. How can we enter into such a thing, and having all these writers coming from other cultures, foreign writers—they don't know what they're walking into here. They think they're walking into a debate grounded in contemporary Scotland, but are they, I don't think so, they'll be attending an event co-organised by a body subservient to the British State's Foreign and Commonwealth Office, at an international book festival based in North Britain, at least that's how I see it.

RG: Putting aside all your work obligations, and so on, if you could read any novel right now, who would you choose?

JK: I would just go for contemporary writers. Some of the younger short story writers I like. I can't give you any names, also because I don't want to, because it's quite unfair in a way. I would like to read more contemporary prose altogether. There's far too many projects of my own, far too many, too many stories, all kinds, novels, essays, plays. Christ almighty! And then I've got two grandkids.

RG: Is that who the book is dedicated to?

JK: Carly and Dylan, yes.

RG: You're a family man.

JK: Well, that's always been part of my life, family.

22

2013

Interview by Seth Satterlee

This interview originally appeared as "Time, Space, and Other Problems" in *Publishers Weekly* on May 14, 2013.

In *Mo said she was quirky* James Kelman enters the consciousness of a London blackjack croupier.

Seth Satterlee: Helen, the novel's protagonist, works in a casino but we don't see her at work until close to the end. Can you talk a little about deciding to begin with her cab ride home from work, and end where you do?

James Kelman: The story begins with Helen, this young single mother, who works five nights a week in a casino in the West End of London and she lives in the south side of London. So she needs a car home every evening, every morning really, five or six in the morning. So she and two of her female colleagues, they're on their way home and the taxi stops on the banks of the river Thames. It takes a while for the traffic lights to alter, and during this time two homeless guys appear. And Helen realises that one of the homeless guys resembles her brother, whom she hasn't seen for twelve years. He's a few years older than her, but as far as she knew he was somewhere else in England and she didn't expect to see him here in London, so part of her anxiety begins from that notion of, "Is it or is it not my brother?"

If it is, why is he down-and-out here in London? That kind of brings the story into life, that moment.

SS: Did you choose that arc because you wanted to begin with her brother and leave the casino for the end?

JK: The real kind of eventual technical problems to resolve—and I did resolve them—were to do with time. Time and space, that business really affects all art. Or all art attempts to stay in the moment, and my work usually stays in the moment. The immediate past, so it's like, the present tense that's just recorded. That's what makes it past tense, is the act of recording it. So it's a movement on from … it's not a first-person present-tense novel. Nowadays contemporary literature has taken a step back. First-person present tense. That's the crucial thing, present tense—which I find not powerful; it's weak. And, in fact, it's almost like a step back from late-nineteenth-century drama, you know. In the way that prose was going through the great writers, Kafka and others this way. It's kind of naive, I find it. It's philosophically naive. And it's not rich in the way that the verb [*snaps his fingers*] can be [*snaps again*] very rich.

SS: Even from a publicity angle, it seems people like to consider the work stream-of-consciousness, as much as that term is thrown around. For lack of a better term, the book seems to be a "working woman's" stream-of-consciousness.

JK: Except that it's not stream-of-consciousness.

SS: Because it isn't in the first person?

JK: Not necessarily. It's simply that that's not what it is. Stream-of-consciousness is a very tired phrase. It's a nineteenth-century phrase. It suggests that my work comes within the English literature tradition, and you can pare that down to the Anglo-American tradition, which is basically Standard English Literary Form. My work doesn't derive from that tradition. It has an influence within it, obviously, but my work comes from the Scottish literature tradition, which is a distinctive tradition. It comes from a different intellectual tradition, it comes from a non-empirical behaviorist tradition. It's a tradition that took seriously Descartes. And also took seriously ways of attempting to combat Descartes's scepticism and move into something other than that. It's an intellectual and philosophical tradition more akin to the French tradition. It tries to find a way of bringing together external reality and the subjective perspective and perception. And what you find in the Scottish literature tradition is an attempt to bring together the external reality and the subjective perception of it. A way of trying to pull together the external reality through the internal subjective being. You've transformed the external world and you've shaped it through your own take on language. That is part of the Scottish tradition.

SS: There are pinpoint moments in the novel where the external world collides with Helen's thinking. Either she's looking at pictures, or looking out of a window.

JK: You cannot over-exaggerate that, how important that is, because that is a very, very difficult thing to do. Some critics who deal with my work, and other similar work, don't get that. They don't realise that that kind of transition has happened, into the outside levels. Suddenly you are looking out a window, and it's a third-person narrative. And you've got to there from some anxiety state, something driven from Helen's psyche … into her perception of the street outside, the idea of the street outside, in a kind of objective sense. It is a very difficult transition to do. This might sound absurd to you, but it cannot be done if dialogue is framed in a way that separates it from narrative. You know how our tradition uses inverted commas? Or we might look at Kerouac and Joyce using the dash for dialogue. It doesn't matter what punctuation or technical devices you use, as long as it is separate, then that transition I'm talking about, it cannot be done. You can't just add in "she wondered." That's the sort of thing that distinguishes it from so-called "stream-of-consciousness," which is always an internal subjective state of being almost as though it's a random thought process. I don't like the use of the phrase for different reasons, but one is, it suggests a non-edited process. If you look at Molly Bloom, for example, you'll see it's totally worked out. It's so precise. And it has to be. You cannot be imprecise and lazy. Many students don't get that. They think it's enough almost to talk into a tape recorder. [*Laughs*]

SS: Since so much of the book takes place in Helen's momentary thinking, how did you decide when to place her into scene?

JK: It's not always a decision at all. My technique is always to stay in the pulse of the individual. So it's within the moment for the individual, within the breath, every action … it's a kind of tracking. I tend to see it as a handheld video camera, but this video camera can take in sound, and it can take in touch, and smell, all the five senses. And you have to stay within this moment and never jump ahead of the character. So using that kind of technique developed by someone like Kafka, that kind of subjunctive mood. And there are things … in my early work, I used to do it in a very studied way. In an early novel of mine there were no abstract adjectives or adverbs. Everything has to be concrete. You can see the blue sky, but you can't see the beautiful sunset. That's impossible because that's a value. There's no value-laden language allowed in that. And Kafka does that to some extent too, as part of that kind of mood, there's no judgment being made within the text; there is no mediator between the thing itself and the audience. Most unlike the Anglo-American tradition, where, I mean, no one appears to notice the God voices are fucking racist or anti-Semitic. You go, "Hang on a sec … " Like Evelyn Waugh, you say, "This is racist, the God voice is a fucking racist bastard." [*Laughs*]

SS: Helen inhabits a fairly masculine environment. She wonders about the patrons frequently. As a man, was it difficult getting into the mindset of a female protagonist?

JK: Well, to some extent, but I have two daughters. So some of it becomes a basic artist at work here. You know, I've got a granddaughter now too. And I've got aunts, and a grandmother, and mother and all this. This is stuff that you've internalised, to some extent; every artist should do this. As you know, once you break it down and think, "What does an artist do?" Forget about being a male writer. The person first and foremost here is an artist. It doesn't matter if you're male or female. One of the things that you do instinctively is to observe, if you're any good at what you do as an artist, you're always observing. And subconsciously, you don't have to note it all down with pencils. I never carry a pencil anyway. Although you tend to when you begin, there's nothing wrong with doing that, but gradually you take everything in, and then when you sit down to go to work you've amassed a tremendous amount of knowledge and information. And that applies to a male writing about a woman, as it does the other way around, which we're more used to. George Eliot wrote great works with male central characters; we take that for granted. Or the Brontë sisters.

SS: So it's that same artistic process of staying in the moment with the character.

JK: In that sense, writing about a woman for me is no different. As I was saying to someone on the radio: it might be stronger, writing as a man, because you pick up information writing about a woman that perhaps a woman writer might ignore, because she's so at home in that world. A male's normal response to the novel is, "I don't believe that level of anxiety, is that true?" Or if I would say to my daughters, "How many times a day do you say you're sorry? How many times do you apologise to a male during the day?" He barges out a door you were going in, you say you're sorry, he doesn't even pause. We have three T-shirts; well, that does us ten days. [*Laughs*] Five pairs of socks, if you even wear them. [*Laughs*] If you look at what a woman has now, and she might not even realise until we say, you know, "Why?" That question "why" might not rise, but to the external observer it's different. For me, it was much trickier to work from a blind human being like in *How Late It*

Was, How Late. A man who goes blind and it's not congenital. That in a way was really difficult, although it's a similar technique you use. Just stay moment-to-moment, never get ahead of the character.

23

2015

Interview by Scott Hames

This interview is previously unpublished.

Scott Hames: You're continually asked the same questions in interviews, and you're very consistent in your responses over the years. But I think I've noticed a slight difference, in the past few years, in how you feel about being located within a Scottish literary tradition—would that be right?

   James Kelman: I think it's knowing more about that tradition and the outward-looking side of it. In general the Scottish tradition is looked on as ... not necessarily parochial, but that such an approach only looks in terms of itself. So a Scottish context means that you look only at Scottish work, rather than looking at what would be the influences on a particular era. And the more I've looked into that tradition the more you see how Scottish culture is influenced by different thinkers, like most intellectual traditions anyway, and at a certain period you'll find people are influenced by certain individuals, it doesn't matter whether they're at home or abroad. So philosophically they'd be interested in obviously Descartes in Scotland, and then Berkeley and Shaftesbury, people like that. The same applies in literature. So you look at the turn of the nineteenth century, the influence of German literature, whether that's philosophically or whether it's in literature, in terms of Goethe's influence and stuff. And you'll find that quite a lot of writers of that generation will be influenced coming from that same international area.

SH: The difficult thing in regard to your own critical reception has been that in the attempt to carve out a separate academic discipline of Scottish literature, you get perennial border skirmishes. Who is part of which tradition, and whether it's legitimate to see Scott within the English tradition or yourself within contemporary British writing, and so on. Most of the critical work on your fiction up until probably ten years ago emphasised a pretty limiting sense of its "Scottishness," which more recent critics (including me) reacted against. And now it seems I was maybe on the wrong side of your own position. Have your views changed from when, in interviews in the '80s and '90s, you seemed very reluctant to see writers like Grassic Gibbon as part of your own genealogy as a writer?

JK: No no, that still stands, that's still valid. It's really as simple as that I've come to read more in that tradition and kind of tried to take on the philosophical context and even the sociological context. And I've seen … it's almost like there's been a wrong notion, there's been an inability to look at the vernacular tradition in Scottish culture, you know? This is something that I was not aware about until I started to get into Scottish philosophy. I didn't understand that, because it's never remarked on. I thought that the significance of that aspect of the Scottish tradition in philosophy is very seldom taken on board. I don't see it in literary criticism but then I don't read a lot of literary criticism.

SH: How do you relate the sense of a vernacular tradition to philosophy?

JK: Well, it's part of like … have you read much of George Davie? Or people working in that area?

SH: Yeah.

JK: Well, it's about seeing the importance of what was going on from about 1690, from that period of Presbyterianism. Scottish intellectuals and those involved in the education system, what they thought was important was to try and both teach and make available to the public a vernacular-based learning ... vernacular-based textbooks for a start. That's quite a modern thing. During anti-imperialist struggles that becomes a crucial point—in the face of the imposition of the colonizer's language people are trying to make available technological advances and even simple information to the indigenous population. You know, things like, how do we read the instructions on a label, if it's all written in English and the local people don't read English? What do we do here? The early Indian National Congress for example, and I think I'm right in saying this, they saw how important it was to try and get the technical stuff written in a language that people could understand, along the lines of brown or red equals live, black or blue is neutral, people learn how to mend a fuse, they don't blow themself up. And that in a sense was the problem three hundred years ago, thinkers in Scotland were dealing with. From that period, the 1680s and throughout the eighteenth century, there's a constant struggle between language as it was used by the Scottish people (including Gaelic) and a standard-ised English which the merchant and upper classes probably rushed to embrace because it was the imperial voice, the voice of exchange and capital. This is more documented later, in relation to Hume and so on. But that crucial thing about the need for ordinary people to be able to communicate, to take part, to make use of their own language—it is a striking part of what was going, it is so essentially democratic, and would have helped create something else, an enlightened people, with a belief in their own ability to think, a self-confident people—a very un-Scottish concept. Maybe I'm reading it wrong.

Francis Hutcheson was a great man and much more should be done to make known why somebody like me says such a thing. But none of it had any influence on me as a young writer. It was only later on once I started to read thoroughly in relation to that, which would be the mid to late 1980s. It didn't really have much of an effect, no effect whatsoever on my writing, but it just changed my attitude towards it in a way. But it's consistent with the way in which the Scottish culture and the Scottish cultural tradition, and that includes literature, have all been inferiorised because there's never—the context, the proper context is so rarely seen. Without taking it on board or without looking at the implications of what comes out of that, it's very hard to understand how it is that so much creativity could have come out of Scotland, and that includes the scientific creativity. Unless people understand the nature of the individual's thoughts and also the external thought, and that marries in with the perennial philosophical issue. Eventually, in a way, it almost culminates with Clerk Maxwell, his whole method of what he wanted to achieve as a scientist, which is really, once you are aware of that, that's an integral part of the Scottish tradition. Because that includes that philosophical thing about how do we get ... like the problem that Chomsky deals with: how do we get from interior knowledge to the external world—how do we know? That has a real bearing in these issues. But it was much later before I became aware of all this, and again, if you'd gone back in time and thought, well, what would have happened if I'd gone and read that—really nothing! [*Laughs*] In fact probably the opposite and I wouldn't have been working the same way. So what I perceive as my tradition, it's very much what I would have said back in my forties, I wouldn't change that position. It would have been the same as I said in my twenties because I didn't do any reading in the Scottish tradition. None of it was important to me—nothing. I didn't read Grassic Gibbon until much later, way past the point of influence. Then it was just ... it was like reading some of the good short stories of Robert Louis Stevenson or something. I didn't have any interest in it, not technically, not really, that had gone.

SH: You extended that context further back than I expected. I was interested that you talked about the seventeenth century and Presbyterianism, which has sometimes been a tricky area for nationalist criticism, wary of the sectarian implications of making the Reformation central to Scottishness. But elements of what you were saying there about the democratic aspect of validating indigenous language, placing a philosophical and spiritual emphasis on interiority, on the individual's own self-experience—I mean, I have Norwegian and German students who read your work and they go, this is the most Protestant book I've ever read! Do you see yourself in those terms at all?

JK: Well, I would just see it as being kind of anti-Episcopalian. So, part of that is anti-hierarchy and basically anti-authority. Well, authority is okay as long as it doesn't interfere with your spiritual life, to use that seventeenth-century distinction—which is more like how people felt, and in some ways that has been maintained. I mean that's the strength of that tradition.

SH: It's good to hear you say that. As you know, there's a long history of Scottish writers and artists oversimplifying the Presbyterian legacy, reducing it to something anti-aesthetic, repressive, totally patriarchal. Of course there's something in that but the strengths of the tradition kind of get washed away.

JK: Yes, I know. Well, they do but in terms of philosophy ... in terms of philosophy they don't. Because what it gives rise to is something else and it becomes a really political thing and it becomes an essentially egalitarian position, because that point I made in that essay on the anti-parliamentary tradition.* This is the strength of Francis Hutcheson's teaching to me, how the emphasis is laid on respecting the position of the other person. Because it's the only way that we can understand the world, is through ... thought as expressed in the behaviour of other people. In a sense that's a move on from Descartes and that's the position that the Scottish philosophers like George Davie who'd kind of show ... were involved in the same areas as the

---

* "From a Room in Glasgow," a 2010 online article for Christie Books.

Dutch, German ... that's coming from that same position, the importance of the anti-atomistic thing, you know, this way in which it's to do with, well, the way that ... I'm thinking here Descartes as well. So Descartes, Berkeley, Thomas Reid and people who are also aware of getting involved in things like optics and sight because they're aware how you need each of the five senses to be able to understand the world, which is kind of anti-Anglo-American and that's, you know ...

SH: Rationalism?

JK: No, it's also because how do we know something? It's not through sight or ... it's not through one sense. It's not in this atomistic way, it's because judgment's based on a ... it's almost like a ... you know, different things are happening at that level of judgment—sight and touch are all entering into it together. And what comes out of that in a sense, is like a radical position. It becomes a real Rousseau-type position. The case then becomes self-evident. Truths then become self-evident because they're shared with human beings, unlike the Anglo-American imperialist position, which demands the right to know what's good for you. And again you can look at that philosophical position as giving rise to that. So it's along these areas that I've started to think or develop my own kind of ... well, my own understanding really, not my own position, I don't have a position. I just want understanding of it because they're essential philosophical issues.

SH: This is why it's almost impossible to write an accessible student guide to your work.

JK: [*Laughs*] Well, of course the problem with so much of the way that literary criticism is taught nowadays and has been for the last 120-odd years is because it is specialist in that sense. And I remember when I went to uni, and I went when I was thirty, a mature student, a writer, a father, you know, and I'd been through quite a lot in different ways. And I remember some of the lecturers who had no knowledge whatsoever of philosophy. I guess I wanted to assume certain things but you weren't allowed to; in fact, lecturers who hadn't done any philosophy were not only … it was both timid and very hostile: "Don't come in here with that, that, battering us over the head with that." And I might want to refer to David Hume or something, or Wittgenstein or whoever I was reading a lot of at the time. And that in a sense wasn't allowed, unless you were fortunate enough to have a lecturer in literature who had studied philosophy to some extent or even read it as somebody who just enjoyed it.

SH: That's interesting. As I'm sure you know, English as it's taught at universities now is full of philosophy, but seldom the figures you're talking about. A "proper" engagement with philosophy in English has led in the opposite direction of where an emphasis on Descartes, for example, would point. What we sort of spoon-feed first- and second-years is a deep suspicion of Descartes. The idea that there is some kind of unmediated access to your own inner life, that you have a kind of continuous and secure, stable subjectivity and the rest of it—practically the only philosophical position most of my students are confident about is the radical questioning of the autonomy of the individual subject. I can see similar questions being posed in your work in various ways, but I also see you as having a strong allegiance to that Cartesian model. Do you see yourself as a traditional humanist in that way?

JK: No, I don't. When I was teaching Creative Writing out in Texas, and I did it again in California, I gave them Descartes. But I gave it from the literary perspective of trying to grasp how important an influence it was in literature. Because once you read that, "the Method" and stuff, you realise so many writers have been influenced by it. I'm not talking about philosophers. And nothing to do with what comes out of it. It's not looking for anything to do with the philosophical position. It's to do with the importance of the individual vision and perspective and that's the crucial thing, and that in itself is the anti-authoritarian thing in Descartes.

But it's not to do with what's right or wrong, about what comes out of that or the nature of judgment. That in a sense is not important in terms of its influence on literature. In terms of the humanist position, I don't hold any position on any kind of movement, I really don't. I mean what I see there is simply a grappling of different areas of thought, trying to come together. So in terms of humanism, I would just … I mean certainly the things that were happening politically as a consequence of philosophical thought politically in the eighteenth century, and going through the early nineteenth, people were taking from that, from different directions. I see humanism coming from a different tradition, trying to make sense of a kind of essential egalitarian position, which is not … the necessity of another individual human being, that is not part of that tradition in thought. Or rather it was maybe earlier but it was done in [shoved aside] throughout the eighteenth century. But at the same time, people who have the correct—you might say the correct kind—of moral or political approach, want to make use of that. They want to make use of the political position or the moral position of somebody like Rousseau, right, but they can't really come at it, because philosophically we're going to attack them in terms of theory or knowledge or something like that. I mean a lot of, for example, the Scottish Common Sense tradition is still really suspect for people on the left. They really don't like it, they can't cope with it. They can't cope with notions of, eh, the shorthand might be original sin. They can't cope with the idea that it's anti-utopian or anti-totalitarian and people will never be perfect. They find it difficult to cope with these positions as part of a materialist way of looking at things, you know, they can't. So I mean always, without going into it, I just look on humanism as being a way of coming to terms with what's happened with other traditions, really.

SH: That question of "another" is really prominent in this current collection of stories [*If it is your life*], the question of a shared or shareable reality, all these isolated themselves. A lot of characters and voices in this collection seem very explicit about that—just thinking of the story "Our Times," where I see the "our" as being really a question. There's these separate spheres for the characters and although the narrator concedes at the outset that there's nothing morally objectionable about Charles, this "upper-middle-class guy who was a genuine goody," the realities of the two characters will always be separate; there's no possible consensus or shared values. "I was aware of Charles's existence but was fortunate to have an independent circle of friends I could describe as 'mine' rather than 'ours.'" That seems to be a real tension throughout the collection.

JK: Yeah, yeah. Obviously I enter any fiction in a different way from the essay, so these issues are … I only work through consistencies within a story. I'm not making any position consistent throughout. So I mean, the only thing it connects with for me in that formal way in my work really, over the last couple of years or the last couple of collections, would be working in the first person. The first-person narrative is the only thing that I see as being a shift, as I wouldn't have used it before, but then there are the kind of struggles I'd already gone through and developed the way I wanted to develop, so there's no need for me to be doing these kind of things, working in that way. I don't have that type of interest. It's more important for me to deal in first-person narratives and try and get beyond an interiority—interiorisation, I suppose. That's the more difficult or technical issue, in terms of writing fiction.

SH: That takes me back to *Kieron Smith, boy*, where you very subtly sort of disperse this first-person perspective across different perspectives and different time-frames without it really being noticeable until you go back and look at it. Is that kind of experiment with the first person something that you've concentrated more on recently?

JK: No, I gave it up to find a different way through. I had to work through developing a third person and making the two coincide so that the interiorisation of the character's thought became basically the same thing as the third-party narrative. These are issues that I had to then find ways through or resolve. At the level of technique I felt I really resolved that in my first published novel [*The Busconductor Hines*]. So I didn't have to go back and do it, although I just made it more the case. I just fine-tuned that in a sense. *How Late It Was* is really just a fine-tuning of that whole thing to the extent that people assume it's a first-person narrative, and in a sense it is, but a first-person narrative by the narrator, not by the central character, which is a problem for some critics; that kind of confusion has arisen. But really, for me it's just been, it's just the actual thing itself, the life of the individual character is down there without any mediation. I feel I don't have anything up my sleeve. As I've mentioned to people, doing what I'm doing with *Kieron Smith, boy* wouldn't have been possible without *Translated Accounts*, without the moves that I was making within that.

SH: I remember when that novel first came out I was really thrown by it, as a lot of people were. But subsequently, I can see more and more continuity between *Translated Accounts* and your other work. Even in the language of some of *If it is your life*, where this Orwellian coinage of "securitys" from *Translated Accounts* appears as this almost natural verbal form.

JK: Yeah, yeah. One of the problems is that a lot of criticism does come from people who don't have any kind of direct or personal experience of these areas of society. It's like the person who said, "Kelman asks us to believe that the police could let this man go without any money." What kind of world do they come from? They come from this really middle-class, upper-middle-class life of security where you can always get a taxi someplace, or you're never without the means to do something. And in a way, that maybe relates to the other story in a sense and becomes part of the political thing, or the problem. Once you get to that kind of irrevocability, or the necessity of the other human being, it doesn't therefore mean that you're in some nice cosy universalist world, you know.

SH: We're all in this together, yeah.

JK: Of course, most literary fiction is based on that, whether it's Ian McEwan or ... everything deals with that universal position, whether it's Hollywood movies or ... everything. It's very hard to get into the real world as it is for most people, which is a world of insecurity and high risk and everything you do is being watched and you bump your head against bureaucracy at every turn and the terrors and drama of everyday life is contingent on the everyday economic and political reality. So I mean, it really is foreign territory for a lot of critics, because of their own domestic world; therefore they think it's fantasy.

SH: Another possible reaction that comes out of it is a kind of voyeurism. Not the way that you represent the area of social life you represent, but some of the writers you've influenced, for example, people like Irvine Welsh, have been accused of peddling a kind of exploitative "realism" which is exoticising, which is about taking a middle-class leadership on a sort of tour, visiting the zoo. Part of that comes undoubtedly from a linguistic technique but I wonder if you're aware of that being a danger in how your work is perceived? Not that you can control that.

JK: No, I can't. I might react to it if I was being given a question if I was doing a reading or something; I might react to that and try and look behind what's going on within that or relate it to other reactionary positions. This kind of work is just a reminder to many people that these areas of human experience exist and some just don't want to be confronted by it and want to find a way—not to dismiss it, because they cannot dismiss it, but they want to find a way of showing that it's somehow invalid. Or they know about it but don't want to be involved or engaged. Like in some of the Booker Prize criticism I had. I mean, once you get by the vitriol of Simon Jenkins, the blinkered nature of what he was saying, there is a bourgeois critique underneath, which is "Look, we know these people exist. We don't see why we should have to engage with it in literature.

Literature is ours, it's not to do with them, these areas of experience." And some of the questions that come from that, or the inferences, are put to me quite often, for example, "Who do you think reads your books? Who buys your books? The people you're writing about never read a book, so why worry?" That's what lurks beneath that position. That reaction is at the basis of so much of that hostile response to my work and to the work of people like Tom Leonard, not so much Irvine. Some people might say that with Irvine Welsh and some of the younger writers, but not so much, because there's a universality position in Irvine, because we have these things that are universalised, so young people are always involved in dope or in booze or in music or these things that enter into the lives of the upper classes and the lowest lower classes. There are these things that we all share together and so on and so forth, royalty and servants all in it the gether, that load-of-crap sort of empathy is not always available in my work, I think, I hope.

SH: I wonder if that's partly a generational thing. I think for Irvine Welsh...

JK: There's no criticism, I'm always talking about perceptions of it, it's nothing to do with the actual writer himself. I mean that's a bit like the way they used these quotes I made last year at the Edinburgh Festival, why they were picked up wrongly. I don't knowingly or often ... I don't intentionally, unless it's in the pub, condemn or make criticisms of other authors. There is perceptions of how their work is used, so I'm not going out and attacking people like J.K. Rowling or McCall Smith or people like that. It's always to do with media perceptions of them, not them and their work but the manner in which the establishment takes them up.

SH: I think most people assume it's Ian Rankin you're having a go at.

JK: They assume it's Ian Rankin because he had a go at me. People like to think there is a sort of feud, it's nonsense, but if somebody attacks eventually you defend. I didn't start off attacking people. I just got sick of it happening. It's silly to think I would be involved in that kind of stuff. Why would I? I couldn't imagine anything like it happening in England. It only happens in Scotland, because of the way that our entire literature is turned into a genre. People can't distinguish between a Scottish cookery book and a Scottish novel. Why on earth should discussions on Scottish literary fiction be obliged to include McCall Smith, Ian Rankin or J.K. Rowling? I don't know, unless our literature is being viewed through a little-English perspective which cannot see a Scottish literary tradition in its own right. Why do they confuse writers of detective fiction with the way I write, or Alasdair Gray or somebody, I don't know. I don't understand it.

SH: I think part of it has to do actually with the way critics and publishers and reviewers have artificially inflated the sense that there is some kind of common Scottishness about this work which makes it all related.

JK: I mean, you would never do it with Russian literature or German literature. They might do it with Spanish literature, I think, or there's a couple of other literatures that are kind of small or seem to be quite self-contained, you know, as some of the better writers seem to be. I don't know because I don't read them but they're supposed to be writers of detective fiction. I'm sceptical about that because usually that is to do with publishing a translation. I know that my own work is less and less translated and it is read abroad but usually nowadays it's read in English. I know that from people in France and people whom I'm in contact with in Poland and Hungary and places, who are amazed that my work isn't translated but they know because of how my literature is looked at in their universities abroad. And it really is turned into this kind of Scottish genre in a way they never do with English literature or American literature. I imagine it started with African American literature and then they will look at Chester Himes and Zora Hurston or something, or Ralph Ellison, and look at it in the same way and you go, why are you doing this? And that becomes the same issue as the one I raised about Norman MacCaig [in the "From a Room in Glasgow" essay]. And unfortunately so much of Scottish literature and the way it's looked at within Scotland is the same, because of the Anglo-American bias, because they come from the same context. So, you know, Scottish literature within Scotland is a specialist area, and that is part of that inferiorisation. That is why people like Ian Rankin and Alexander McCall Smith and ... it's nothing against them, I don't have any problems there. Why would people think I would have any worry about that, about other writers? I can't understand that. It's always to do with perceptions and how they are related and how these are the standards and the criteria seem to be the same. How can it be the same? Why would you deal with Van Gogh and Jack Vettriano in the same ... why would you think that? I mean, they would never do it in these other cultures, why would they do it here?

SH: I think some of it has to do with boosterism in Scotland, critics and journalists insisting that there is some kind of common Scottishness they can write a story about, you know.

You mentioned a few African American writers a moment ago, and that has opened up in the last few years as a kind of alternative perspective on your work and various other Scottish writers. There was a very interesting anthology published in the States a few years ago called *Rotten English: A Literary Anthology*.* The way it handles Scottish writers has its limitations, but the editor points out that "half of the novels that won the Man Booker Prize over the past twelve years are in a non-standard English." What was happening in various areas of the English-speaking world, in experimenting with— whatever we want to call it, idiom, vernacular, dialect—what was going on there, is the premise of the book. It takes an interesting cross-section of contemporary and earlier writing, and various critical essays, and tries to work out how can these

* Edited by Dora Ahmed (New York: Norton, 2007).

writers be taken out of their own local or national tradition in order to be related together? Writers like Tom Leonard are to the fore, Irvine Welsh as well. You're clearly a big presence in the background but oddly you're not excerpted. Do you have any views on whether leaving your own local culture out of the frame and focusing on language and linguistic difference, certain effects of authenticity—is that a valid way of forming connections between your work and others, do you think?

JK: Well, that's the way I've always connected. It's never been to do with Scottishness at all, it's always been that. So that relates to what we were talking about in the beginning in a way. That was my position in my twenties and I still hold to that. I mean the only reason I talk now about the Scottish tradition is because I've become aware of it. It was never ever a taught tradition—well, maybe as a subdepartment of something else. I mean I have always related my work to that tradition right from the early '70s, and these were the writers that I was look-ing to. Not that I ever felt a proper influence by then, I mean it was just writers that I shared things with. I always felt I shared that with Tutuola and Sam Selvon. That for me is quite straightforward. What was interesting and what remains interesting is how African American writers have never seen these connections. That for me is an interesting thing. It's a real interesting thing about American culture altogether, the way African American literature is viewed within it. It's not seen as part of the ordinary vernacular tradition that Faulkner is a part of. Why have they not seen Richard Wright and Faulkner in this way? That extraordinary bias that you find yourself in with American culture, you know, that kind of elitism, "high" thing, racism, which is similar to what we share.

SH: It's interesting you should mention that. Another recent book, by the French critic Pascale Casanova,* uses

---

* *The World Republic of Letters*, trans. M.B. DeBevoise (Cambridge, MA: Harvard University Press, 2004).

an American analogy to talk about your work. In a slightly undercooked way, she lumps yourself, Tom Leonard and Alasdair Gray together as a "Glasgow School" and says that your collective influence on Scottish literature—for her, you three create a new kind of Scottish literature—is the equivalent of Twain and *Huckleberry Finn*. She quotes the Hemingway line about "all modern American literature comes from one book by Mark Twain," and then says: "With *Huckleberry Finn* the literary world and the American public became aware of the existence of a peculiarly American oral language—and therefore of a distinctive 'Americanness,' a national differ-ence resting on all the dialectal variants of the American melting pot, a joyous, iconoclastic distortion of the language bequeathed by the English." And this is what she says you, Gray and Leonard do. On yourself in particular: "While remaining within the English language, [Kelman] managed through the illustration and defence of a popular language—affirmed as a specifically Scottish mode of expression—to create a differ-ence that was both social and national." What do you make of that comparison, of that reading of your work?

JK: Right away, the problem I see with that is to look at Twain completely within that American tradition, an homog-enous tradition. That's as bad as the ones that want to look at me or Tom or Alasdair in that Scottish thing. I mean who's Twain going to be influenced by? Really, like any other writer of that period, he will know Scott intimately, he will know all of the work, he'll know *Heart of Midlothian* and all that stuff. He will know the Brontës, he will know *Wuthering Heights* and he'll know all the validity of that individual ... not just the experience but the individual, the language of that indi-vidual. So for people like Twain, it's just a case of bringing that to bear within his work. That is an English language tradition that ... it's almost like they were unaware of impe-rialism in a sense; again, America and Canada is different from talking about Africa and India, in the sense that most of the Indigenous people who are forming American society, leaving aside Native Americans, have come from that English-language-based culture. So not only is it their first language, it's the first language of their great-great-great-great-grand-parents, do you know what I mean? So they will see themselves as being part of the tradition that produces Scott, Fielding and everybody, and all that Twain is doing is using that. I mean, Twain will have read Laurence Sterne, so I'd see that just as a misreading, a wrong reading of Twain, do you know what I mean?

SH: Sure. Although ... this is a side issue, but within the American context, part of what makes Twain's work so extraordinary compared with Hemingway is that he's cutting against the grain of what Webster does with English in the US, which is almost the reverse of what Standard English does in Britain. Noah Webster is very, very clear that it's necessary to the Republic that there is a democratic common speech and that it's not a class-coded speech, it's for everybody, and that provides a context for what Hemingway wants to see as "modern," possibly analogous to the deep history of the Scottish vernacular tradition you mentioned earlier, that democratic aspect.

As I said before, you seem to have given the same interview dozens and dozens of times. Is that a source of frustration?

JK: Yeah, because, well, for one thing, you get used to picking up and realising there's an agenda. And having being interviewed for more than thirty years, you get attuned to that and realise, hang on, there's something going on here. And often that is to do with the pigeonholing, and often that can be simply seeing my work in terms of that Anglo-American tradition which must put you in with, kind of, Alan Sillitoe—nothing against Alan Sillitoe but they will always begin from that position and it's like you think, Christ, I was having to talk like this when I was twenty-eight to people. Why am I still having to do it, you know?

SH: So often, it's like they've never read your fifty earlier interviews where they ask the same questions.

JK: A lot of what I say, then, becomes ironic but it's too laid-back for them to realise, you know, until eventually it explodes into … they realise that I'm being very hostile. Takes a while for them to realise. It was kind of implicit from the third sentence.

SH: The bit of this edited collection* that I found really difficult was introducing it without falling into exactly that pigeonholing thing. But I also had to summarise it, to give an overview of that kind of lazy journalism.

JK: I won't read it thoroughly, so it doesn't matter. I will glance at it but I won't read it thoroughly. It's not … there's nothing in it for me. It can only ultimately be negative, there's no way it can be anything other than negative. And it's nothing against yourself or what's going on or anything. It can't be anything other than negative.

SH: I get the sense that you've had such a clear sense of what you're doing as a writer, and what the philosophical underpinnings for it are, that any alternative way of explaining your work you just regard as kind of irrelevant.

JK: The problem, I think, for the artist is that it's always retrospective. You may have moved on completely from the work in question, you may even have turned a corner and it means that you've really moved past that. And there's not really much you can say about it, you know? You can talk about the way it was, but you've already gone beyond it. And obviously me talking to you about the first person and what the alternatives are—I just feel that, the alternatives are things that I worked through fifteen and twenty years ago, longer, twenty-five years ago. Sometimes I see things that are said about my work and … see this collection, this new collection of

* Scott Hames, ed., *The Edinburgh Companion to James Kelman* (Edinburgh: Edinburgh University Press, 2010).

stories, for example? Some of the stories I began maybe thirty years ago. There's always the assumption made by critics that you work in this linear or chronological way, simply because of when something is published, and that of course isn't the case at all. And you can't imagine people making that mistake with other types of artists. They can with writers because they're used to looking at writers in a generic kind of way, the kind that brings in the writer of detective fiction, different types of writers together. If they produce a detective novel every year they assume that's the way that other writers operate, and it's not. The writers who are engaged in … in a sense, the higher art form, the timing is more to do with technical advances you've made as an artist. It's when you're equipped to finish something and when you have to leave something and walk on. So a better analogy is to think in terms of an artist's studio. You know, if you want to look at maybe the work Alasdair's working on and if you've been a friend with him for thirty years, you think, well, you've been working at that for thirty years and Alasdair might sigh. [*Laughs*] That's the way artists operate. I mention Alasdair because he's also a visual artist and you see it laid out, but that's the same if you were talking of Johnny Taylor, or people like that, it's the same. And then they may eventually finish it because they've turned a corner that has allowed them to go back and do something. And when musicians talk about their work, they will say the same. You know, why were you able to finish that piece of music now? Why? Because I finished that piece. That's a piece that I started like two years ago. Completing that piece has allowed me to finish that stuff I started forty years ago because the thing that stopped it, I needed to make a technical advance. That's what's going on.

SH: That development is kind of immanent to your own practice, it's not something that comes from outside. But just to follow that through, do you think only artists can really illuminate the work, not critics? It's impossible for a piece of criticism to show you anything new about your own work?

JK: I don't know whether that's the case and I wouldn't ... I would only take that on personally and not generalise from it like other writers. Not all writers are forced into reflecting about what it is they do. Writers like me are forced into that position because of hostility. You're forced to look at what you do. Whereas if that's not happening ... just go back to look at a guy like Ian McEwan. It's like, you've never been in a position where you've been forced ... from early on, your work has been accepted and you could always just move on from there. You've not had, like myself, hostility. As soon as somebody says, "I'm not going to publish your story because it's obscene," the first thing you do is go back and look at the story, what the hell's going on with the story. Every time you get that hostility, it forces you to look and reappraise it, so you become ... you have to become quite secure in that sense. It's not so much to know what you're doing, it's to know that you're doing it honestly, you know?

SH: Right, you become highly self-conscious of what you're doing.

JK: Yeah, you become very self-conscious in a sense. But even then, that's always a retrospective thing too because you've got to think clear to approach the work in freedom. And to approach in freedom means you can't be self-conscious in that way. It's got to be kind of non-reflective or something, as Sartre would say. You've got to have the freedom to enter into it in that way, otherwise you would never do anything. It has to be non-reflective, that's what it is. But you have to build up the experience and the faith to do that, because in spite of it all, you've got to continue working. You know what I mean? And that becomes something you have to fight for. And the reason I was saying about Ian McEwan, I don't think a writer like Ian McEwan has to reflect on what it is he's doing, simply because his work has never been attacked, apart from in ways that maybe don't matter too much. So he's never been forced into saying, "What am I going to do with this work?" He's a nice guy, and I'm sure he would be able to find ways of dealing with it—but it might have made him a better kind of artist in a way, if he'd had to do that.

SH: Do you think that's been your experience?

JK: I think that's the fact. It's just been continual hostility right from day one, so that is what faces you all the time.

SH: Do you think you're better for it in a way?

JK: Yeah, you have to. Yeah, because you have to develop a strength through it. When I'm teaching much of my method is based on that, showing students the necessity of developing strength. Because what you're going to meet with, if you're doing work that's any good, is a lack of response. So what you have to inculcate and develop is that sense of validity and worth and not to take external criticism in such a way that it will stop you working, as some artists have. Some writers can't cope with it and it really stops them in their tracks. So that experience of my own is what I try and make use of. So in that sense, okay, I would say it makes you stronger in what you're doing, it really does, if you can get by it.

SH: I don't think you've had to win over academic critics for some time? You haven't had continued hostility?

JK: I don't know, because I don't ... I mean, it would be news to me. If someone points me to a piece done on me I might look at it but I don't really read it thoroughly. I just don't find it ... I can't do it. I don't know whether other artists or writers do. I certainly don't dig it up. I mean if it's a foreign critic I'd be more liable to look at it. I can't imagine it being the kind of criticism where they say he's not a writer at all, that type of immediate kind of Booker Prize response. I don't think that's really ... you'll know, my position there was to have been scathing of critics or academics because there are so few of them who raise their heads above the parapet to defend the work. I mean there's very few do that. So my hostility to or criticism of academics would be that they never ... they didn't look for ways to enter into the public domain or public discourse, and not just about me. Thinking of my essay on Rushdie.* Rushdie thought I was attacking him and I wasn't really attacking him. I was attacking him in a different way. It was a criticism of these usual stereotypes, you know. But who I was attacking really was literary criticism or academic critics who did not come out and give proper arguments against what was happening at that time. So they allowed the racism to really start to dictate the context in which the fatwa was discussed, and how that whole thing against Rushdie was being treated; they allowed that to become "freedom of expression." It became very dishonest because of it. So to me, academics should have come out then and nailed that argument about freedom of expression and just taken it away from the whole kind of racist thing, because it fitted in with the anti-Islam agenda, you know? So anyway, I can't imagine that academics have been particularly ... how would you say, like ... like criticism premised on the fact that I was involved in bad art or something; I can't imagine that nowadays because it's been verified from outside the culture, and once it's verified from beyond, they have to grudgingly ...

SH: Not so grudgingly!

JK: I had it recently from a young writer who was reviewing something of mine and felt obliged to acknowledge or say something about my own response to critics. You know that way where, "For all that, Kelman can still ... ," begging a question, that still goes on a lot. Can't be bothered with that. It happens in reviews, it doesn't really happen in—I can't imagine it happening with academics very much these days. But as I say, I don't really go into it.

SH: Fair enough. That brings to mind a character from the title story, "If it is your life," who is an academic. And the student character says the best you can hope for in an

---

* "English Literature and the Small Coterie," first published in 1990 and collected in *Some Recent Attacks: Essays Cultural & Political* (Stirling, Scotland: AK Press, 1992).

academic is sort of, not too posh an accent and a similar taste in philosophy!

JK: Oh yeah, yeah. [*Laughs*]

SH: And even he's an elitist shit.

JK: Yeah, but I mean that's a character.

SH: I'm not taking it personally.

JK: No, but it's really important for me to say these are characters, they're not my judgment at all, because that'd be very dishonest of me to come out with that, because it's not the case. I mean that story is written from the perspective of a twenty-year-old or something.

SH: There's a criticism of using "workers' language," as Theodor Adorno calls it, that provides an interesting critique of your work. The idea from a Marxist standpoint is that legitimising a class language cannot but legitimise the social violence it reflects. The idea of a specific, valid, working-class culture would be reduced to a vector of economic forces, including language. So Adorno says, in a fragment called "Not Half Hungry," that "the language of the subjected…domination alone has stamped."* So you can't celebrate a class language without celebrating capitalism, because that's what generates the social division that the language reflects. I can imagine that wouldn't cut very much ice with you, but does that Marxist line of criticism have any bearing on how you see your use of language?

JK: No, I just see a lot of stuff that appears to be Marxist takes exactly the same value system as that elitist value system we saw with the Booker thing; basically the assumptions are the same. So I would be hostile to that. Because the assumption again is the same idea, that in order to discuss Plato you need to have a different type of language or something.

SH: He goes on to recommend "the strictest linguistic objectivity," like there is some kind of language, some higher

---

* See *Minima Moralia* (London: New Left Books, 1974).

form of German that can resist and keep a distance from social exploitation. Writing can do this in ways that speech can't. He also seems to be criticising Brecht, arguing that "Proletarian language" has a phony warmth and authenticity that can't help but endorse social relations, that it's in bed with what it seems to oppose.

JK: Oh·yeah, yeah. I don't take exception to that viewpoint, I would go along with that. That is what happens. But I would just see that as being where working-class experience or language entered literature traditionally, so I would agree with that. But I mean writers like myself have been working in a different way linguistically. I've been working against that always. Trying to get as far as possible within working-class experience as expressed through working-class language is basically a function of that same division. My fight there is like narrative and dialogue; it's like when I first got rid of quotation marks on dialogue, or my first use of the first person before that, as a way of taking on that struggle. You know, to show the fact that all areas of experience are available within this … the life experience as we see it through language. Anything then can become possible through language, and there is no … I mean, so that division is kind of gone in terms of what I'm doing. That to me is like … there may still be some people, Marxist theorists, who look on things that way. I would just regard that as being very … it's not even so much outmoded, it's just a failure to take on what's been happening in language, it's a failure to take on what's been happening in English language literature. It's a failure to look at English literary working-class voices as being part of the English language tradition, rather than the English high literary tradition. In other words, not relating what I do with people like Tutuola or Saro-Wiwa or Selvon or Zora Hurston. Once you do that, then I think that type of Marxist argument is gone. I don't think there is any validity there; it's redundant. I would think students would show that up. The existence of this body of literature kind of shows how invalid that position is.

SH: I have a related question. If I could put it simply, do you think you're at all romantic about voice? Do you see voice as the locus of authenticity and the place where the subject is kind of fully present to itself?

JK: Well, it depends, because it's just a function of individual stories really. And that may apply to one individual in a story I made but it's not some kind of … there is no position that I hold in relation to that. I don't see that at all. The only thing I'd say to you is that, back to that idea, people don't exist without their language. I mean, people are always struggling in terms of issues around language and their own authenticity. So I don't …

SH: I should put it another way. The way your work is often read, it's as though vernacular language somehow embodies the identities of people. That language is somehow lived rather than used. Whereas the strong emphasis that you make on technique and on artistry in language insists that you use language and you don't live it in some unselfconscious way.

JK: And you're talking about me as the artist, rather than within the stories?

SH: Yeah.

JK: I don't see that as something that affects me as an artist at all, and certainly not as a human being. Unless you want to rephrase it or something. Maybe I'm not getting it.

SH: People come to your work and they see the non-standard features of language you use and they can't help but read that through the filter of their received knowledge of, in particular, Scottish forms, Burns and so on. And because of the very romantic residue of "voice" that you get in writers like Burns and Wordsworth and in quite a lot of the English tradition leading up to your period, there is an established way of reading non-standard language that places a premium on authenticity, immediacy. And I can think of all sorts of instances in your work where you militate against that, where you experiment with distancing and defamiliarising effects, and you scramble our usual ways of processing vernacular language. That's the area of your work that particularly intrigues at the minute, but there are other areas in your work that do seem to lend themselves to that kind of romantic reading. That what you're getting in non-standard language is real and direct access to the interiority of people who are somehow extra "real." And that people who use the standard language are these kind of empty bourgeois shells, who don't have the same textured solidity in the world.

JK: This takes me back to your earlier question. Part of why I avoided first-person narrative was simply because I saw it as romantic and I didn't want to ... that for me was wrong. And I wanted to get from ... instead of romanticism, I wanted to get to existentialism. I'm not happy using the term "vernacular," I use it simply because that's the way it's used, because we're talking about the external world is reality, right? Now, as soon as the external world is vernacular, the thing ceases to be romantic —that's the way I look at it. As soon as I start to move into a third-party vernacular form, that has defeated that position, as far as I'm concerned. These first-person narratives I've engaged in for the last, eh ... probably since before *Translated Accounts*, because the earlier collection of stories was similar, *The Good Times*, I'd already made the move then. So I don't regard from that period, these first-person narratives as being part of that romantic thing, in a way that I would have looked at it maybe fifteen years before that. But that was before having worked through and transformed that vernacular into reality, into the external world. And that for me was the strength of Dostoevsky, making a move away from that, you know, so what the character does is move out of the romanticism of that first-person voice, no matter how strong it is, and Dostoevsky manages to make it jump somewhere. So I don't see it as romantic in that way; that is, it's truly existentialist. And I see it that way in the first-person narratives that I'm using now. I don't mind literary critics or reviewers who are obviously—they're doing their work—who think the barrier is gone or see it as being solipsistic. I don't resent them saying that, I just think they're wrong. Simply they haven't realised the fact that that might have applied twenty years ago but it's not the case in these first-person stories. Certainly it may be the case in one or two of these but only individual stories, it cannot be said about … well, I know as a writer that's not the case, simply. Maybe they haven't read as attentively as maybe they think they have done. They fail to see … and it's not even to do with distancing. You know, there is that kind of thing as an artist: you're always in a paradoxical position of wanting to have real life on the page, and you can't do that. You're always creating and it's always art you're creating but that's always part of what it is. So you can't say, "This is reality"; well, it's not, it's a fucking story! But at the same time, it is. It is that kind of … that distance should not be there.

SH: But as soon as you start treating the external world from that vernacular point of view, you're relativising perspectives.

JK: Well, it appears to be but I don't think it is. The fight in a sense is against relativism.

SH: Or undoing the myth of objectivism?

JK: I don't go along with that position either! [*Laughs*]

SH: I'm interested in viewing your work in aesthetic terms rather than sociological terms. In teaching your fiction I emphasise the fact that vernacular prose, vernacular fiction, involves self-conscious stylisation. So in other words, the areas of your work that seem the most realist and direct and unmediated are, at the level of your own technique, the most self-conscious and the most stylised.

JK: Well, I mean, that's your own judgment, you know? [*Laughs*] I see it in different terms for myself.

SH: I think of novels like *You have to be Careful in the Land of the Free*, where you do have sections of this almost surreal stylised universe that we're seeing through a very unconventional perspective. And we perceive this world through a highly idiosyncratic, highly colourful language, which mediates all our access to that external world.

JK: That's true, but the thing about it is, although it's mediated, I accept it has to be in that sense. It's a first-person narrative but it's only mediated to the extent that somebody might come up behind me and slap me on the head while I'm talking to you. And if it's a first-person narrative, there has to be some way of that being expressed. The technical thing is how I can express being slapped on the head without it being a value judgment or without it being ... it's not a relativist position. There is something that's going on here that is part of the real world. It's part of the reality of that character's existence, being in the bar or wherever he is being, as the character's walking through that world, you know? And to see it as mediated through him, it's kind of flimsy in a way. It doesn't mean therefore it's an evaluation coming from this character. That in a way becomes almost trivial, simply because it's been recorded by the character. I'm glad in fact you used the term "relativism," because that for me is a mistake. That's part of a fallacious premise that the Anglo-American tradition brings to bear on this, you know? It's almost like you're trying to reach something that is coming from a different philosophy and you're trying to use your own terms to look at that and you can't really be okay with that, you're wrong. You're trying to cope with existentialism coming from a tradition that has really ... this is why English literature has never been comfortable with existentialism. What writers in the English literary tradition are existentialist? How many? You know? How have they coped with what's come out of Russia and Germany? If you take away somebody like Laurence Sterne, you're into real romanticism, you're into Thackeray writing a short story like "Poor Boots" ["The Fatal Boots"?] and you think he must have read Gogol. This is the best English literature can do, coming from Gogol or from Goethe. It's that Anglo-American intellectual failure to see what's going on with Scottish philosophy and at the heart of continental literature. That's what I see. The fight is always to get out of relativism and scepticism; that's what the struggle's always been. That is a real kind of intellectual failure and I just see them unable to take off the blinkers and entering into a defensive position, and it's like an unwillingness to actually acknowledge something, you know what I mean? And because of that, so much of what goes on in contemporary literature escapes them; they can't quite grasp it. And they still approach things in a very elitist way, and in an imperialist way, because they still use these terms to try and cope with it—"vernacular," "dialect." And there's a certain point where you feel as if they haven't caught up with Einstein, they haven't caught up with Clerk Maxwell, they haven't really quite managed to understand what's going on there.

SH: I think many people reading this would be surprised at how strongly your impression of literary history is driven by philosophy and specifically epistemology, that's the driving force to literary development.

JK: I think it's a mistake not to, because literary development, unless we go back and we talk about storytelling, that's a different type of tradition, but if we're talking about literature, well, we're going back to the seventeenth century or thereabouts, we're not really going back to Chaucer. We're going back to the seventeenth, mainly eighteenth century. I mean, somebody just reviewed … the publisher sent it as a good review and it was like the person, they weren't dismissive but they were basically almost dismissive of some of the work, and for me it was like, you haven't understood your own tradition even, you haven't understood the importance of meditation in prose. I mean, I'm not a fan of Eliot, as you know, but you think of some of the stuff even Eliot would be trying to celebrate, some meditation … the problem in English literature or Anglo-American literature is a failure to actually deal with meditation, because they can't. Where is that nowadays in

English language literature? It would be dismissed as so-called vernacular or romantic because it's the individual, it's intro- spective. If you're dealing with prose or if you're dealing with tradition, the idea that they would not be influenced by philoso- phy in that period can't be taken seriously. You're talking about quite a recent thing, about 1870 or something, you know? The whole way in which the individual is taught changes. I mean, when I was in Texas, some of the academics there were really into rhetoric and that way of looking and you think, yeah, I mean relating that to the eighteenth-century Scottish tradition, you can see why, you can see where these divisions come from. Anyway, that way of looking at literature is not really what I do and I don't think it … well, a lot of writers do but I think only in the third world tradition, not in other cultures.

SH: In terms of that progression, do you see any connec- tion between your work and what we call Modernism? Part of the reason critics often, and I include myself, locate your work in that way is because what we see in Modernism, among other things, is a serious engagement with philosophy at the level of form. And although you can see that it's a fudge—if you look at literature responsibly you'll see all sorts of writers doing these things in all sorts of different periods—the way we customarily divide English literature up into periods, what you're doing seems to be in the same neighbourhood as Joyce, Kafka and Beckett and they're Modernists, so you must be a Modernist. I understand the limitations of that but you would insist on a different and philosophical way of aligning yourself to earlier writers, is that right?

JK: Yeah, that's a term that develops out of academia. You rightly point out that's the way you will tend to look at it and as soon as you introduce Kafka and Beckett into proceedings, you think, well, hang on, one's writing in French and one's writing in German, how do you relate that to English literature? What is it that you're seeing there? And then of course that raises all manner of questions about the nature of translation, but if you leave aside translation, what is it that academia is finding in the work of Beckett and Kafka that makes them ... they don't hijack it but they've kind of gone into that work with their own perspective coming from that high Anglo-American tradition which is a late-nineteenth-century construct, and I don't think it has a great deal of validity, not once you start to look outside of that context. I don't think it can deal with ... you will not deal with James Hogg and people like that. You can't deal with that type of writing.

SH: You mentioned academics hijacking or appropriating or exploiting literature to fit their own agendas ...

JK: I don't see it as an agenda, I think it's to do with how they have been taught themselves. And they're taught from within that tradition and it's hard for academics, unless they've come from other traditions, to break out of it. You know, if you're taught coming from Cambridge and you're always taught through a Leavisite kind of perspective or something, it's hard to get beyond that and challenge the canon, so they will always see things as operating for or against, or on one side or another. And then if you come from outside of that, it will be wearying, accepting that they control our ... they control the higher education.

SH: But outside the really sniffy British institutions, the orthodoxy is anti-Leavisite. Our students are taught, frankly, a pretty shabby, not very powerful rebuttal of that legacy from the first day. And what it can lead to is a pretty flimsy fetishisation of the political: these writers were marginalised by that horrible snob and we should celebrate them for that reason alone. And I actually find that more limiting.

JK: Yeah, so did I.

SH: Has that been a factor in your own work?

JK: Yeah, I suppose similarities again with your Afro-American writer, or African writer, being genre-ised again, so the value of what you do is not seen, because the blinkers are on.

SH: What can you do about it? Not much.

JK: Eventually you just stop.

SH: That seems like a good place to stop. Thank you very, very much.

24

2016

Interview by Ernest De Clerck

This interview took place in Leuven, Belgium, on May 10, 2016, the day before James Kelman would give the Servotte Lecture at KU Leuven. A translation of it was published in the December issue of *Deus Ex Machina*, a Belgian literary magazine. The theme of that issue was "Angry Young Wo/ Men," inspired by the sixtieth anniversary of the publication of John Osborne's play *Look Back in Anger*.

Ernest De Clerck: What is your opinion of Osborne's *Look Back in Anger*?

James Kelman: *Look Back in Anger* has nothing whatsoever to do with me or my culture. It's essentially an English thing and the only way it could affect Scotland would be through an Anglified Scottish university system, a university system where things that are Scottish are inferiorised, or made to be localised in their own country, parochial. In that sense *Look Back in Anger* is mainstream bourgeoisie. Politically and culturally it has nothing to do with me. It is not in any way relevant.

What I wanted to do as a young writer was write about my own community. Not about somebody else's community. And the English language forces you to work in somebody else's community.

EDC: How do art and politics blend for you?

JK: Art and politics are inseparable. Especially when you work with language. In a sense, it cannot be divorced from politics. Language is value-laden. You cannot work in a value-free language. It's hardly possible to do it in a formal language such as logic, never mind in real language. Usually people don't understand this is the case. They accept what mainstream culture dictates to them. At first, everyone thinks language is value-free. Then they discover it is not. The whole roots of sexism, racism, elitism etc. can be found in language. And usually when writers begin writing, they don't realise that. Until somebody from a culture, a marginalised culture, asks, "Why are ye attacking me?" For example T.S. Eliot is anathema to me. So it's ironic I should be involved in a lecture with a former academic who was very much in favour of Eliot. For me he was part of that rigid authoritarian standardised form that is very prejudicial against our culture. Elitist and racist. For me, as a young writer, I wasn't interested in reading Eliot. Or John Osborne. That for me was no more than a little argument within the mainstream. The establishment will always have little arguments amongst themselves. It's like party politics in Britain. It's not really radical. They don't really know what you mean by radical. They think to be radical is against the monarchy or something. They don't know the history of radical politics. They don't understand that.

EDC: Perhaps they don't wish to.

JK: They don't, because they hold power.

When I went to university I was twenty-nine. I was a bus driver and had two children. I wasn't interested in reading people like Eliot or other English writers such as Evelyn Waugh. They were utterly racist. But the university wanted us to read them so on ye go. Their language was supposed to be the standard form. It was supposed to be an unbiased and objective form of language. When you show that it is actually full of value, then you can start to reject it. Then you can point out the writer of that good poem is on the far right, an elitist and a racist.

Once you realise as a writer how value-laden language is, you realise all the possibilities that you have. It's a great lesson. Every sentence becomes a possible story.

EDC: Would you say Waugh and Eliot are political writers?

JK: Ignorance is no excuse. Evelyn Waugh was, I think, very aware of what he was doing. He was aware he was being anti-Semitic, racist and elitist. In other words, he would assume that if you came from a different or "lower" culture you wouldn't be intellectually capable of taking on certain things. For him it would be an absurd idea to have an African American read Plato. Eliot and Waugh would believe a black man reading Plato is an impossibility. A contradiction in terms.

Many people aren't even aware of the fact they are being elitist or racist. It's the internalised prejudices of the culture, and the language they use. It always takes you by surprise. In Waugh it's an active emission of racism and elitism. If you compare that to the great Scottish philosopher David Hume. You might wonder how on earth someone like Hume could be racist. People would immediately say, "Come on, ye're talking about 1740, someone's going to be racist in 1740." Well, hang on. What was the intellectual establishment he was part of in that period? More importantly, what books are on his shelf? Eventually, you will learn that Hume had omitted certain areas of knowledge and the potential inferences from that. Omission of knowledge is almost like a recipe for imperialism. You convince yourself that other people are not people.

EDC: There is a clear distinction between your approach to politics in your fiction and your nonfiction.

JK: The fiction must always work in terms of itself.

I don't have a great knowledge of the literature of Belgium. But I've been reading up on it. When I was young I really liked Maeterlinck's drama. I read his plays like *The Blue Bird* and *Pelléas and Mélisande*. He seemed to me to be at the very high end of European literature. His work stands up with the really famous writers of the period. There was this story he wrote when he was twenty-four. It was based on a painting. It's really spectacularly good.

But the interesting thing is that the story is like an ekphrasis. As a teenager I wanted to be a painter. And as a writer I wanted that same freedom a visual artist or musician has. In other words, I just wanted to make the thing right in terms of itself. And make it stand like that, so you could walk round it. In that sense, questions to do with value were very important to me as a young writer. I wanted every value to be self-contained in the artwork.

But Maeterlinck's story is spectacular. I'd compare him to Chekhov. The crucial thing for me is how his verbs operate. What I wanted to capture in my stories was a moment in time. It doesn't mean you have to use the present tense. Sometimes you use the past tense. There are a lot of different types of past tense.

What attracts me in a painting is that there's no commentary in it. There is no description of what is going on. All you have is the thing itself. And that is what Kafka does. That is the greatness of Kafka. The reader brings the evaluation. That's the amazing thing that comes out of the great nineteenth-century work. It doesn't happen, however, in Anglo-American writing. Unless with unusual individuals. It's not a general thing about their culture. It's almost as if they never learned to be sceptical.

The writers of the '50s and '60s in Britain were never part of a radical literary movement. I was never convinced by them. They weren't doing anything. All they could do was have a different view of the same reality. They weren't really sceptical about that reality. They all believed in the same thing. All they wanted was their share of the goods, of the spoils. It's like King Leopold or something. They just wanted their piece of the pie. There was no critique.

EDC: Can politics be dangerous for an artist?

JK: As I said, art can't be separated from politics. But it can be separated from the artist. Yet the art can never be anything other than political. There's no need for the artist to do anything. Except do the work properly. And that is a political act.

EDC: Still, many people dismiss your work because they dismiss your politics.

JK: That has cost me many readers. And I still have no money. [*Laughs*] I think my last novel sold about a thousand copies in the whole of the UK. What I'm saying is, what the artist needs to be aware of is that your work cannot not be political. Art is always political. If the artist decides to engage in politics as a human being that is something else. There is no extra need for the artist to do so because you do it in your work. If you do your work properly then you should be challenging value everywhere.

As soon as you compose a painting or a story then you're moving into some unique area and are creating a unique thing; you are making a statement against an authoritarian system. Because the existence of that one human being that creates something original goes against what the system is. The system wants to put people into blocks. Each time you create a work of art it is a unique thing and to do that is to engage in an extremely political act. I would never be critical of any artist who does not engage politically because if they do their work properly then they are doing what they should do. Never confuse the art and the artist.

The establishment does not want to accept all art is political. They want to find a way to say, "We can discuss pure art here." A university system for example is not really political in that sense. That's why you can have the most fascist and racist writers being studied by students in universities. They want to be able to say, "This is not politics, it's aesthetics!" So, that's the kind of stuff you want to attack. It's not even difficult to attack.

EDC: In your case public opinion doesn't separate your work from its artist.

JK: That is correct. And because of it my work gets marginalised. In Scotland I'm quite a big name but not in the whole of the UK. You won't find my books in any store in England. It has been difficult at times. By marginalising you they take away your ability to earn a living. And then you have to do other things to survive. Then again, that has always been a problem for artists who want to stick by what they do. But when you assimilate you get commissions, grants coming from the government, you're invited to places etc. I will not attend literary events backed by the British government. I wouldn't be involved in that. And that's just part of the way it is. It is not heroic on my part. There's nothing I can do about it. It's simply because I do my work in this particular way. See, I don't want to write about somebody else's parents. Like John Osborne, his life doesn't interest me. I would rather go and drive buses.

EDC: On the other hand, those that like your work are particularly supportive of it.

JK: Yeah, well, that's true. An obvious reason has to do with what you're engaged in. So if as an artist you engage in something it always comes down to formal things and techniques. To do what I do is very demanding. Most writers know that. Even the ones who don't care for what I do. I make some writers uncomfortable. They know my formal techniques are of a very high level, and they don't criticise my skills but still many people have problems with the formal aspects of my work.

Compare the situation to that of a young painter. You want to know how Cézanne put the paint on the canvas. "Aye, he's cheating, he put it on with his finger." And then you realise there is no paint police, who cares how you put the paint on. It can be with a knife, or a finger. You learn all kinds of things. You learn that you're free. You're free to say no. Or you're free to question and challenge. Generally speaking, most people assimilate for whatever reason. They don't want to challenge. They may not be confident enough. That's how you get stories about existential policemen seventy years after Raymond

Chandler. And even Chandler wanted to do other things. He would rather be Sherwood Anderson. He only wrote his detective stories in order to make some money.

EDC: Is it any better these days for Scottish writers? When you compare it to when you first started writing and publishing?

JK: Yes, it is. It's better and healthier because it's stronger than it was forty years ago. There was not the same self-esteem when I started. Generally speaking Scottish writers were always inferiorised. Irish writers never had to experience that. Scottish writing is linguistically more complex in terms of literature. Some of that's to do with the nature of the Irish, Scottish, Gaelic or other Celtic languages. It's even difficult to talk of Scottish language literature because there's so many different varieties. There's a huge difference between the language writers use on the east coast—think of Irvine Welsh—and the language on the west coast. That makes a difference in phrasing, syntax and rhythm. But if you take Scottish literature overall then it's better nowadays. Even me saying all this, people would be nodding heads, aware of what I am saying. Forty years ago that wouldn't have happened. That has to do with class as well. And once you get involved with class, very quickly you go back to language again. Gaelic, for example, is considered slang. While it isn't. So if you're working with how people use language in Glasgow, there's Gaelic in it. In individual words and in phrasing. In England, people may look at you, surprised, at that idea.

That's something I've never been able to understand. Why people didn't read my work and Tom Leonard's work and a couple other people's work. Why would you not buy it? Why would you want to dismiss it? Why would you not understand there's different ways of using language? This prejudice has dismissed a whole body of knowledge.

I've been in the States. And the way Afro-Americans are using language in New York City is influenced by Irish Gaelic. Sometimes there's a great Scottish connection as well. Often it's taken for granted as *jazz*, or something like that. Even the word "dig?" is Gaelic for "understand?" The Gaelic speakers and African Americans lived in the same communities at a time there was discrimination against both.

What do I and Dizzy Gillespie have in common? Both our grandmothers were Gaelic speakers and neither of us can speak it!*

EDC: When we speak of angry young (wo)men, how would you describe that anger?

JK: I see it as all wrapped up in a society like this one. If anyone who comes from the European "white" races is sceptical about the rights of authority, then somewhere, somebody will call him angry. Being called angry is synonymous with "Why are you rocking the boat? Why are you disturbing the peace? Why have you got to talk? You're not a refugee, you're not black, you don't have to worry about anything, you're one of us." I don't quite see society in these terms because then you're assuming a white nationalism. I don't respect it and I don't even know what it is. I don't know how you can identify yourself with authority, with the monarchy, with far-right politics, Saxe-Coburg or the Queen of England or anything. There's nothing quite wrong with the Queen, I just don't see why she should have so much power. Or why people seem to think they are entitled to use this power. All I'm saying is, on what grounds can you verify why you're entitled to that? In my country they would go, "Well, in 1604 there was a treaty between Scottish royalty and English royalty and ..." The ruling class just wanted to consolidate power, that's why they joined forces. The best way of doing it was to create a monarchy and that's that. A deal done between thieves.

In a sense, what happens in our society—in this kind of white European society—is that anyone who is sceptical about

---

* Not a grandmother of Dizzy Gillespie as far as I'm aware but a female ancestor.

the right of authority is considered "angry." And the burden of proof is on you then. "What's wrong with you?" they'll ask. The whole idea of the burden of proof being placed on you is because you're white European. No one would object if the person was black. People will even be surprised if you were not angry. To be able to pose the question "Are you angry?" to me indicates a kind of conformity to state politics. Why would you not be angry? It is very difficult for me to realise that you might not be angry.

EDC: Who are the angry young (wo)men and what are or should they be angry about?

JK: In a way this relates to what I said in my last reply. The only way you can put that question is if you assume everything is okay. And it's the kind of question you could not put to someone who maybe came from Somalia. If I was a writer from Somalia you could not raise that. The whole basis of what you're doing is structured on a very right-wing view of society. It is that same imperialist view you sense in John Osborne's work, and in the work of all the writers of the British establishment from around that period. Because it's wrong just to say English, it includes Scottish, Welsh and Irish too. I taught for a while in America. These students would faint (with pleasure) if someone from Cambridge or Oxford patted them on the head. You can't believe how passive they are to upper-class English society. They would just assume that anyone from Britain likes the royal family or something. They have absolutely no knowledge of the culture. And why should they?

In a sense it's very hard to kind of look at the world without looking at imperialism. The only way in a sense to do it is to omit it. You could only ask me that question through ignorance.

Why would a young person not be angry? The one time in your life that you can be angry about society is before you get corrupted by the necessities of that society. When you start a family and so on. Then you're no longer allowed to speak for yourself, so you're forced to assimilate, take on a job or a career.

The only point at which society allows you to be angry is when you're young. So how would it be possible not to be angry as a young person? And then we're back to that question about scepticism. To be sceptical is to be angry.

EDC: Don't many young people now seem inert? Many people express their anger on social media, but when it comes down to really do something people don't budge.

JK: If you're engaged as an artist or a writer you don't have to. You are already doing your part. I think it's hard. I don't want to give an argument against the position of the artist who doesn't actively engage in politics. But it's not as easy as it sounds. On the whole, most artists, in my experience, are a disappointment when you meet with them. Many of them say they're not involved with politics. In fact that means they have absolute politics. They are rejecting the need to be critical. That is political.

People want to earn their living and live their life. And there's the politics. Everything you do is political. People that say they aren't political are actually political, but just very establishment.

When you say people aren't doing anything, that's wrong. Then you are the one that isn't doing anything. What you're not doing is seeing. People are doing things all of the time. You're just not aware of that. In a sense there's no excuse now because of the web. You have access to all the information.

Once you're helpful to somebody or some cause, then you're doing something.

The following additional question is previously unpublished:

EDC: James Wood wrote that your short prose was more effective than your longer prose. What do you think about that?

JK: I don't really think anything about that. I'm always glad people take cognisance of the work. My short stories aren't readily available everywhere. I would never be critical of those who read them. It doesn't really mean that much to me what they write about it. It's not something that can affect you much as a writer. I do different things. Sometimes people say things that are just kind of silly. And unfortunately I have to respond to these things. The person who said the thing is blatantly prejudiced. Just say it was Julia Neuberger. There are professors of literature that have said things about me while, basically, they had simply lost their temper. They've lost their temper because of the work I done.

For a start, I should not have to respond to those comments. You can't respond to a prejudice. All you can do is demonstrate it is a prejudice. It's just blatantly elitist and racist. The thing is that others would be better to respond on my behalf. It was quite clear to me about what I was doing as a writer in my early twenties. It was a real source of surprise to me, to find out I was not supported by people of the literary community, or people who "knew" literature. Then you realise that whether or not they know what you're doing, you yourself do know. And you don't want to be responding to silly things, if you can go on doing what you do. People that want to attack will come and attack.

I often don't find out I have been attacked until other people tell me. But you can't defend against prejudice. Anyway, I've just got to get back [back to work].

25

2017

Interview by Robin Lloyd-Jones

This interview was originally published in *Autumn Voices*.

Despite James's willingness to meet up with me for an interview, a combination of ill health and full schedules on both our parts made it too difficult. In the end, James suggested that I email him my questions and he would reply in writing. Here is the resulting dialogue:

Robin Lloyd-Jones: In an essay for the Scottish PEN website you said that the marginalisation of your work continues. Could you expand on this, please? Do you think actual hostility to your work is at the level it was?

James Kelman: The hostility is nowhere near the same level, although it would be inaccurate to say that it does not continue. A general marginalisation occurs anyway at the Brit level for Scottish writers who fail to assimilate. And not only Scottish writers. A recent example is the level of hostility directed towards the tennis player Andy Murray when as a young fellow he identified as Scottish. He had to learn to identify as British in the first instance, and allow his Scottishness to remain secondary. This frees the media and establishment and allows them to push the oneness of the "one nation" argument, by inference its unity, its indivisibility. What's new?

RLJ: A lot of criticism you received in the past was vicious and personal. Were you hurt at the time and what are your thoughts about it now?

JK: Not so much hurt as dumbfounded. So much of it was obvious nonsense; these peculiar, anti-literary notions trotted out by established literary authorities. I thought it instrumental that one of the more vociferous was quickly promoted to higher editorial positions within quality newspapers, Simon thingwi—then later selected to chair a Booker Prize panel. In 1989 I was on the Booker short list and awarded the prize in 1994, yet none of my last five novels has even made it onto the long list never mind the short list! Another unprecedented achievement.

RLJ: In *The Red Cockatoo*, Mitchell and Rodger have a diagram, "The Network: Kelman's Political & Intellectual Firmament."* To what extent has this network changed since then?

JK: I don't know about "The Network," which appears an imaginative construct by the authors. I had no involvement in writing the book. People do move on, move away, give up, burn out, expire, drap deid.

RLJ: The same authors comment that the 1980s and '90s were the most intense period of your political activism. What are the reasons for the level of intensity dropping since those two decades?

JK: As I said, I had no involvement in writing the book and can say little about the authors' perception. However, very few people ever get paid for these forms of activism, although those who police or punish the activists typically do earn a wage.

I was an unpaid full-time worker in the struggle against the British State's abuse of people suffering asbestos-related diseases. I relied on my wife as breadwinner, and also an advance from a publisher. Eventually I had to stop it all and

---

* Mitch Miller and Johnny Rodger, *The Red Cockatoo: James Kelman and the Art of Commitment* (Dingwall, Scotland: Sandstone Press, 2011).

earn some money. I needed to be writing, needed to repay the advance.

These economic pressures remained. Eventually I couldn't find a way to earn a living in Scotland. In 1997 I applied to a university in USA which I knew was teaching my work and I was given a job in their Department of English Literature. I was offered the chance to continue there but was tempted back to Glasgow University in 2002, working with Alasdair Gray and Tom Leonard in a three-way split of the Chair in Creative Writing. The universities of Glasgow and Strathclyde were involved jointly in the Creative Writing set-up.

After I arrived it dawned on me that we weren't being welcomed with open arms! A wee while later I realised it was worse than that. Altogether it was a lousy experience. I resigned in 2002–3 and haven't set foot in the place since. But one day I'll tell all!

RLJ: Do you still call yourself a libertarian socialist?

JK: Forms of anarchism are the only way ahead.

RLJ: You have written in the past about the essential working-class experience being intimidation, provocation, sarcasm and contempt. To what extent do you still experience this personally?

JK: To a certain extent.

RLJ: An article in the *Guardian* (July 2016) says of you: "Being a professional irritant is at the heart of how he describes his creative development." And you are on record as saying, "Good art is usually dissident." Do you intend to continue being an irritant and a dissident into old age? Have your motives for writing changed at all as you grow older?

JK: I do my work as best I can. The only motivation is survival.

RLJ: You are currently campaigning for the Kurdish people. What led you to this? Of all the injustices that exist in the world today, why did you choose this one to campaign for?

JK: I'm not currently campaigning at all. I don't look for campaigns. I reject that way of looking at it. We learn to deal with injustice in our own individual ways but most of us learn to live with it. The ruling elite and leisured classes come not only to live with injustice, they value it as the cost of their own survival, which is contingent upon survival of the State itself.

Injustice affects the lower orders in a different way. I use the term "lower orders" very loosely here; referring to working-class people, immigrant groups and diverse minority communities; racial, ethnic, linguistic, religious, and groups such as single parents, people with health issues, learning disabilities. The question of "choice" remains but the context shifts. Injustice is no longer indirect, but thrust upon us; it is happening to us or those closest to us. Each day is a minefield of exploitation and humiliation, not only for ourselves but for our families and friends. Allowances aren't made for writers. A working-class writer is a working-class person. In the United Kingdom the reality of class is thrust upon us.

On the situation in Kurdistan itself, perhaps you are thinking about a talk I gave in Edinburgh in 2016, at the invitation of Scottish PEN. You should know that as far back as 1990–91 I was invited by Kurdish people to talk at the University of Edinburgh. I accepted the invitation. My interest extended beyond then, at intervals. In 1997 I attended the inaugural Freedom for Freedom of Speech assembly in Istanbul. I launched my novel *Translated Accounts* at a joint benefit night in support of the Stephen Lawrence Family Campaign and the struggle of Kurdish people. The situation in regard to Kurdistan is a nightmare for the political authorities in Europe, USA and beyond. Anyone can read up on what's happening but find your own way: disregard the propaganda, the disinformation, the lack of information and the downright lies. Be creative and do the obvious: go and check out what Kurdish peoples are saying themselves ("peoples" plural).

RLJ: How do you define creativity and has your definition of it changed over the years?

JK: I don't think I define "creativity" other than as an infinite set of activities pursued by any member of humanity. Perhaps in earlier times I might have attempted to find a way of "arguing" that every human being is creative. It is now forty years since I first had to deal with the work of Noam Chomsky (1977) in a course on the Philosophy of Language. His stuff on "creativity" irritated me at first. It seemed too constrictive. I realised that I just had to come to terms with reality, that I am a human being after all, and my "creativity" is a function of that. Wittgenstein made the point that "If lions could speak we wouldn't know what they were saying." Yet Wittgenstein's work on "language games" is very relevant, how they cross boundaries yet remain sealed off—which leads me to field theory and so on. Yet in art ... I remember a great short story by Doris Lessing, the South African writer, a rather brilliant story written from the perspective of an actual creature—so there ye are, logic and reason defeated by a good piece of art. Wittgenstein would have approved.

RLJ: In general, has the nature of your creativity changed as you get older?

JK: No, as with impatient non-swimmers, we just jump in the deep end and swim for dear life. Those of us with a little more patience lower ourselves into the shallow end and paddle about, wondering whether to risk it, but how do we define "it" is an interesting question.

RLJ: What aspect of ageing do you fear most? Has this found expression in your creative work?

JK: I don't fear the ageing process itself but I'm kind of flummoxed by the idea of relying on other people, apart from Marie, whom I've relied upon for the past fifty years. I accept the right to die.

RLJ: What, from your own personal experience, have been the most negative aspects of ageing? How have these impacted on your creativity?

JK: I don't find much that is "negative" at all, although younger folk might presume it can hardly be otherwise. Some older people despair, or simply bemoan the fact that things are not, after all, "changing for the better." This suggests they could have done better themselves, or adopted a different outlook. It applies most regularly to people engaged in party politics from a moral or ethical perspective (rather than selfish or personal interest). They come to suspect they've been party to a fraud or hoax, and maybe discover they've engaged in the fantastic notion that the British political system will evolve, that it will come to alter itself sooner or later, if only we commit to the process in spite of all common sense—a kind of teleological, pre-Enlightenment view of existence.

RLJ: For you, have there been any gifts and unexpected joys that accompany ageing? What are they and have they found their way into your writing?

JK: "Gifts" and "joys" relate chiefly, but not wholly, to my family, immediate and wider. I love to watch my grandkids take part in things with other youngsters. I realise that my last three novels have been influenced by them.

RLJ: What have you been reading recently?

JK: I tend not to read books individually but as part of a field of interest, most recently trying to understand some basic factors in the work of Immanuel Kant. I delved in and around this area, beginning with about four books. Obviously he was very aware of David Hume's work but he was also aware of Hutcheson's work on morality. Thomas Reid's position on judgment and perception, and non-Euclidean geometry, would have been of great interest to him if he had known it. Scottish thinkers have made important contributions to Kantian studies, e.g., Kemp-Smith and H.J. Paton. It was through William Hamilton that Clerk-Maxwell and James Ferrier were introduced to it.

Before delving into Kant I had been doing the same around Clerk-Maxwell, enjoying the line back through the Scottish tradition in philosophy, a tradition which includes seminal thinkers like Descartes, Newton, Shaftesbury, Leibniz, Spinoza and George Berkeley—not to mention George Buchanan, Plato and Pythagoras. I'm here belabouring the point that the Scottish intellectual tradition is generalist by application, internationalist in approach.

It's not a massive leap to see a connection between Clerk-Maxwell's work, McLaurin's use of Newtonian method, and the mechanistic implications of Kant's work on the Moral Law.

It occurs to me that this sort of leap may be evidence of advancing senility.

One area of interest from around five years ago concerned my grandmother from Lewis. Reading into this side of my family took me in all directions but for a so-called radical like myself it's been interesting to see how little I knew about our own history. I always looked forward to retiral age so I could read more. I forgot that writers don't retire. Nor do we stop reading. If writers do retire it may not be a function of age. I should say that I never need to stray beyond my own home for books. I have a decent collection, plus broadband. And if I cannot access something in that way I make it up, or leave it alone.

RLJ: How do you envisage the remaining years of your life? Do you see yourself continuing to be actively creative into even later life?

JK: As I've been suggesting, I see creativity a little differently, as an inseparable aspect of the thought process; in others words we cannot help but be creative.

RLJ: Of all the things you have produced as a writer since passing seventy (not necessarily published), what gives you the most satisfaction and pride?

JK: I don't know about "satisfaction and pride." Every book is an issue to resolve, yet remains at issue during the editing process. Sometimes the work is never finished. A couple of my published works contain errors that will never be resolved. At the same time I don't wring my hands about it. It's a pity but it cannot be helped. The editorial process has altered drastically in the last fifteen or so years, with the advent of word-processing systems. The areas of literary endeavour which appeal to myself have very little space to breathe. There is a lack of knowledge among writers that I find surprising. Many seem unaware of what is possible in literature or why some writers may have felt obliged to develop formally in particular ways—e.g., drama and the problems of time and space. It seems not to occur to some that the central issues of their epoch exist in their own areas. There is an intellectual passivity, a docility; a worrying lack of scepticism, suggesting the dangers predicted by George Davie on the push to specialisation.

RLJ: What advice would you give to writers who aspire to continue being productive into old age?

JK: There is the practical matter of doing the work: get the first hour or two in every morning "before the day begins." With luck ye might manage more later, but even if ye don't that one solitary hour—preferably two—will keep ye going till tomorrow. A close friend of mine—Chris Harvey—published his first book past the age of seventy, and lately has published his second. He's lived fifty years in Scotland and retains his Berkshire accent, having failed abysmally to assimilate to Scottishness. We argued on philosophical points fifty years ago. Nowadays we tend to nod in agreement, but I'm waiting for one of us to double-click on the nod. Our children and now our grandchildren are acquainted; perhaps they argue on other matters.

RLJ: What haven't I asked you that you would like to say in relation to writing/creativity in later life and the changes that ageing bring?

JK: We just have to keep doing it. Creation is survival. Making art is life. There seems so much to do but I have to confess, it's exciting. Why is that "a confession"? Who gives a fuck, on we go.

26

2018

Interview by Jim Gibson

This interview was originally published as "Just Writing Stories" in *Low Light Magazine*.

Jim Gibson: You are renowned for having quite a rigid approach to tackling your writing. Can you give us an insight into how the process of sitting down to create is for you?

James Kelman: I don't see myself as "rigid." I just need to ensure that I do the work. It's how I earn a living. Life in general has a habit of eating into my time. If I don't get to work while I can then people and the outside world break in and that's that. I start generally between 5:00 a.m. and 6:00 a.m. The process begins when I switch on the computer. I have worked on Mac systems for twenty-five years; presently this is an iMac, 8 GB, 2.7 GHz Intel Core i5. I open three items immediately: my Finder, Gmail account and Firefox. I go to Firefox firstly: I check out the *Guardian* football, *Racing Post* horse-racing and world-snooker pages. I go to Gmail secondly: I check emails, and see if there's anything cheery. If it's all gloom and reminding me of obligations then I stop reading. After about ten minutes I go to the Finder folder: I start/resume work from the last point, usually the evening before. This will be fiction of one sort or another or nonfiction of one sort or another.

This morning I finished the final draft of a novel I've been working on for a long while, a few years. While working on this I was also involved in other stuff. Presently I have quite a few projects on the go. I jump between them, nonfiction as well as fiction.

JG: Do you feel that the writers' own experiences matter to their work?

JK: This seems like a trick question! Of course it matters. How could it not matter? Do you honestly believe that a billionaire and a homeless person will write the same story? It is totally ludicrous. At the same time the English establishment pretends otherwise: ignore the economic, health, cultural, educational and social reality; the riches, pomp, privilege, hereditary wealth and so on. Forget all that. Underneath "we are all the same," nice white English people who are willing to lay down our life for the sake of "Rule Britannia": a united front against "johnny foreigner," "the outsider," "the alien," "the immigrant."

JG: How do you view the craft of a story or novel with regards to the conventions that are in place?

JK: That is what they are, conventions. Artists must break these in order to create, to take the freedom to begin from our own unique perspective.

JG: How do you think the short story compares to other art forms and in what light do you view your own work?

JK: It is no better and no worse; it is simply an art form in its own right. But it certainly suits people who have to work in other forms of employment in order to survive. The short story has much in common with drama. It is no accident that Chekhov, Babel, Hasan Manto and Bashevis Singer were also at home in drama. Nineteenth-century prose fiction in general moved towards the immediacy of drama. In that context the Standard English literary tradition is lagging behind others.

JG: As a Scottish author, do you think different countries and cultures approach the telling of working-class stories in different ways?

JK: I'm not sure about how it happens in other countries outside of those who come under the collective title of the

United Kingdom. Scotland is similar to England and Wales. In each of our three countries class functions at a level other countries probably cannot comprehend. But Wales and Scotland differ also from England in ways very many English people cannot comprehend either. It makes issues of culture quite mysterious to them. I don't think the majority of people in England, including people of the left, grasp certain fundamental distinctions, beginning from what it means to say that Scotland is a country. Class is a root issue in Scotland as in England and Wales but in both Scotland and Wales we encounter questions relating to imperialism; the Anglification and colonization not only of our cultures but of our wider societies. This makes matters very complicated.

English culture is intrinsically elitist and hierarchical in a way that it isn't in Scotland. I find it horrific how obedience to the upper classes, to royalty and to aristocracy enters each of our three countries; the acceptance of hereditary wealth and privilege. To a minor extent this is challenged in Scotland. I'm sure it is in England too but very little news of it crosses the border.

I left school at fifteen, a working-class boy, but I was always a great reader. To say to me when I was twenty-two years of age that I was writing "working-class" stories would have left me pretty well dumbfounded. I was just writing stories. If one of my characters read Plato, James Joyce or Franz Kafka; enjoyed Richard Tauber or Paul Robeson while not gambling horses, playing snooker or going to the greyhound track then so what, that to me was my culture; "working-classness" was a label applied by an establishment that was essentially elitist, hierarchical.

Different writers treat matters differently. As a side issue, I don't accept the notion of "working-class" writer. In fact I reject it altogether. If other writers are happy to identify as "working-class writers" then so be it. I want to write about anything under the sun. It is hard enough trying to write without carrying all that baggage to do with "representation" and *forced* identification. What happens if you are gay, working-class, black, atheist, Lancastrian, six feet eleven inches and female? Usually what happens is that other people want to pigeonhole the writer. Let them do it. The writer shouldn't pigeonhole his or herself. I don't even want to use the phrase "working-class stories." What are we, a different species. To hell with that.

JG: Reading is as important to a writer as writing and it often takes you on a journey from one author to another. How has your literary journey been over the years?

JK: An absolutely wonderful, exciting and crazy adventure. I'm just about to turn seventy-three years of age. Calling all you young people, get into art immediately. Go and live your own life. Fuck them all.

27

2018

Interview by *thi wurd*
Literary Journal

This interview was conducted at the Mitchell Library café, Glasgow, in February 2018 with Brian Hamill and Alan McMunnigall.

thi wurd: There was a thing you said in *A Lean Third* about having ideas but resisting ideas. I'm interested in the process of how you write. I was thinking about it in terms of something like jazz improvisation. Would it be related to that? Do you work within structures the way a jazz musician might? With someone like Charlie Parker there would be a particular chord sequence and he would hit a note on the chord. For Parker there would be structure into which he'd improvise. With your method do you go fresh to the page and completely improvise?

James Kelman: It's a good way of looking at it, in terms of jazz. The thing that would make it similar is that there's a point there where you're actually in the story, there's a voice, each character is a voice. You can look at the voice as being the basis of whatever it is the jazz musician begins from. They have a structure or a kind of skeletal thing, a very skeletal basis, and they can go within that and improvise within that. But they cannot go outside it. Sometimes in my working process if I've been spending time revising something and not managing to get it right I discover that it's a different story. And that will eventually happen, after a lot of work. I just need to take this bit out and cut and paste it somewhere else, probably a new story because it's actually another voice. That's also a thing in music and in painting, it happens across the board in that ideas sort of crowd in, and each has a different context. You can think of the tree diagram idea. Trees move into each other but they are separate in a sense. If you've been working and trying to develop something and you keep hitting a stone wall, often it's because it needs to be taken out altogether, the bit that's blocking progress. It's another story. Another piece you've got to work on and develop.

tw: Is it an intuitive thing while you're actually working?

JK: It's a bit more than intuitive, simply because you're working through something. If it has become inconsistent it's not like jazz where you resolve it within the piece because you realise this character is a different character. If you're working in the first person, then that first person becomes a different first person. You get into a way of looking out for that.

tw: Say that you were working on a longer work, a novel, would you continue to work at points when you're away from your desk? I mean, if you were walking in the street, would you still be thinking about it?

JK: I try and avoid that, right from the earliest stage. Put it this way, there's never been a point from being a young writer where I ever allowed myself to work something out, I kept it for the page. I was always working for other people while I was doing my own art. Because of that I was always involved in the process. But I was very aware of painting and music and how crucial the working process was itself. The working process is like mental arithmetic—you can use that as an analogy—the teacher always wants to see the working. You don't just have $a = 2$, that's not what is wanted. It's about how you arrive at $a = 2$. There's a big, long sequence, paragraphs, symbols and semi-colons, open brackets and blah blah blah. So that's what you want to get, how you arrived at $a = 2$, all that working through process. A lot of people never ever grasp that point about art.

They might do when you talk about painting and music but they don't really when it comes to literature or writing a story. There's so many misunderstandings about how it all happens because so often writers take what critics say about the process of writing and they believe what the critics say about what they do. But writers are the ones that do it. Critics don't. Why would you take somebody else's point of view before your own about what it is you yourself are doing?

tw: I was at uni when you won the Booker Prize and you said in an interview that you were surprised when Sammy in *How Late it Was, How Late* went blind. I remember a lecturer saying that this was ridiculous. How can Kelman say that? He's making that up because the writer must know because he's the person writing the work. But I understood what you meant.

tw: It's the point that Flannery O'Connor went into some depth about, in the story "Good Country People," where somebody gets their prosthetic leg stolen. She said she didn't know the leg was going to get stolen until she saw it on the page.

JK: So many critics don't understand the actual process, they don't understand existentialism either, or are maybe scared of it, the creative impulse itself, it's beyond their control. They're so bound by a kind of theological approach, Christianity or otherwise. It's like scholastic philosophy or something. There is always the existence of God, overriding everything, an ultimate external control, so fate and providence, the existence of the end result. Artists have a problem with theology at a certain level. The critics don't really understand this level, generally speaking, where it is you're coming from. This is a central problem with the Anglo-American tradition in a way, because although it seems to take on these issues of art it doesn't. They can't really deal with a writer like Goethe. Some critics would regard it as a contradiction that artists might make it up as they go along, maybe just see it as naive or primitive. It's nothing to do with being primitive, we just don't have this skeleton that we fill in. These writing courses and PhDs in Creative Writing seem to believe we do—write an essay to go along with your novel, to say how it began, where it came from and how you saw it developing blah blah, to what extent it accords with your original intention. It's utter baloney, have they ever read *Notes from Underground*? I'd be beating my head against a wall trying to explain how it really happens, they don't get it, not the real stuff anyway. They don't want to either because it means it's beyond control, not just their own but ultimate authority.

tw: It's funny how far that sort of critical approach is from what an artist would actually be doing. When you were younger you've said that you maybe benefitted from the freedom of not going to university, at a young age you were obviously teaching yourself and learning from other writers. In terms of that being a way of working was it an immediate thing when you started to write?

JK: I was writing when I lived in London. I came back to Glasgow with Marie, so that would be the very end of 1969, November or December. Right away I was working on the buses and doing shiftwork and I was into that way of working, that I developed and maintained all the way through.

Existing on not an awful lot of sleep and if you're lucky catching up later. Making use of that shiftwork pattern and I still really do the same thing. I got into the way of working at four, five, six in the morning and I'm still working that way. When I was going to work, working shifts, I was continually having to break off my own work. I soon realised that I didn't want to continue with a story if I knew what was going to happen. I wanted that to happen on the page, "what was going

Payslip January 1974

to happen" was the very stuff, the thing itself, the drama. I was very much make it up as you go along, that's what you do, for me, that was it. And subsequently everything made sense. I started tutoring in the mid-'70s. I was twenty-six or twenty-seven. I'd be away tutoring and the thing was it started to make sense to me once I started to talk about the process. I'd be like a sort of critic at the same time. I could say to people, look, I want to surprise myself. It's quite obvious you maintain mystery if you don't know what's happening. If you're writing and you don't know what's going to happen then how can a reader? If you don't nobody does. It could be that it becomes inevitable, but that's fine. And maybe it becomes predictable in some ways, but it doesn't mean that it's pre-conceived.

tw: So there's a freshness?

JK: Yeah, and you're keeping the drama going because really you can't do otherwise. That would lead me into talking about writers, especially Kafka. I used to really enjoy Kafka's journals and looking at Kafka's methods and methodology it was consistent with my own learning experiences of doing the thing and how I'd be talking about the process itself.

tw: So you'd be interested in writers talking about their methods?

JK: I was always interested in writers talking about their methods. When I was reading artists' biographies I was interested to read about that, someone like Delacroix—whoever. I'd been reading artists' biographies since I was young, maybe to do with my old man and my grandfather being picture-framers, gilders and restorers. There's a wee interview my old man did with a local newspaper in the early 1970s, done in his last work-shop, in Whiteinch. It was a pretty hopeless place for him as it meant no passing trade. He was used to the west end. He liked Gibson Street and Otago Street, Park Road, Bank Street, Great Western Road. Being out in Whiteinch was a bit of a night-mare for him and he took a job at the Kelvingrove Art Gallery soon after. But anyway, the journalist was interested in asking him what kind of paintings had been through his hands and he mentioned a couple he'd worked on: Constable, Fantin-Latour, a Botticelli of some sort, maybe an etching, a wood cut, I don't know. My grandfather was friends with J.D. Fergusson and people like that, because he did work for them. And old paintings too were getting restored. I would see these things in the house, I was used to it.

tw: You were thinking about how artists work?

JK: Well, you can't help that. When he mentioned Fantin-Latour I remembered being interested; my father would say, Jimmy I've got a Fantin-Latour. I found it was the sort of thing I could spend time looking at, just how he did it, flowers. Another thing I saw close up were Rennie Mackintosh watercolours and they were really brilliant, studies of flowers too, petals, very delicate, barely anything. You don't associate Rennie Mackintosh with these small watercolours, an old friend of my father had maybe three of them, an art collector, he lived in a flat in Cecil Street, I think he had stuff by Josef Herman, he collected East European artists as well as Scottish, David Wilkie and people, I think he had a Sam Bough. It's also being aware of the tremendous craft that people don't associate with artists and writers necessarily, what all goes into it, and how they live their life. I would try to explain to students about Van Gogh and the life experience he was coming from before he started painting, before he allowed himself, and talk to them as well about his brother Theodore, the family connection. It was stuff I knew when I was their age. My grandfather hung paintings and exhibitions so the likes of Van Gogh's family is interesting to me, and that side of things, other artists and getting things going. My old man was the youngest in the family. He had four brothers and one sister. My grandfather would get a couple of the older brothers and they'd hire a van because they had to take an exhibition down to London, and they were going to hang it down there. One of Van Gogh's portraits is of a guy my grandfather did work for, a Glasgow gallery owner. That side of it was something I grew up with. I took my own interests from that after about the age of twelve, probably even before. Durand-Ruel too, in my teens, I thought he was great and I thought at one time going to Paris to learn about art-dealing, there was a college there. My father was in favour of that, and my elder brother out in New York, we talked about it. Instead of taking it further I went to Manchester and worked in a copper factory. Just nonsense. But I maintained an interest, so I would know about Van Gogh and Gauguin, Cézanne and Zola, that kind of thing, Tolstoy talking about Chekov, Turgenev and Dostoevsky, Gorky's pen-portraits, Kafka reading a new story by Aleichem to his friends, making them laugh, that kind of stuff. I found when I started tutoring that the students all liked to hear about the lives of the artists, that's why I'd say instead of the *Lives of the Saints*, we should give young people the *Lives of the Artists*—every student wants to be an artist. Because you can get drunk and have a lot of sex and it's all really exciting, travelling about having great conversations with kindred spirits, or so it seems, then also the reality, the poverty, people in poverty trying to create, doing their work, great great artists whose work doesn't sell, and those that do and these things also I wanted to know, how did they live, who got a bowl of soup from Pissarro's wife, who helped Utrillo, so then heroes, Degas, Cézanne, Modigliani, Rodin, all that. These are the fantasies that bring the artists. Gradually you realise it's not the case at all or you become a drunk, an addict. The bars are full of drunk guys who want to talk about art and literature. That's what separates them out and you see the number of people who actually do the work gets smaller and smaller. You find that's who you associate with. You get kind of impatient or bored with people who just talk about it.

tw: You said that you don't work things out away from the page?

JK: I try not to do that. Sometimes it can't be helped. An example I could give, a way of thinking about it, is dreams and nightmares; I've made use of them in the past. Never look for a meaning, just get it down, as it happened, only as you remember, don't stray from the thing itself, it's already formed, fully formed. And once you think about that it gives you an insight maybe of why you don't want to get into resolving things away from the page. I'm distinguishing here, dreams and nightmares from ideas, that you have this kind of worked-out thing in your head, the idea, that you just have to transfer to the page. No, it's not like that. How do I write down the idea? No, it doesn't work that way, the ideas don't exist in that kind of skeletal or Platonic-style form—not with my work anyway. Other writers maybe see it that way. It's quite primitive I think, not as sensitive as Keats talking two hundred years ago. I would rather hear somebody talking about God moving their hand, or guiding their hand, the difference between moving and guiding, because that'll lead you to the creative spark more quickly than the other way, eureka, I've got an idea, and now I'm going to go home and write down the idea on the page. And that's the poem, gives the idea its material reality, or something.

tw: A lot of people see writers as resolving things. It makes me think about Katherine Mansfield talking about Chekhov, the fact that she felt he was a writer who asked questions but didn't try to answer them—that he didn't need to answer them. But you do see different strands of fiction, where you see writers resolving things. Or writers answering questions. I wonder in the process you've described if it opens things up?

JK: If you're working with the thought process of characters anyway, you have to pay attention to what it is you're doing. If you're working with a thought process then that's what it is, it's not like finding the end result of the process. Or what is the end of all this, like $a = 2$. If it's a process then that's what it has to be. Right from the early questions you raise as a writer, at the earliest point of beginning one story as opposed to another, you really want to make use of that. You never want to jump ahead of yourself really.

tw: Is it in a sense being out of control in the way it could be in jazz?

JK: Don't think of the first day, think of the second, third or fourth day. You've got to rely on the fact that it's there, it exists, the thing you're working on. But you're also making it. You begin from somewhere. It will change and you will work through that because you're a writer and not a visual artist. If you watch the wee film of Picasso working and completely changing a painting, then at any stage you could have said stop, and taken the thing away while in process, because there's an image at every stage. But that's the way that painting operates, a way that the visual arts operates that literature doesn't. In literature you do finish up with a finished thing, the working is part of the actual story. Whereas in painting you go and see something that's finished. The artists may have done sketches and so on towards that but it's finished. Sketches in pencil and crayon beforehand but what you see is a finished oil painting. But in writing it's all there really, not all, okay, but a great deal of it, because that's what the story is. I don't know if other writers work in that way—I'm thinking of contemporary writers. I'm more comfortable talking about the writers that interest me. So if I'm talking about people, whether it's Beckett or Joyce or Dostoevsky or Chekhov or whoever the hell it is, and even writers that I'm not that bothered about—say Hemingway. At least Hemingway knew enough to give bits of good advice to people. He said finish your day's work half-way through a sentence. That's a good piece of advice because you can expand on that to students and you can ask, "Why would he say that?" And it leads to picking up on the thought, because in order to finish that sentence, you have to get back into the train of thought that led into that. You can begin from that with students. A lot of Hemingway's technique was derived from being a journalist. You tend to forgive him stuff because where you can see it's also useful.

tw: I'm always interested in process. I remember you saying in response to the question "Do you use notebooks?"

that if you forget something you're trying to remember then trying to remember it can be more interesting than going to a notebook.

JK: The way I'm telling you about working is the reason I write so many stories that are variations on themes. It's always a good analogy talking about the workings of painters and musicians. As soon as you talk about variations on themes we might know about it from poets, and we can accept it from painters and accept it from musicians. But people are less willing to see that it also applies in prose fiction. If you see a writer like Beckett, you know that's the way it is. Think of Flannery O'Connor too, some of her stories are similar to Chekhov's, and you'll say, Christ, that's a variation on another story. So you can have six variations on one story by Flannery O'Connor, or one finished story by Flannery O'Connor. Which would you rather have? There's no argument really. Why would you want to have something that's so finished! That's a thing you can take from Kafka's journals, you see how he's working through things and he'll come back to the same basic story or storyline. And to my mind he should just have had a good editor, and if he'd had a good editor and if he was showing his work then somebody would have said to him that story's finished, that's why you've given up, because it's finished. Whereas Kafka's not seeing them as stories, you see that he wants to move on to get to the "real story," but he's just moving through variations. And you think to yourself, but that is a finished story. It's only a page long, but thinking of Martin Buber, *Tales of the Hasidim*, Kafka's coming from that tradition, and you're thinking why weren't you just finishing those wee variations, and putting them all together? These are just one-page stories, one paragraph even, they're brilliant! Our own culture hardly has room for that whereas Kafka's tradition does. Except maybe the Gaelic tradition, we might have it there.

tw: I was interested to hear you talking in Edinburgh last year about syntax.

JK: When I was working more in phonetic transcription, thinking about what goes on in spoken language, I became more interested in syntax. The difficulty here is that I'm going to speak as who I am just now but talk about how it was when I was twenty-four, twenty-five or twenty-six when these things were not worked out. The last story in *An Old Pub Near the Angel* is "Nice to be Nice," which is in phonetic transcription. By the time the book came out I was writing "Remember Young Cecil" and seeing there were different things I needed to be doing in my stories. It wasn't so much a transcription of the speaking voice as to do with how you framed the actual unit, the unit of breath, just trying for local rhythms of speech, ways of speaking, to do with phrasing, to get the more precise meaning. An obvious example is "ye cannay dae that but." It's realising that "ye cannay dae that but" is different from "but ye cannay dae that." There's a different meaning. And if you just use the so-called correct grammar you can't convey that meaning, and the phonetic transcription is not relevant to that. You can hear straightaway that there's a difference in what's intended by that. So even before you get to looking at language as an area of study you realise that there's a different set of techniques and skills, whole different ways of getting meaning through how language is used by people speaking—orature as distinct from literature. Things that are obvious, but it wasn't straightforward to be doing it, not then. People weren't writing in those ways. Or if they were I never came upon it. I didn't know about Grassic Gibbon at that point. I hadn't read anything by him. People were aware of it here but I didn't know about it. I didn't know Tom Leonard at that point. I'd never seen his work and not heard of him until Anne Stevenson referred to it, which would have been 1972.

tw: So were you working it out as you wrote?

JK: Aye. And paying attention to what was going on with American writers. You'd be aware of the ways American writers would be using language and how they'd talk about it. You'd just assume it was valid to be doing the same thing, as a Scottish writer, especially when you were involved in the types of stories I was doing. The things that made them exciting were the actual characters involved. The richness was to do with an old guy talking. If you take away the old guy talking there's nothing there. You have to find a way to get the guy talking. You can't do that in an ordinary third-party way. You've got to give the story in another way. You cannot "describe" what the character is doing but be right in the middle of it. These things were clear and seemed obvious to me from just about the very start. I liked these very English kind of adventure stories when I was young, Somerset Maugham, where an "I-voice" first-person character— Maugham himself—is travelling on a train in a foreign land and he meets a strange person who tells him a strange story. Except I wanted to write it where the "I-voice" first-person character was the strange person involved in a strange story right there and then—a good introduction to Gogol, or Hogg.

tw: When people first read your work there was the issue of class prejudice concerning the people and cultures in your work. Did people have a problem with how you rendered your fiction in terms of syntax?

JK: Right from early on and it's not changed that much. It's remarkable how much of that hostility is still around. And the lack of understanding and the desire not to comprehend. To try to maintain a position against it.

tw: That's a good way of looking at it.

JK: You look at the continuing marginalisation of a writer like Tom Leonard, I mean, I'm reading an interview in a recent Scottish literary mag and it's weird they could speak about such stuff with a straight face. And there's an actual sense that they don't have any true awareness of where things are and have been in Scottish literature for the past how many years. They're either Scottish or based here, critics, academics, poets, one was French, I think. It's weird kind of late 1950s bourgeois aesthetics. You realise that there's a denial somewhere, if you can be bothered working it out.

But going back to the point about early reactions to the work. Thinking of the poet and radio drama producer Stuart Conn, who was very generous to other writers. I got to know him because our kids were in the same nursery. Stuart was good, he did *Poetry Now*, working for BBC Scotland, he did good things. He commissioned stuff from people, Tom for instance, Alasdair, and myself too. That's how I got the commission to do the *Hardie and Baird: The Last Days* play for radio, it was Stuart got me it. Another thing he recommended to me was to try John Calder. That'd be the mid-1970s. I'd done an early version of *A Chancer*, enough to show somebody. I sent it off to John Calder. I was pleased to do that because Calder was publishing good stuff. I sent off *A Chancer* but he just seemed confused by it. He wrote back about it being written in Glasgow slang or dialect and wouldn't sell because of that. And really it was written in English—only not in standard form. It used syntax and phrasing differently, but I thought that was already happening in some of the stuff he was publishing.

tw: Were you shocked at the time you got that response?

JK: It was a surprise. It seemed to confuse him. I thought with him and the Scottish connection he would have settled more comfortably into the rhythms of the language, then too, him being used to Beckett and Burroughs, Trocchi. I was using language in those ways, so I thought, developing phrasing, or just paying attention to the rhythms, getting different meanings through the syntax. I didn't understand why he would have said what he did except through a lack of knowledge about how language operates other than Standard Literary Form. Okay, it was a backhanded compliment, his confusion, I knew I was getting the phrasing right.

tw: You expect him to be reading at a better level.

JK: Aye, it made me think maybe it was Marion Boyars who was doing the work at Calder and Boyers. I just assumed it was Calder but maybe it wasn't.

tw: And Calder in the '70s was publishing Selby.

JK: Yeah, he had such a great list.

tw: I can see why you would have sent to him. It makes a lot of sense.

JK: Yeah, it made sense when Stuart suggested it.

tw: It's amazing how different for the reader a work like *The Busconductor Hines* could seem. It felt so different on the page. Some readers immediately responded to it. I'd never seen anything like it. To me it felt revolutionary. Were you aware it was going to be different?

JK: Fortunately my work was attacked at an early age. It was good because when you're attacked consistently it forces you to look at what it is that's the problem. You become more of a critic. You start to realise that certain things are triggers. These are the things that are offending people. You come to learn it's not just the word *fuck* that offends people. You realise there's something else going on, especially when there isnay any *fuck*s in the story but they're still offended. So how come, what are the triggers, why are they so upset? Back when *The Busconductor Hines* came out some things were a surprise to me. But sometimes the thing that surprises me most is that there isn't a proper fightback and the writers are left on their own. People who might support are still uncertain, they don't rely on their own judgment, they aren't strong enough intellectually. People tend to not want to take on the establishment like that. The Saltire Society was a classic example when they also attacked me after the Booker Prize and you think, what the hell's going on here? Are they so inferiorised, so uncertain intellectually that they can't come out and defend these positions? They're just part of the tradition, and it's our own tradition.

tw: It would be difficult to defend the position against your writing. In saying that, there are critics and journalists who respond to your work.

JK: Aye, but it would have been easy for journalists and critics in Scotland to have defended me, because if they're throwing my work out like this they've obviously never read certain short stories by Scott and Stevenson then James Hogg for Christ sake and of course they've read them, and Grassic Gibbon, of course they've read them. Burns for Christ sake. How can they take seriously some of the things going on with McDiarmid? They could have defended me quite easily but they didn't have the confidence to do that. In a way it's quite sad. But thinking of Tom Leonard again, that's what they do, and they're in danger of allowing a major figure like Tom to go unheralded altogether, I mean, what the hell's going on and why, that's a fucking crime. Why are these people in denial? There doesn't have to be any conflict between that and the stuff they herald to all quarters. Why can't they look at work done in their own country by their own writers and confess the truth: it's the real thing, it's the McCoy.

tw: I think the denial thing's important. I don't think they're just stupid, I think part of it is that there's something hostile there.

JK: I think that was clear with Kenneth White and the satire thing I did. I had to respond to him it was not personal, it was not like defending against a personal attack, there was none of that. I was just offended, and amazed—the great people who were at that event, the Self-Determination and Power event, the discussions and debates, everything. I'm not too bothered about critical attacks from other writers, usually it's just stupid. With Kenneth White it was stupid, just silly. His attack on the event came after it and he obviously knew nothing about it apart from it somehow being in opposition to some of his own positions, or so he thought, and maybe it was. Whatever, it was foolish, facile—and huffy too! The person who doesn't want any positive development in his own country unless he's at the core of it all, the central figure, the elemental force. That adolescent position, close your eyes and the world disappears. Waxing philosophical without doing the work, excruciating. The utter presumption, the arrogance, finishing off Thomas Reid! Give us a break.

tw: It's like the way these things work at the uni. When I was an undergrad in 1991 I was reading a lot of your work. You're one of the artists that I liked, but straightaway there's a clipping of my wings. In a tutorial I made a positive comment about reading your books. The reply was a subtle "you're wrong and here's what's right." Sometimes the response would be overt. I remember a tutorial in which I more forcibly said what I found of value in your work and the lecturer asked to speak to me outside in the corridor. We went out and this very posh-sounding lecturer, speaking in a high register, said, "It might surprise you, but I'm from a very working-class background and the things represented in those novels are everything I've tried to get away from in my life. My mother was an alcoholic, and when you're in tutorials saying you like this stuff, it's deeply aggravating to me." I could not believe this situation. Again when I went to do my PhD, I was doing it on Chomsky. Chomsky was allowed because he was an academic, a professor at MIT in linguistics, and although I was writing about his political work, they could cope with it. But any "deviation" into talking about you or Tom and I'd get my wings very slightly clipped. I wonder if the whole thing operates like that.

JK: But that tutor sounds about as honest as you could hope for. You'd like everybody to be as honest as that. But if he was more self-analytic he would come upon why he was doing it and maybe go home and blush or something like that. I mean, some of them do keep people down but he doesn't sound to me like that. Any good occupying force would do that, you would choose the local aristocracy to be the boss. That seems to be the situation generally in Scotland. But you just look anywhere, there were periods of my work when I was very excited and influenced by Camus, because if you are a young artist and you're looking around and being influenced by things, there are people in authority who will recognise that and react to it, and some really resent it and find it threatening to their own position. You would probably do better if you were down at

Oxford or Cambridge or something. Here in Scotland I used to experience that when I was at uni. That's why I ended up having a hard time. A couple of local academics couldn't cope with the idea I might know the same as them in certain areas, even although I was near enough the same age (I was thirty when I went), whereas if you were dealing with a lecturer who was Oxbridge taught they could say, well, we know what you're doing Kelman, but the other ones were too insecure, they found it too difficult, they kind of knew what you were doing but wanted whatever it was to be part of what they were about themselves, why they were as they were and who they were. People find a niche for themselves and keep it to themself at all costs. Acceptable rebels, outsiders who've made it to the inside, and hoist the keep-out signs. It's like the one black guy who's "gained entry" into white company. As soon as he sees anybody else who's black he doesn't say hullo, he doesn't acknowledge them, and really just wants them out, sees them as a threat to his own position.

tw: There's also the fact there's so many people—deep readers—who really love your writing and are so influenced by it. You always meet other Kelman readers, that's there as well.

JK: I am aware of that, it's good you know, it's good at times too if you're feeling down. Although I don't actually feel down. In fact I never feel down about that kind of hostility. It's just interesting to look at it. After *Translated Accounts* came out I wondered why certain things had not happened. Whereas a few people abroad seemed to understand how it worked people here didn't seem to at all, talking generally, it's like they didn't know how to read it. I did a talk in Brussels and the students there were excited, wanting to discuss things to do with it. Somebody in Poland was trying to get it published there, but saying maybe it was too close to home. Only one country has published a translation of *Translated Accounts*: Russia.

tw: There seems to be a perception with some people of a kind of threat and they've got to deny this. They have to work to deny it. I always feel certain people could admit the merit of the work but they don't. But I think the people who are into your work are deeply into it, and into it at a level of language, it's just so deep.

JK: So they're not going to be offended in that case.

tw: There were those articles written in the aftermath of the Booker, where people wrote about Sammy Samuels being a drunk, and he isn't drunk at any point in the novel. So why would they go to some elaborate effort to think of a way to demean this character, and it wasn't even in the book.

tw: I remember at the Booker Prize ceremony, the TV panel in 1989 and in 1994 making almost the same quote about being stuck in a lift with a drunk Glaswegian.

JK: Yeah, or Germaine Greer saying it's like Billy Connolly without the philosophy, that and the snobbery of the Irish critics, the only-one-in-the-room mentality, colonials—only they know what real rebellion is, anybody else is an imposter. But to whatever extent they've had to assimilate, that's what they've done and they resent anybody that hasn't, or who thinks they haven't, so they set out to scorn and ridicule them as pretentious upstarts. Look, he's wearing a tie. The insidious thing was class, the open class attacks I think is what took me by surprise, especially from them, the Irish guys—I can't remember their names. Once you start to look at these things you can see what it is that's a threat, really, it's straightforward, class and imperialism, that colonial inferiorisation, the usual, it's a form of psychosis. The Booker Prize is an interesting one because of what happened with *The Busconductor Hines*. I could understand the hostility to *A Disaffection* in 1989 because it was on the short list but *The Busconductor Hines* had nothing to do with anything back in 1984. But it still got attacked, and by the guy who was chair of the judges, so you think, why is this guy attacking the novel? Why is he even talking about it! It's got nothing to do with anything. And my tutor in philosophy at the time, 1984—I was doing an honours year at Strathclyde

Uni—was Hywel Thomas and Hywel knew the guy, his name was Richard Cobb, a professor. And Hywel said, he's a great guy, you'd like him, you'd get on with him, he'd get on with you. So you're thinking, well, how come he's on the attack. Hywell wasn't defending the guy but like you know, well, he was defending him! The same kind of argument they give for a football player who dishes out racist abuse and is defended by the footballing and media establishment: oh, we all know this guy and there isn't a racist bone in his body, it was just how he behaved, it isn't the real him, it was just the heat of the moment.

Excuse me! And Alick Buchanan-Smith, the Tory MP, he raised questions in Parliament, asking why was the Scottish Arts Council supporting novels like this? But where these attacks did have an effect was on me earning a living because of course the Edinburgh Uni students, my publisher at the time—Polygon—lost their publishing grant for my next novel, *A Chancer*, although good on the students, they still managed to publish and get me an advance—five hundred quid it was. And some bookshops wouldn't stock my books at all.

tw: You wouldn't think that would be the case in the 1980s, it's not like everywhere you go you see *The Busconductor Hines* assailing you. Why are they taking it to that level?

JK: I don't know, it was a tricky period politically, things were going on. At one point Renfrewshire education authorities were trying to ban my work from the school libraries or something, which was weird after me working there as a writer in residence. What's interesting there was to be mentioned in the Booker Prize like that for my first novel and five years later to be on the short list for my third, five years later to win the thing with my fourth. But then every novel since then—and I've written five of them—not one made the long list. Maybe that's another record.

tw: I know. It seems you provoke certain people just by saying you like James Kelman's writing. And then the same people say, "We love Beckett. We love his language. We love literary art." And then if you say, "I like this James Kelman novel," all of a sudden there's a negative reaction.

tw: What makes it especially interesting, I can imagine in the '60s, if you said you liked Selby people might be uncomfortable with it because there's really graphic and horrific content. Although it's daft, there's a logical basis for opposition there. But if somebody says they're really opposed to James Kelman … for what? There isn't anything that's in the books that could be construed as offensive.

tw: It is class, isn't it?

JK: Yeah, well, if you think about the last sixty years in publishing, at least from Lawrence's *Lady Chatterley's Lover*, you know it can't be the word *fuck*, so what else can it be?

tw: I think it's to do with some of the things you talk about to do with assimilation, about the fact you're overtly not assimilating to the dominant literary culture. And when you think of all the Scottish writers, talented writers, who do assimilate comfortably into that culture, you see them in the *Guardian* and stuff, but you overtly don't assimilate like that.

JK: It's kind of gone back the way. Writers you would have thought were better than that, they assimilate as well, basically do as they're told. A lot of the ground that was won twenty, thirty years ago or more has not been taken on.

tw: I thought around 1995–96 was an exciting period to be a reader. I really thought things were moving in a direction where if you were working class and wrote in your own voice or from within your own culture, that was going to be a good thing. I thought things were opening up and then it seemed to close down.

JK: Well, there are different things that happened, you know. Political things, obvious things, except people didn't seem to notice or think important. After the Booker Prize the chief guy at Dillons Bookshop, the biggest apart from Waterstones in Britain at the time, said they weren't going to stock my books. People wondered if the hostility would have any effect.

Any effect! What do you mean? They've said they're not going to stock my books, so now they are not stocking them. Is that not an effect?

These bookshops aren't stocking my books. So what that means is they're not stocking my books. So how do we sell them? There was only bookshops and mail-order in those days. No online purchasing or fuck-all. So yeah, it was worse than the '80s.

Then the knock-on effect on your own publisher, your own marketing people, they lose confidence in your work, and ye can't blame them. They can't go in and sell it to Dillons and these other bookshops because they know in advance they won't take it. They've already told them! Then the sales and marketing squad meet the man in charge of the budget, and he's going to say I'm only going to give you x amount instead of $x(yz)$ because there's no point in giving you big marketing budgets and all that promotion stuff, festivals and launches and so on.

A massive knock-on effect on your next work too. These things are straightforward for anyone to look at, facts and figures and dough. You don't have to dream anything up, these are the facts. It isn't something inherent to the actual book. You don't have a big sticker on the cover saying "Don't Stock Me at All Costs." People would say to me, why are you irritated? And I'd say, my wife's just been into a major bookstore in Glasgow—this happened in the 2000s—they've got every Booker Prize winner on display except mine.

People say, what do you mean? And I'd say, well, every single Booker Prize–winning novel of the last so many years is in the window except mine, and that's here in Glasgow.

And they'd say, pardon? What are ye trying to say?

Nothing, I'm just saying it, every single Booker Prize–winning novel of the last twenty years is in the bookshop window except mine.

What do you mean?

I've just fucking told ye!

Why are you getting upset.

I'd say, I'm not getting upset, it's you that getting upset. I'm just telling you the situation, don't blame me for it. First the denial there's any significance, any correlation, after that the irritation. Write a novel like that and what do you expect. A novel like what? I don't know. Where does that logic lead. A woman's been raped and the cops look at her clothes and ask how come she was alone in the park? A black guy attacked and battered and the cops asking how come he was walking down the street, didn't he know it was dangerous?

Searching the victim for why they've been attacked, ignoring the people responsible. That's how it is and it's been the situation for a long time. Ultimately you've got to ignore it, as an artist, because you have to get on with the work and the best line of defence is attack, write another one, if the last one offended ye wait till ye see the next one, and you're also thinking, isn't it great to get out of this place and just get treated as a writer, an ordinary writer. It's not just me. I don't know how young writers get seen in this country, totally marginalised or having to defend yourself, walking into these bookshops knowing you won't see any good stuff on the shelves, and you want to ask the bookshop people, is there nothing within your own culture that warrants a space in your shop? Apart from stupid fucking murder mysteries. Mind you, I was in touch with Duncan McLean recently and I saw the last two pamphlets he's done up in Orkney ... I don't know if you see any of this down here?

tw: Is he writing fiction again?

JK: He's doing a bit like what he did with Clocktower [Press] only in Orkney.

tw: That's great to hear.

JK: It's actually a bit like *thi wurd*. Writers local to Orkney and he's also trying to do pamphlets. He's done one of his own recent stuff. There's poetry too, essays—one of his where he's talking about Frank Sargeson. I'd forgotten all about Frank Sargeson and I remembered I had a collection of his stories. I went away and found the book and looked again at them, the first time in years, seeing what he was doing back in the '50s and '60s. I don't think I read him until about 1980. I never heard of him when I was young. The edition I have was published in 1975.

tw: Someone gave me one of his collections in a class about three or four weeks ago and I've only glanced at it. It looks really interesting.

JK: Well, as soon as you see it you know it's interesting, you can see some of the things he's using formally.

tw: It's amazing how you can see it visually on the page sometimes. The person gave me the Frank Sargeson book and I looked at it without even having my glasses on. I could just see on the page that it was going to be interesting. I saw that he didn't use speech marks. I put it in my pocket and already I was thinking, this is going to be good.

JK: The democracy is there on the page straightaway, and 100 percent quality. There isn't any enclosure of people. Some of the things there if you just scan you think, "What's different about this page?" These speakers are all the same. There isn't any God voice. The God voice is the same as the person speaking. He's a New Zealand writer and you can think of New Zealand in lots of different ways. You can think of colonialism or the labour movement or the socialist movement, it's so strong there. That was where the National Health Service began. It's also where they had a tremendous feminist movement, very strong at the turn of the last century, a solid socialist strand there. And that New Zealand writer who won the Booker Prize?

tw: Eleanor Catton.

JK: No, I'm talking about the woman they attacked, the critics, years before me, a smashing writer, immediately interesting, as another writer just, technically—Keri Hulme, a really fine writer. There isn't any enclosure of people. Some things there if you just scan down you think, "What's different about this page?" These speakers are all the same, everybody's a human being. No God voice. That's how ye get attacked by the establishment. Nobody has that superior authority, that RP voice in total control, imperial master, The Voice of English Literature, it isn't there, fuck them, and that "fuck them" is there on the page.

tw: Can I ask you a little bit about the new novel that we're publishing the first chapter of in *thi wurd*?

JK: An elderly writer letting off steam … it's not exactly a fashionable subject, a book by a grandpa about a grandpa, maybe it's just for other grandpas. At least it's got a happy ending. Which I can't divulge here, and don't even divulge in the actual novel.

tw: Will it be coming out next year rather than this year?

JK: What a question.

28

2019

Interview by Brian Hamill

This interview is previously unpublished.

Brian Hamill: *How Late It Was, How Late* is written in a similar, close third-person style to your previous novel, *A Disaffection*, with one distinct difference being that there appears to be another entity, another voice, within the narrative of *How Late It Was*; at one moment the voice emanates directly from Sammy (like it does consistently with Patrick in *A Disaffection*), but then it seems to be the voice of another, of someone who knows Sammy well but is not actually him. Is this a fair interpretation, or is this just Sammy's way of conceiving and speaking of himself? Is it possible to say why you chose this particular narrative method for Sammy's story? What is the significance of the "other" narrative entity who refers to Sammy in the third person?

    James Kelman: A man who knows Sammy well sits in a Glasgow bar with other men who know Sammy well, and narrates the story to them. Every voice, and perspective, is part of the guy's narrative. The narrative makes use of literary and oratory methods, techniques and devices.

    BH: *How Late It Was, How Late* is such a linguistically rich work, with incredible voice, rhythm and music. I've seen you mention in interviews and in your own essays how much you enjoyed the work of Caribbean and African writers when you were a younger writer—artists like Samuel Selvon and Ken Saro-Wiwa. Were novels such as *The Lonely Londoners* and *Sozaboy* important for you in developing the prose formulation of voice for this book, or was their significance more in what they represented, the refusal to assimilate to English RP for the language of their narratives?

JK: I was already involved in my own work in my own way. The crucial thing for me was recognising kindred artists involved in identical, and related, issues, struggling with language as an effect of linguistic and cultural imperialism. I came upon Selvon's work in the mid-1970s, and others such as Tutuola, and many others; Saro-Wiwa's work maybe ten years later. He was later for myself, but just one of many. The important connection was New Beacon Books, bookshop and all matters literary and political, and the connections through anti-racist struggles.

BH: In your afterword to the new edition of *An Old Pub Near the Angel*, you wrote:

> I tried and rejected the present tense; locked into one dimension, behaviourist, static, lacking mystery, deterministic, non-existential. Just fucking philosophically naive, like science fiction or world-weary detectives trudging the mean streets humming a piece of Mozart, to a backdrop of the theme from Johnny Staccato: the mental masturbation of the bourgeoisie, that was how I felt about the "I-voice" present tense. Avoid it at all costs. Go for richness, sophistication, infinite possibility: use the past tense properly, discover its subtlety. Learn yer fucking grammar! Do not be lazy. How does the verb operate in other language cultures?

This is a really interesting point for aspiring writers like myself, as so much of the literature you encounter is written in first person, present tense. I guess I'd just like to ask you to explain this a little further? What is it specifically about that narrative mode that you dislike or that you think does not ring true?

JK: It is difficult to be more specific! It is one-dimensional, philosophically naive, making certain untenable assumptions about "objective reality" and naive in its apprehension of drama, and how drama works. It is impossible to know the work of Kafka, Beckett, Hamsun, Joyce, Camus, Sartre (and countless other noteworthy writers, including James Hogg) to continue for long in that "first-person, present-tense" mode.

BH: Did you try to write in this mode early in your career and if so, what was it that prompted you to move away from this?

JK: I didn't try to write in that mode, I did make stories using the device. The "first person, present tense" does have its uses. It is simply another way of making a story. I am arguing that it is a very limited device and fails to deal adequately with more sophisticated work.

BH: Could *How Late It Was, How Late* have been written as a first-person, present-tense narrative coming directly from the mind of Sammy, or would this have been untenable?

JK: Not untenable, impossible, an absurdity.

BH: I've read in different essays and such like where you've discussed your artistic method over the years, and how the first draft relies on a level of improvisation when faced with the blank page; that you don't like stories to be pre-conceived or planned out before the act of writing that first draft commences. There was something I mentioned during the interview we conducted for issue number 3 of *thi wurd*—about how Flannery O'Connor said she didn't even know the character in her great story, "Good Country People," was going to have her prosthetic leg stolen until she saw it happen there on the page. Does your own level of "improvisation" extend as far as this too; when writing *How Late It Was, How Late* were you unaware of what was happening until it was actually occurring during the writing of that first draft? Did you only know the book would close with Sammy exiting Glasgow once you/he had reached that point, or was there always a fatalistic sense of this being how his story must conclude?

JK: I created the story from nothing other than myself.* I sat down and began writing and the first sentences remained the first sentences. From thereon I moved, going more deeply, shaping and clarifying, staying with the moment, allowing the character to enter properly, within his own situation, his own existence, never jumping ahead to describe actions, never knowing more than the narrative.

BH: One of the most important artistic achievements of the novel is how innovative it is in terms of representing the actual conception, flow and integration of the human thought process. Sammy can be thinking one thing then consciously drop it, or get distracted and forget, or fail to relate it to what he had been thinking of immediately before, etc. The novel is full of aborted thoughts and sentences, of confusion and resignation—I've never read another book that gets as close to a representation of organic human thought and expression. Do you feel like you got especially close to Sammy as a human being, in terms of his voice, emotions and psychology? Was this something you hoped to accomplish with this novel, or did you just find yourself experiencing Sammy's consciousness very acutely as you wrote?

JK: I never have an overview of a story. It cannot work if it has to conform to some template or preconception, or intellectual plan of action. The best I can do is refer back to Question 1, the idea of a story being told by a close friend or acquaintance of the central character.

BH: The American writer Hubert Selby Jr said this in an interview in 2003, with regard to the writing of his great novel, *Last Exit to Brooklyn*:

---

* But I do remember that I had been reading *The House of Hunger* by Dambudzo Marechera (1952–87), a wonderful writer from Zimbabwe.

I also knew that if I wrote the way I was being directed to write, that I would look like a barbarian, a primitive, and if I didn't succeed perfectly, I'd look like an idiot. But, I had no choice. Anyway, that's where it all started. I had to find the means, as they say, to be loyal to these people, to be true to the nature of their lives.

I think it's fair to say that *How Late It Was*, much like *Last Exit*, is a novel that is innovatory and/or "experimental" in terms of its language and syntax—at least when compared to the conventional English novel (although of course the modes of innovation are very different across the two books). A significant feature of Sammy's thoughts and his language, which is very distinctive, is how the text deals in repetitions and fragments of sentences. Were you ever concerned with how you were managing to represent this in prose, both in terms of its artistic efficacy and how it may be (mis-)interpreted by readers/critics?

JK: I see Hubert Selby's work as within a tradition and my own is also within a tradition; these traditions are related closely and cover concerns associated with existentialism, anti-imperialism and the elemental rights of every human being.

BH: A beautiful moment in the book occurs when Sammy is becoming frustrated and depressed at his treatment by a "Medical Officer," who is noting down his answers to a succession of questions, and he suddenly starts singing "Always on My Mind" inwardly to himself. It's then as though the music has buoyed him; the effect of just the thought of the tune and the words at that juncture. How important is music in this book, to Sammy, and to you as an artist? Do you consider your work in prose fiction to have any relation to songwriting?

JK: Sammy has endured years of imprisonment, a married man with a child. I cannot imagine music not being of fundamental importance to him. Music is art. Within art people encounter all that there is, and this is an aid to survival for those experiencing deprivation. Literature and orature are concerned with syntax, phraseology, rhythm, grammar: so too is music.

BH: This is a quotation from your interview with Roxy Harris in a 2009 edition of *Wasafiri* magazine:

> A professor at the University of Texas at Austin—she's an African American woman who had made certain links with my work—began teaching *How Late It Was* and then constructed a course to do with Virginia Woolf and James Kelman.* These links and this course would have been unthinkable or seen as absurd in the UK. It often takes someone from outside the culture to see that there are things that can be shared, that can be talked about.

Cairns Craig in his influential essay on your work, "Resisting Arrest," also drew a comparison between yourself and Woolf, and I remember seeing it stated in a book review in the *Independent* in 2012, that (with reference to *Mo said she was quirky*): "James Kelman's latest book could have been written by Virginia Woolf." I think many people might find this a surprising comparison. One of Woolf's many dubious statements about those outwith her own social elite was her disdain for "working men attempting to write"—this seems like an antithetical mindset to that of your own work. Do you appreciate the artistry of Woolf's novels on a technical level, independent of her worldview? Do you see significant parallels between *How Late It Was* and Woolf's work?

JK: I haven't read Virginia Woolf's work. On the wider issue, I don't find it easy to section off myself in such a way as to applaud technique, disconnected "artistry." It would become a matter of style. I do not see art operating in that way. I don't see much difference between that and finding it worthy of

---

* Professor Mia Carter.

comment that Hitler had a very neat moustache, Stalin had a rather stylish hairstyle, that Churchill had a very fine rhetorical delivery when he made the case for chemical weapons to be used on the civilian population of a great chunk of Kurdistan in order to rob them of their land, their oil-rich land.

BH: Roland Barthes wrote:

> For the purpose of achieving an ideal digressiveness and an ideal intensity, two strategies have been widely adopted. One is to abolish some or all of the conventional demarcations or separations of discourse, such as chapters, paragraphing, even punctuation, whatever is regarded as impeding formally the continuous production of (the writer's) voice—the run-on method favoured by writers of philosophical fictions such as Hermann Broch, Joyce, Stein, Beckett. The other strategy is the opposite one: to multiple the ways in which discourse is segmented, to invent further ways of breaking it up. Joyce and Stein used this method, too.... To write in fragments or sequences or "notes" entails new, serial (rather than linear) forms or arrangements.

By way of comparing *How Late It Was, How Late* (and by extension, *A Disaffection*) to your more recent work, those great novels of the late '80s/early '90s were not demarcated in any way other than space-breaks, whereas *Dirt Road* (2016) was presented in distinct sections, and your new, as-yet-unpublished novel *Creative Chronicles* [published by PM Press in 2022 as *God's Teeth and Other Phenomena*] is given in a succession of shorter, titled chapters. Is this a conscious development in your style of novel-writing, to move from one continuous flow to something that is more formally structured, or is it simply a choice of medium made to suit each particular character/story?

JK: I don't find Barthes's point here of particular value. Joyce, Stein, Beckett are great writers but they operate in distinctive ways. Stein and Beckett moved much more deeply, and successfully, in relation to time and space, in my opinion. It was what Joyce aspired to.

There is no "style" in my work. These are technical matters, they are necessities. Another writer once remarked to me that he quite liked the way I didn't use quotation marks. He did not grasp "necessity," that the movement between the external and internal was impossible where dialogue was separate from narrative. It derives from necessity; finding ways to go more deeply.

BH: You've never written a sequel to any of your novels, never revisited or developed further any of the characters. Is this because you perceive sequels to be akin to commercialism and lacking in artistic integrity, or is it more a case that each novel feels like a finished concept in itself once it has been completed? I've always thought there could be a great second book about Sammy, especially seeing as we never actually meet either of the other major characters in the book—his partner Helen or his old friend Charlie Barr. Did that idea ever appeal to you, or is the concept anathema to how you work?

JK: I see this relating to Question 4. My stories generally begin from one human being. It might be said that the creation of this one human being is the story. Once the human being is created there is no second story. All that might exist from thereon is a series of situations and experiences that this character, the fictional human being, encounters. Any sequel would begin from an already realised character. There's nothing in it for me, speaking as the artist, the creator. I've got too many stories to write, too many I want to write; my life is full of my own projects. If anyone ever wants to write a sequel to any of my novels I might not object, get in touch with my agent!

Author's Note: The interviewer here was Brian Hamill, a young friend who died in 2022. Brian was very familiar with my work and could have interviewed me on various areas of it.

He discussed this with me from time to time and he had a few ideas in that direction. In 2019 he chose to do one on my novel *How Late It Was, How Late*. This was the first work of my own that he encountered. He had been involved with *thi wurd* magazine but later struck out on his own and was soon building a formidable reputation as the publisher, founder and driving force behind the Common Breath, a dynamic small press based in Glasgow. In less than two years he published five works that exhibit clearly his passion for literary art, and his generosity.* He was a writer first and foremost, though perhaps too modest to admit it; keen to gain every ounce of technical knowledge possible, and I responded to him with that in mind. He is sorely missed.

---

* *Good Listeners*, a collection by Alan Warner and Brian Hamill; *The Middle of a Sentence*, a short prose anthology; *Waiting for Nothing*, by Tom Kromer; *All to Blazes*, selected stories by Frank Sargeson; *passing through*, poetry and prose by Tom Leonard; and *Look at Me How*, a limited edition work by A.L. Kennedy.

29

2022

Interview by Rastko Novaković

Rastko Novaković is a writer and filmmaker. He has been active in the anti-war, housing and trade union movements in former Yugoslavia and the UK. This interview, "Existence Is a Guerilla Campaign," originally appeared in *Salvage*.

Malignant bureaucracies, class hatred, the revanchist rump of British Empire—they were all on the wane we were told, but presently they are alive and virulent. These are the cold winds that blow through half a century of James Kelman's writing, huddled around a warm poetic of everyday resistance.

A fine stylist and experimenter, with a honed ear for voice and uncanny way of writing stream-of-consciousness, an elegant essayist, an artist with an infectious passion for existentialism, country music, anti-colonial writing and social justice. Over the years, Kelman has also been active in the community, fighting the commercialisation of public spaces, supporting victims of asbestos poisoning (in his youth, he worked making asbestos-boards), the striking miners, exiled and brutalised Kurds, those resisting racist attacks—by no means an exhaustive list. He speaks alongside and with others, because he sees that being a writer also means taking responsibility, acting in solidarity. He shares this feeling of social conscience with Noam Chomsky, with whom he published a book this year: *Between*

Thought and Expression Lies a Lifetime: Why Ideas Matter, which charts their exchanges over thirty years. With an avalanche of books, new and old, some revised and reconstituted, to be issued in coming months and years, Kelman is still breaking new ground and remains relevant to our present moment.

A couple of recent books passed by without fanfare or much notice—some of the finest fiction I've read. *Mo said she was quirky* (2012)—a novel about a day in a young woman's life. She tries to just get by and fit in, but ends up unravelling when she faces some ghosts from the past. Delicate and tough as nails, like all of Kelman's work, this is monumental without any fuss. The short story collection *That Was a Shiver* (2017) is a wild set of escapades, greatly varied in length, style, interest. From one page to the next, it shifts between abjection, bizarre humour, unbearable social situations, precise philosophical investigations, intimate portraits and meditations on what writing and language is. These stories are free and fresh and they confront you with strange and believable realities which are hard to forget.

Kelman's latest novel, *God's Teeth and Other Phenomena*, is a synthesis of genres in which an ageing writer, Jack Proctor, departs for a writer's residency at "The House of Art and Aesthetics," which he promptly rebrands as "House of Snottirs." Night-time he writes his stuff, probing the meaning of it all, and during the days he gigs in the culture industry, facing students and administrators who mostly have no idea what he's talking about, what he does or why. He is expected to teach Creative Writing in workshops to the young and the mature, novices and pompous MA students, to do readings, opine on the influences of "T S Hitler," shine and grin as the "Banker Prize" winner that he is. It is a nightmarish farce on a grand scale, but also a deadly serious exposition of what writing is. As Eimear McBride says: "This is a book about how art gets made, its murky, obsessive, unedifying demands and the endless, sometimes hilarious, humiliations literary life inflicts on even its most successful names." This is a great and irreverent novel.

Rastko Novaković: The novel describes the kind of exploitation artists face daily—I think this will strike a chord with young writers, but also with workers everywhere. You have written about art administrators and the culture industry for thirty-odd years; what is different nowadays?

James Kelman: Nowadays I concentrate on making my work available, sorting through everything, revising, refining and finishing. This has led me to one in the top rank of indies— PM Press—based in Oakland, California. I needed one willing, able or interested in taking on the corpus, and at my stage there has to be a corpus. Most of my work had gone out of print. Here in Scotland a couple were willing to consider a new novel, a new collection of stories, even an autobiography, but none offered the chance to get all my stuff in order—fiction and nonfiction— new, old and revised. I found this not only invigorating but relaxing. I've been free to get on with it, wherever it leads.

RN: "The Kelman Library" is what they call it and it is exciting that all your different forms of writing are brought together: political essays and interviews, traces of your long engagement with different struggles, your political and philosophical exchange with Noam Chomsky, long and short fiction etc. You've resisted the compartmentalisation of your work into art and politics, so this is something to celebrate. Can you talk a bit about commitment in art and politics?

JK: No art is apolitical. Artists are people. Everybody has a position. Sometimes they commit, sometimes they don't.

RN: Proctor is totally isolated in his work as a teaching guest writer; there is no camaraderie and he is overseen by people "whose primary experience has nothing to do with the process and who know nothing of the process" of writing. You really dwell on the absurdity and violence of it all and you contrast it with the freedom of his nocturnal writing. There he is more free to confront the constraints we all face without having to think on his feet. Can you comment on this?

JK: Those who control art and artists know nothing of the process: it is irrelevant to what they do. Jake Proctor wants to get on with his work. The story begins with him at his desk, interrupted in mid-sentence. That is how it is. His partner is not to blame. No one is to blame. For many artists life is a series of interruptions. It has a detrimental effect, not just psychological, it is an assault on the digestive system. In my happy days as a smoker, it meant settling back, prising open the tobacco tin and rolling a smoke. I learned to relax. The struggle to regain the train of thought becomes enmeshed in the story itself. Sometimes interruptions allow positive twists. We move sideways, in the process dumping the boring stuff.

RN: Often in your books the characters get tripped up in an almost supernatural, nightmarish way—oppression is often precisely analysed, but it is also cosmic. Jack's resistance to his "proctorship" in the culture industry is a scrappy, messy guerilla campaign. Which artists did you learn to fight from?

JK: I think your first sentence leads to areas that arise in the work of Franz Kafka. In *The Trial* Joseph K's struggle is not so much against authority but his inability to deal with reality, with what's under his nose. The "unseen hand" is not supernatural, it's the expression and manifestation of a repressive authority. For the vast majority of humanity, existence takes the form of a guerilla campaign. There is no one artist, no one individual. I was open to all influence as a young person. I was fortunate to be beyond ordinary schooling from the age of twelve. I attended school but didn't get involved. Learning from thereon took the form of guerilla warfare. The wheels of authority grind us down in the never-ending struggle of the ruling class to eradicate, and eliminate, the will to learn. This cannot be eliminated but it is eradicated. People forget they can question, but the recognition that it is possible is rediscoverable.

RN: I also had a feeling of being in a nightmare of being tripped up at every point, not wilfully, but as a result of the world's complete indifference. There is always this existential moment and Proctor has to face it, on every page. Can you talk more about this?

JK: I had to get to grips with the "I-voice" as a young writer. Nobody is more central than the "I-voice." In the English literary tradition the general function of the "I-voice" is to tell a story about unfortunate other people. That was the way I found it. The "I-voice" occupied a position of authority, a sort of social worker. I wanted unfortunate other people to tell the story themself. The difficulty here is that "I-voice" characters must live to tell the tale, otherwise who writes the story. It's okay for believers in the supernatural. Their characters "may pass on" to the next world, or dimension, or stage, or level, maybe a cloud—a place where they can "look down." They then communicate the story by some extraordinary transcendental communication with a publishing editor who writes the preface: Dear Reader, This is a story by a poor unfortunate soul, self-penned by himself, found in an iron box chanced upon by a Novice Monk at the last stroke of Midnight, buried beyond the sacred walls of All Souls Cemetery …

This issue is structural to my earliest stories. I wanted the drama to be 100 percent. Don't take it for granted that the "I-voice" character survives. What if somebody sticks a knife in his guts? Dear Reader, I am dead, some dirty bastard fucking killed me! My first collection was put together when I was twenty-five. I've been battling ever since, finding ways such that the story doesn't end with a strangled cry piercing the penultimate page but reaching as close to it as possible— thinking here of that wonderful story "Voices," by Vaikom Muhammad Basheer.

RN: It's clear from Jack's adventures that as a writer you can never graduate, but also that you can never retire. What are the implications of this?

JK: State-sanctified writers "graduate." They are helped earn a living in the Creative Writing industry, doing bits and pieces in the popular media, script-writing, copywriting. A few write books about writing books. Every writer seeks to earn a living at what they do best, which is write. Those who fail to fit or adjust to establishment requirements rarely graduate and rarely retire. They work to survive, like most of humanity. There are no "implications" that I can see. But there are inferences. One seems obvious. There is no intrinsic economic value in writing. Books considered "good" don't sell themselves.

RN: The USA and UK State is working overtime to control what can be said (and therefore what can be thought) about the war in Ukraine. In Scotland there is a similar process with the drive to another independence referendum. What are your thoughts on this?

JK: The State never stops. Propaganda, disinformation, misinformation, counter-information; revised versions of everything. The term "Fake News" seems to describe this but doesn't. It reduces the impact by suggesting it is either the work of nasty individuals, or a form of conspiracy by a network of nasty individuals.

I see no similarity to the independence question in Scotland. This concerns the effects of imperialism, an intransigent class system and a lack of will to change. Since the UK exit from the European community the lower-order public are getting used to zero rights. What are civil rights, citizen rights, human rights? Basic values derived from solidarity, empathy and a vision of shared humanity can no longer be taken for granted. In a number of areas it is against the law to organise. The US model forces lower-order people to survive in thrall to the existing order, and take solace from a world to come.

RN: What I see in Scotland is this using of nationalism (and sometimes its purest toxic form of ethno-nationalism) to shut other conversations down and to shut out the socialist and trade union movements. And with the latest pronouncements, to hitch an independent Scotland to militarism and US hegemony.

JK: Scottish people are in the same boat as most ordinary people: they dream the American dream, which is a dream of freedom. They can no longer emigrate to the country but accept the propaganda which suggests a value system that allows an escape from the suffocating world of privilege, hierarchy and class servitude—the British system.

Independence bestowed as a gift, an act of charity, from a right-wing State—are ye kidding? It's not the case of hitching to militarism and US hegemony, there's never been anything else in my lifetime, and it ain't going away. I've nothing to say about the labour and socialist movement as it stands, the leadership appease the bully. It's a hard fight but it will have to come.

RN: For many years you've been interested in tracing the inner movements of will, emotion, action, commitment. In this novel you seem to be trying to get as close to that Einstein statement as you can, "My pencil knows more than I do," to write yourself in the act of writing. Is there a political aspect to this?

JK: Einstein's period embraced the idea that human beings cannot be other than human beings. We can reach, but cannot move beyond. The "reaching beyond" is what matters. Einstein's work, like that of other people, helped set the conditions for greater exploration, and tied in with that is a call to the individual. This is the mark of that wonderful tradition. Individuals each have a position, each has a perception of what is, at any given instant. And many will develop a perspective. This is a premise, I think, but it is always revolutionary. How come? It should not be revolutionary. But it is, because of the suffocating control exercised by authority.

There is no fundamental right to authority. That right is grabbed by other human beings, then sanctified, by other human beings.

RN: This book feels very much like your credo, but so much of it is about doubt. The title itself is an invitation to blaspheme. You make fun of Jack by having him strike up the poses of a preacher. Often his sermons go badly! There is a call to overthrow everything, including the hero of the novel. Do you recognise that this is at odds with a lot of contemporary fiction which is about self-affirmation?

JK: Organised religions call for an extended form of something we already know. This can be a form of glorious comradeship where individuals are wholly free or we can bask in the warmth of a King of all Kings, one who has acquired the riches of the universe and allows his innermost trusted servants a share of the spoils. All you have to do is accept his right to authority and convert others to the cause.

The State seeks to control everything, including our inner life; our imaginings and reflections, our creativity. Every area of thought. This includes the worlds following our death, the ones we create for ourselves, usually in the form of a shared community. Even here the State seeks control, in case our imagined worlds lead us to wonder if some of that might be put in place before we die. The religious cops find methods to stop people making sense of their own suppression; perhaps there is a greater good, one that justifies inhumanity. Those of a mathematical bent seek a logic to account for the illogicality. New religions develop. Eventually the old authority will be expelled, if they don't look out. People will confront the leadership, or even go directly to the King: no representation, I'm an individual; no mediation between me and the King.

Authority acts to stop doubt, even to stop people pausing in the act of acceptance. A pause suggests uncertainty. There is no right to be puzzled. Kids are punished daily for this: Mummy, what is hell? Sssh. But mummy ... Sssh. But ... Go to bed! Oh but Mummy ... Any more out of you and I'll wake up yer father! The truth of the religion is its application in reality. Blasphemy survives by order of the State.

I have a term for the act of rejecting the idea that John Smith is King of the Universe. This term is "exshite." Anyone who disputes that John Smith is King of the Universe is guilty of exshite. The person who so exshites is known as an "exshiter." If I ever take control of the legal system of this country I can have it enshrined in law that "exshiting" is illegal. Anyone found guilty of so "exshiting" shall be hanged, drawn, and quartered. That's probably a bad example, it fails to reveal that the most crucial question is begged. The existence of the King of the Universe is unchallenged. How such a being is identi- fied by a sub-species such as humankind is only of academic interest.

The "self-affirmation" industry finds methods to show as balanced that which we know to be imbalanced. "Self- affirmation" is an apology for inhumanity, to show that a certain amount of that is necessary. Why does a sportstar earn $10 million a month for whacking a ball, and an auxiliary nurse who works six ten-hour shifts a week in the contagious wing of a hospice earn less than the cost of living? The question does not arise. The "self-affirmers" demonstrate that each person can be a successful human being. Accept what you have and do it the best you can. The status quo rules. Some of us are billionaire tyrants, some of us are down-at-heel beggars. It is all part of a glorious strategy that will be revealed in the world to come. Never lack in self-esteem, and keep yer hand out my pocket. That is the American way. Be thankful for what you've got, because we can take it anytime we like, and we made the law to enforce it.

RN: A lot of your work is about the resistance to the King of the Universe. You always start from the fundamental posi- tion of La Boétie (who only spoke a folk truth), which is that the ruled prop up the authority of the rulers. Where around you do you see resistance which gives you hope? Or inspires you to write and engage politically?

JK: It depends how we access information. If we pay atten- tion to what is happening outside of the establishment media we find people are resisting tyranny 24–7, all over the world.

There is no inspiration in my writing. Inspiration is a myth perpetrated by those who exploit the work of artists. Art begins from work, that's where it proceeds and finishes. Those who don't work at art don't make art.

You have to pay attention to what goes on in imperialism. The mistake is to assume a level playing ground between ruled and rulers. The ruled are ruled by a variety of rulers. The imperialist's first point of contact is the previous leadership. Clan chiefs, tribal chiefs, religious leaders etc. The imperialist makes the previous ruler an offer he can't refuse. They will kill not only him, his wife and kids, but his entire community, and anything else they see potentially dangerous. The old chain of command continues. Only the leadership changes. The old chief is now subordinate. The imperialist force is now in place. Old rivalries are encouraged, invented and enforced. It takes people a while to work out the reality of authority, who exactly are the enemy. Class solidarity is learned. The rise of fascism is showing the depth of these cultural differences. The return to myth and legend is an attempt to distinguish one community from another, to say what is unique about us, and why we deserve to survive. It takes a while to work out that we have to look at what we mean by "deserve."

RN: The drama in this book sometimes comes from the sliced sentence or a single set of quotation marks. It's a great feeling to skip a heartbeat or just drop off a cliff as a reader. Has this been a problem with publishers?

JK: Since 1972, when a printer refused to print my first story on the grounds of blasphemy and my use of the language of the gutter.

RN: I feel that the battles you've won have been eroded; a lot of writers don't understand the importance of doing away with quotation marks around reported speech and how much that focuses the writer and reader on writing a character's voice. The left internationally has bought the idea of censorship and stewardship and enforces it zealously, leaving the right to define the terms.

JK: No authority trusts art, the left included. Creativity like scepticism is dangerous. It certainly pissed me off as a young writer that art was seen as a mark of a bourgeois sensibility. Anyone who read for pleasure was frivolous, no matter the book, Arthur Conan Doyle or Isaac Babel, they were all the same. Much of the left still think in these terms. They either deny or disrespect Marx's position on alienation. This is the alienation of the individual, not a class of being, but the uniqueness of each and every one of us. Karl Marx and Søren Kierkegaard were contemporaries. Marx reached to find a freedom for all, and it was a great project, poor old Kierkegaard recognised the utter uniqueness of each human being, including the lowest of the low, but feared it. That's an opinion. I'm reminded here too of Dostoevsky, and Chekhov, where the upper classes have become aware that these lower-order people have inner lives. Dostoevsky's characters look in a mirror, eyes widening. Chekhov's characters shrug, but not in a healthy manner. I think I need to get back writing myself the way this is going.

RN: There is an absurd chapter called "How Long is a Short Story?" where someone questions the right of Jack's very short stories to exist. There is a certain snobbery about "the novel" (and the feature film etc.), but the freedom of theme and form that you achieve in your last collection, *That Was a Shiver*, would be hard to find in most longer pieces. There is also a freedom for the reader. What effect, if any, does this have on your writing?

JK: It has no effect that I know about. I go where the writing takes me, and I've tried to maintain that position, even when forced to stop working in order to earn a living, and I have to go to work for an employer, whether in a factory, as a driver, or as a tutor in Creative Writing. Stories short or long, we have to stop work on them eventually.

RN: People like Diane Williams have a great commitment to this short form (often branded as "flash fiction"), the approach which compresses a whole life-story or epic into a page without the burden for the reader of sitting with a main character for weeks. It also keeps a relationship of writing to music and painting. I was elated to see this in *God's Teeth*, brought back into the form of the novel.

JK: I've been working in the shorter form since the 1970s. As a young writer I was reading people such as Kafka and Borges obviously—also Solzhenitsyn, whose short pieces I thought smashing—people should remember how great a writer he was. But I read everywhere and from as many cultures, ancient storytelling from the earliest sources. I liked stories and that was that. I discovered Japanese short prose from the late nineteenth and early twentieth centuries. That tied in with my own vision, which was to create stories that worked in the same way as any other piece of art, a wee self-contained structure, that began and ended in itself—just like a song or a painting or a piece of sculpture.

RN: Jack never appeals to authority in his teaching and writing workshops and the novel repeatedly questions the foundations and the authority of the "I-voice." Why is it still important for you to question how we know what we know?

JK: He is influenced by Socrates, seeking an authentic dialogue between teacher and student; to enlighten the student by bringing them through stages in a process, a wee bit like doing algebra. We go through a series of ifs on one side of the = sign, answer on the right, maybe drop a line and show where we have arrived. Then drop a line, so if we have arrived here and this is the case, then … and fill the gap. Drop down a line. We come to see what exists, rather than what we thought exists, or what we were told exists.

You can understand from this why Socrates had to be executed. It doesn't matter to the ruling class if any god or gods exist but the authority of such certainly does exist, as applied by ruling authority: priests, mullahs, rabbis, community leaders, chiefs, kings and all manner of leadership. This returns us to Dostoevsky's Grand Inquisitor and to Kafka's land surveyor, "K.," in *The Castle*, dealing with an all-too-real authority, which has no essence, no substance—the Wizard of Oz.

RN: Have you read recent fiction which resonated with you?

JK: Not so much in recent years. The existential drive in nineteenth-century literature, through the earlier part of last century, seems to have dried up. We've returned to a stage where "reality" as presented by authority is allowed unchallenged. We live or die by a value system that is abhorrent, typically upper-class, white-Anglo-Saxon-heterosexual male. In prose fiction this is expressed by a third-party narrative where the "voice" is Standard English Literary Form. And the dialogue can be any voice you like: working-class Scottish, African American, Nigerian, anything. But the voice of the third-party narrative is always the same voice, the God voice of Anglo-American authority. The imperialist is always in control. All the inferiors, women, servants, natives, lackeys, can do whatever the fuck they like, as long as they keep to the margins. This is why writers who insist on hijacking the third-party narrative are dangerous.

RN: You got me reading Tutuola, for which I am grateful. What is it about him and Ayi Kwei Armah that makes you keep returning to their writing? How do you read it now, what's different?

JK: With Tutuola it is the Voice, how to manipulate the language of the imperialist, to return us to an inner place where the free human being exists. Reaching down to there, and moving outwards and upwards, what comes to the surface is the richness, the sense of language as dynamic, the languages and culture of you and your own community, pre-colonizer, pre-imperialist. The story is written in English but what kind of English! Full of all these strange rhythms and syntax, weird beliefs and perceptions of reality, a phenomenological world.

When I first read Ayi Kwei Armah I began to see how bold he was, how ambitious. I feel pretty useless here. I never felt without a community, in the wider sense, I could look to other European literary traditions. Imperialism and colonization are ruthless and brutal and will destroy whichever indigenous form stands in their way. Was he alone? It was just so difficult what he was taking on. Maybe the world was passing him by. I would like to have known him and sat about talking literature and politics, and how to move. I think of Knut Hamsun here, and his movement out of the greatness of his "I-voice" earlier work into something else altogether. Do they have people to talk to? Other artists and people they can trust? An authentic community is so damn crucial.

RN: PM Press will be re-issuing your *Translated Accounts* sometime in the future. You are planning to revise the text. How and why will you do this two decades after it was written?

JK: I have already done this. I had the chance, and thought that the earlier sections might benefit from that.

RN: Have you been able to appreciate translations of any of your work? How important is it for you that these get published and read?

JK: Foreign communication is a lifeline. Community knows no borders. Writers learn to smile and say nothing, let the translator get on with it.

Index

"Passim" (literally "scattered") indicates intermittent discussion of a topic over a cluster of pages.

"stream-of-consciousness"
(phrase), 237, 238–39
Strathclyde University, 40–41,
169, 287, 314–15
strikes, 77, 110
swearing, 24–25, 163, 207–8
Swift, Jonathan: *Modest Proposal*,
28
Swing Hammer Swing (SHS)
(Torrington), 79–82 passim,
87, 89

TAG Theatre, Glasgow, 129
Thatcher, Margaret, 40, 91, 125,
145
That Was a Shiver (Kelman), 331,
340
Thomas, Hywel, 315
Torrington, Jeff, 31, 131, 173;
conversation with Kelman,
79–91; "The Last Shift," 30, 33;
Open Wide Otto (unpublished
novel), 80; Parkinsonism,
86–87; *Swing Hammer Swing*
(SHS), 79–82 passim, 87, 89
trade unions, 105–10 passim
Translated Accounts (Kelman),
138–49 passim, 160, 168–69,
173, 180, 181, 191, 251, 267, 313;
American edition, 158; earliest
attempts, 27; launch, 288;
revision, 343; translations, 164
Transport and General Workers
(T&G), 108, 110
Traverse Theatre, Edinburgh,
111–17 passim, 122, 124
Treasure Island (Stevenson), 81
Tressell, Robert: *Ragged-
Trousered Philanthropists*, 31
The Trial (Kafka), 333
Trocchi, Alex, 234, 309
Tron Theatre, Glasgow, 126–27
TUC. *See* Scottish Trades Union
Congress (STUC)

Tutuola, Amos, 186, 206, 256, 265,
322, 342–43
Twain, Mark, 257–58

Ulysses (Joyce), 36
universities, 23, 27, 38–41
passim, 62, 154–55, 212–13,
299, 312–15; Kelman teaching,
142, 154, 169–70, 212. *See
also* Glasgow University;
Strathclyde University
unions. *See* trade unions

Van Gogh, Vincent, 210, 255, 302,
303

Walmsley, Anne, 211
Waugh, Evelyn, 23, 44, 45, 124,
239, 275–76
Webster, Noah, 258
Welsh, Irvine, 93, 152, 252, 253,
256, 280
White, Kenneth, 311
Williams, Diane, 341
Williams, William Carlos, 19,
23, 35
Wilson, Brian, 124
Wiseman, Sue, 48
Wishart, Ruth, 135–36
Wittgenstein, Ludwig, 289
Wood, James, 283
Woolf, Virginia, 213, 326
Workers City (group), 58, 59,
64–66 passim, 75, 76, 101
Wright, Richard, 212, 256
writers' organisations, 170
writing groups, 82–84, 216–17.
See also Paisley Group

Yiddish literature, 187
*You have to be Careful in the
Land of the Free* (Kelman), 183,
268–69

About the Author

James Kelman was born in Glasgow, June 1946, and left school in 1961. He travelled about and worked at various jobs. He lives in Glasgow with his wife, Marie, who has supported his work since 1969.

ABOUT PM PRESS

PM Press is an independent, radical publisher of critically necessary books for our tumultuous times. Our aim is to deliver bold political ideas and vital stories to all walks of life and arm the dreamers to demand the impossible. Founded in 2007 by a small group of people with decades of publishing, media, and organizing experience, we have sold millions of copies of our books, most often one at a time, face to face. We're old enough to know what we're doing and young enough to know what's at stake. Join us to create a better world.

PM Press
PO Box 23912
Oakland, CA 94623
www.pmpress.org

PM Press in Europe
europe@pmpress.org
www.pmpress.org.uk

FRIENDS OF PM PRESS

These are indisputably momentous times—the financial system is melting down globally and the Empire is stumbling. Now more than ever there is a vital need for radical ideas.

In the many years since its founding—and on a mere shoestring—PM Press has risen to the formidable challenge of publishing and distributing knowledge and entertainment for the struggles ahead. With hundreds of releases to date, we have published an impressive and stimulating array of literature, art, music, politics, and culture. Using every available medium, we've succeeded in connecting those hungry for ideas and information to those putting them into practice.

Friends of PM allows you to directly help impact, amplify, and revitalize the discourse and actions of radical writers, filmmakers, and artists. It provides us with a stable foundation from which we can build upon our early successes and provides a much-needed subsidy for the materials that can't necessarily pay their own way. You can help make that happen—and receive every new title automatically delivered to your door once a month—by joining as a Friend of PM Press. And, we'll throw in a free T-shirt when you sign up.

Here are your options:

- **$30 a month** Get all books and pamphlets plus a 50% discount on all webstore purchases

- **$40 a month** Get all PM Press releases (including CDs and DVDs) plus a 50% discount on all webstore purchases

- **$100 a month** Superstar—Everything plus PM merchandise, free downloads, and a 50% discount on all webstore purchases

For those who can't afford $30 or more a month, we have **Sustainer Rates** at $15, $10 and $5. Sustainers get a free PM Press T-shirt and a 50% discount on all purchases from our website.

Your Visa or Mastercard will be billed once a month, until you tell us to stop. Or until our efforts succeed in bringing the revolution around. Or the financial meltdown of Capital makes plastic redundant. Whichever comes first.

DEPARTMENT OF ANTHROPOLOGY & SOCIAL CHANGE

Anthropology and Social Change, housed within the California Institute of Integral Studies, is a small innovative graduate department with a particular focus on activist scholarship, militant research, and social change. We offer both masters and doctoral degree programs.

Our unique approach to collaborative research methodology dissolves traditional barriers between research and political activism, between insiders and outsiders, and between researchers and protagonists. Activist research is a tool for "creating the conditions we describe." We engage in the process of co-research to explore existing alternatives and possibilities for social change.

Anthropology and Social Change
anth@ciis.edu
1453 Mission Street
94103
San Francisco, California
www.ciis.edu/academics/graduate-programs/anthropology-and-social-change

Between Thought and Expression Lies a Lifetime: Why Ideas Matter

Noam Chomsky & James Kelman

ISBN: 978-1-62963-880-5 (paperback)
978-1-62963-886-7 (hardcover)
$19.95/$39.95   304 pages

"The world is full of information. What do we do when we get the information, when we have digested the information, what do we do then? Is there a point where ye say, yes, stop, now I shall move on."

This exhilarating collection of essays, interviews, and correspondence—spanning the years 1988 through 2018, and reaching back a decade more—is about the simple concept that ideas matter. They mutate, inform, create fuel for thought, and inspire actions.

As Kelman says, the State relies on our suffocation, that we cannot hope to learn "the truth. But whether we can or not is beside the point. We must grasp the nettle, we assume control and go forward."

Between Thought and Expression Lies a Lifetime is an impassioned, elucidating, and often humorous collaboration. Philosophical and intimate, it is a call to ponder, imagine, explore, and act.

"*The real reason Kelman, despite his stature and reputation, remains something of a literary outsider is not, I suspect, so much that great, radical Modernist writers aren't supposed to come from working-class Glasgow, as that great, radical Modernist writers are supposed to be dead. Dead, and wrapped up in a Penguin Classic: that's when it's safe to regret that their work was underappreciated or misunderstood (or how little they were paid) in their lifetimes. You can write what you like about Beckett or Kafka and know they're not going to come round and tell you you're talking nonsense, or confound your expectations with a new work. Kelman is still alive, still writing great books, climbing.*"
—James Meek, *London Review of Books*

"*A true original. . . . A real artist. . . . It's now very difficult to see which of [Kelman's] peers can seriously be ranked alongside him without ironic eyebrows being raised.*"
—Irvine Welsh, *Guardian*

God's Teeth and Other Phenomena

James Kelman

ISBN: 978-1-62963-939-0 (paperback)
      978-1-62963-940-6 (hardcover)
$17.95/$34.95   368 pages

Jack Proctor, a celebrated older writer and
curmudgeon, goes off to residency where
he is to be an honored part of teaching and
giving public readings but soon finds that the
atmosphere of the literary world has changed since his last foray into
the public sphere. Unknown to most, unable to work on his own writing,
surrounded by a host of odd characters, would-be writers, antagonists,
handlers, and members of the elite House of Art and Aesthetics, Proctor
finds himself driven to distraction (literally in a very tiny car). This is a
story of a man attempting not to go mad when forced to stop his own
writing in order to coach others to write. Proctor's tour of rural places,
pubs, theaters, and fancy parties, where he is to be headlining as a
"Banker Prize winner," reads like a literary version of *This Is Spinal Tap*.
Uproariously funny, brilliantly philosophical, gorgeously written, this is
James Kelman at his best.

James Kelman was born in Glasgow, June 1946, and left school in 1961.
He began work in the printing trade then moved around, working in
various jobs in various places. He was living in England when he started
writing: ramblings, musings, sundry phantasmagoria. He committed to
it and kept at it. In 1969 he met and married Marie Connors from South
Wales. They settled in Glasgow and still live in the dump, not far from
their kids and grandkids. He still plugs away at the ramblings, musings,
politicking and so on, supported by the same lady.

"God's Teeth and Other Phenomena *is electric. Forget all the rubbish
you've been told about how to write, the requirements of the marketplace
and the much vaunted 'readability' that is supposed to be sacrosanct. This is
a book about how art gets made, its murky, obsessive, unedifying demands
and the endless, sometimes hilarious, humiliations literary life inflicts on
even its most successful names.*"
—Eimear McBride, author of *A Girl is a Half-Formed Thing* and *The Lesser
Bohemians*

Keep Moving and No Questions

James Kelman

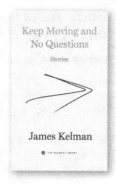

ISBN: 978-1-62963-967-3 (paperback)
978-1-62963-975-8 (hardcover)
$17.95/$29.95   288 pages

James Kelman's inimitable voice brings the
stories of lost men to light in these twenty-one
tales of down-on-their-luck antiheroes who
wander, drink, hatch plans, ponder existence,
and survive in an unwelcoming and often comic world. *Keep Moving and No Questions* is a collection of the finest examples of Kelman's facility with dialog, stream-of-consciousness narrative, and sharp cultural observation. Class is always central in these brief glimpses of men abiding the hands they've been dealt. An ideal introduction to Kelman's work and a wonderful edition for fans and Kelman completists, this lovely volume will make clear why James Kelman is known as the greatest living modernist writer.

"Kelman has the knack, maybe more than anyone since Joyce, of fixing in his writing the lyricism of ordinary people's speech. . . . Pure aesthete, undaunted democrat—somehow Kelman manages to reconcile his two halves."
—*Esquire*